Grace To A Witty Sinner

Other Books by the Same Author

He and She
The Long Road Back
Dictionary of Last Words
Yet Once More: Verbal and Psychological Pattern in Milton
A Milton Dictionary
Endymion in England: The Literary History of a Greek Myth

Grace to a Witty Sinner:
A Life of Donne

EDWARD LE COMTE

Walker and Company · New York

Preface

Despite the overwhelming modern interest in Donne (which
has itself been the subject of a book and is the subject of
the last chapter of this book), the twentieth century has
seen only two biographies: Hugh I'Anson Fausset, *John
Donne, A Study in Discord* (London, 1924; New York, 1925)
and Evelyn Hardy, *Donne: A Spirit in Conflict* (London,
1942). The former, though ambitious critically and stylisti-
cally, biographically follows Sir Edmund Gosse, *The Life
and Letters of John Donne*, 1899. Mr. Fausset's stated aim
was to furnish an introduction "to many who are unable
to possess themselves of Mr. Gosse's monumental work,"
which was then out of print. But Gosse's work has proved
to be in need of much correction, as much correction as
he himself administered to the first biographer, Izaak
Walton. Miss Hardy's 1942 book deserves to be better
known: very few copies (in wartime) reached this side of
the Atlantic. It is continuously interesting and based on
some independent research. However, downright factual
errors (especially in regard to dates) apart, there are places
where I, for one, fail to recognize the picture it gives,
beginning with the opening pages on the treatment of
Catholics in Elizabeth's time and ending with Appendix

III, a graphologist's analysis of Donne's handwriting about which we are warned that it is "bound to be, in some ways, only a superficial and questionable summary"—in which I recognize nothing at all, even of Miss Hardy's version of Donne.

In the last ten years, to say nothing of the last twenty, important light has been thrown on Donne by the researches of such scholars as R. C. Bald, John Bryson, Helen Gardner, Sir Geoffrey Keynes, David Novarr, George R. Potter, I. A. Shapiro, Evelyn M. Simpson, and Baird W. Whitlock. Their recent books and articles add to earlier work by some of these and by R. E. Bennett, Charles M. Coffin, H. W. Garrod, Sir Herbert Grierson, John Hayward, John Sparrow, P. Thomson, and F. P. Wilson. In the days when I was a Miltonist struggling to become a Donnean, I cunningly started a correspondence with Professor Whitlock, now of the University of Wyoming, who has patiently answered my questions and rendered help generously in several forms—reprints, letters, and formal correction and commentary in reaction to my first draft. I have spared him subsequent revisions and of course take sole responsibility for the final result.

This life of Donne is dedicated to the memory of my former teacher and colleague, George Nobbe, late Professor Emeritus of English at Columbia College, who suggested it.

E. L.

State University of New York, Albany

Contents

1 | Man About Town

In 1630 the Very Reverend Dr. John Donne, Dean of St. Paul's and the greatest preacher of his time, fully aware that at fifty-eight he had entered upon his last illness, drew up the final version of his will. He made the usual charitable bequests, gave mementoes to friends, and left rich sums to his children, for he had prospered as a church-man, being the holder of several lucrative livings. Just before he closed the document, having mentioned several in-spirational paintings, he descended to speak of a portrait of himself when young. He had had it by him some thirty-five years; remembering his days as a courtier, he bestowed it now upon a courtier. "Item, I give to my honorable and faithful friend Mr. Robert Ker of His Majesty's bed-cham-ber that picture of mine which is taken in shadows and was made very many years before I was of this profession."

"Taken in shadows"—what did that mean? The pic-ture was referred to more than once in the seventeenth century. But for three centuries it remained unknown.

In 1959 it was found, found just where it belonged, at Newbattle Abbey in Scotland, the ancestral home of the Marquis of Lothian, direct descendant of Donne's "faithful friend." At last we have a handsome and convincing portrait of Jack Donne the Elizabethan, love poet and man about town, as distinguished from Dr. Donne, whom his first biographer, Izaak Walton, revered as a saint. At last we can see young Donne, Donne in his early twenties, plain.

Plain?—he was never plain, at any age. He is far from plain here. Above his dark doublet gleams a lace and embroidered collar, and, without taking too much trouble to look miserable, he is posing as a victim of lover's melancholy. Inscribed overhead is the blasphemy "Illumina Tenebras Nostras, Domina"—"Lighten our darkness, mistress"—a parody of the prayer, "Lighten our darkness, we beseech Thee, O Lord" (*Domina* for *Domine*). Melancholy was one of the four "humours," and this leanly handsome gallant is acting out the most fashionable form of it, the two signs of which, as one could learn from that current comedy *Love's Labour's Lost,* were folded arms and a hat pulled down over the eyes. But Donne does things differently; his bonnet is rakishly set back on his head, lest what Walton called his "melting eye" be concealed. That ungloved hand is sensitive, too, and there must be some books and a quill in the foreground. As an essayist summed up, love "bringeth forth rhymes and songs full of passion, enough to procure crossed arms and the hat pulled down; yea, it is a very fine thing, the badge of eighteen and upward, not to be disallowed." At last we have something visual to pair with a college friend's description of this same supremely confident and supremely clever dandy: "not dissolute but very neat, a great visitor of ladies, a great frequenter of plays, a great writer of conceited verses" (that is, verses notable for their *concetti*—ingenious analogies). What another contemporary observed is also manifest: "neither was it possible that a vulgar soul should dwell in such promising features." But he does not look as if he has plans for becoming a saint.

Still, there were a saint and more than one martyr among his forebears. If he was gay, he was gay against a family background of suffering and renunciation extending through four generations.

The beginning of the shadows was Henry VIII's break with Rome. John Donne's great-granduncle went to the scaffold for the old Catholic faith, the faith in which Donne was brought up. He was Sir Thomas More, author of the *Utopia,* which gave the language an indispensable word. Formerly Lord Chancellor, More could not in good conscience subscribe to Henry VIII's Act of Supremacy asserting that the English monarch, not the Pope, was the head of the Church of England. This great humanist was canonized in 1935, four hundred years after his martyrdom. Besides grace, he had wit, right up to the end; like his great-grandnephew he died a good death in a period when dying was considered an art on which books of instruction and edifying examples were printed. The condemned man on reaching the steps said to the lieutenant, "I pray thee see me safely up, and for my coming down let me shift for myself." He moved his beard from the block on the grounds that "it has never committed treason."

St. Thomas More's sister, who was to be Donne's great-grandmother on his mother's side and who bore the same name, Elizabeth, married John Rastell, a printer and lawyer. In that age of the Cabots, Rastell also went to sea, and, like Caxton, he was one of those printers who wrote. In fact in crude verses he set down the first English description of America:

> Within this twenty year
> Westward he found new landes
> That we never heard tell of before this,
> By writing nor other meanes;
> Yet many now have been there;
> And that country is so large of room,
> Much larger than all Christendom ....

The son of John and Elizabeth Rastell, William, became distinguished in both professions—printing and the law— putting out a loving edition of More's English works in 1557, and rising, just before Queen Mary died, to the

Queen's Bench. However, as a Roman Catholic he went into exile early in Elizabeth's reign.

So did his sister and brother-in-law, Joan and John Heywood, the parents of Donne's mother. In fact all the Heywoods were heroically Roman Catholic. John's brother, Thomas, was a priest who was executed for his faith. John fathered three children—Elizabeth, Donne's mother, who carried her faith into the reign of Charles I, and Jasper and Ellis,who were both Jesuits and therefore risked their lives every time they set foot in England. As part of his campaign of proselytizing, Jasper Heywood contributed devotional verse to *The Paradise of Dainty Devices*, a miscellany more sober than its name.

John Heywood is well known to students of English literature for his epigrams and his comedy *The Four PP's*. Like More in More's *Dialogue of Comfort against Tribulation* (written in the Tower), like the young Donne, he could be medievally saucy at the expense of womankind, a continuator of the Adam-versus-his-crooked-rib tradition. The Four PP's—a palmer, a pardoner, a 'pothecary, and a pedlar—get involved in a lying contest which is won by the palmer when he says:

> I have seen women five hundred thousand,
> Wives and widows, maids and married,
> And oft with them have long tarried,
> Yet in all places where I have been,
> Of all the women that I have seen,
> I never saw, nor knew, in my conscience,
> Any one woman out of patience.

Is this so far in spirit, whatever the difference in style, from Heywood's grandson's:

> If thou be'st born to strange sights,
>   Things invisible to see,
> Ride ten thousand days and nights,
>   Till age snow white hairs on thee;

Thou, when thou return'st, wilt tell me
　All strange wonders that befell thee,
　　And swear.
　　Nowhere
Lives a woman true, and fair.

Heywood could be obscure, too, as befitted a critic of the court. But it is mainly his laughter that echoes down the halls of time: he is "merry John Heywood," "the mad merry wit." Perhaps his last jest was his best. On his death-bed his confessor kept reiterating "the flesh is frail" until he drew from the old man the reply that the priest seemed to be sorry that God had not made him, Heywood, a fish.

But it was no joke to end one's days in Flanders in exile, having left one's property in the hands of an un-reliable son-in-law. So Heywood evidently found the elder John Donne to be, for he wrote Lord Treasurer Burleigh in 1575 that he hoped "it pleaseth your good Lordship . . . to command my son Donne to send me over the arrearages which hath been detained from me," and the latter part of this long plaintive epistle comes back to the point that "my son Donne . . . never sent me one penny yet either of that lease or of any of my living since the time he bought my lease, for he saith he durst not." It may have been that Donne really "durst not," for after Pius V had excommuni-cated Queen Elizabeth, an act so foolish that it even em-barrassed Philip II of Spain, the government issued a "proc-lamation" of all refugees and summoned them to return and began looking into their property. But John Donne the elder seems not to have been, from a couple of other records that survive, a completely scrupulous character. In 1570 he was called before court for failing to have coal weighed according to the monopoly held by St. Bartholo-mew's Hospital, and there is evidence that he participated in the occupation of tenements that had been willed to the poor.

In any case the relatives of distinction of Donne the poet—cultural and religious leaders—were all on his mother's side. His father, also a Roman Catholic, illustrated a different facet of the Renaissance—the upward push of the rising merchant class. John Donne the elder made his way, made his way to affluence, as an ironmonger. The family was originally from Wales, but cannot now be traced. When the son became Dean of St. Paul's he assumed the same coat of arms as that of the Duns or Dwnns of Kidwelly in Carmarthenshire. It is a pregnant thought—nothing like a Celtic strain for a poet. It may explain the voluptuousness and intensity, a quickness of temperament more Welsh than English.

John Donne the elder was admitted to the freedom of the Ironmongers' Company in 1556, and became Warden—an executive official under the Master—in 1574, by which time he had amassed (legitimately or not) considerable wealth. He must have married Elizabeth Heywood around 1562. Unfortunately all family records, as well as the house in which Donne the poet was born, were destroyed in the Great Fire of London in 1666.

The consensus now is that the poet was born not in 1571, or 1573, but in the early part of 1572, a few months before his friend Ben Jonson. The Donnes lived in Bread Street, nearer to the Mermaid Tavern than to old St. Paul's Cathedral (destined also to go down in the Great Fire). John was to be a frequenter of both places, but God's building enforced attention by sheer height, even without its steeple, which had been destroyed by lightning in 1561 and was never replaced. A mile off, pointing heavenward over that crowded port, "the mart of the known world," the precocious child could look up and see the cathedral's tower clock, where, exerting a moral influence, an angel stretched an arm toward the hours ("great clocks, which in steeples chime, / Placed to inform whole towns to 'employ their time"). Through that city of a fifth of a million souls wafted all the smells of life undisguised; it was repeatedly said to be a wicked place, and the senses reported that it certainly needed whatever washing the rain and the winding Thames could give it. With its motley interests, its sensuous and intellectual opportunities, it summoned a child of spirit to develop fast. "Energy is eternal delight."

This was the age of superlative energies, but absolutely without promise of long life. One should hurry, and pluck the day, and be glad that one was not living in "the barbarousness and insipid dulness of the country."

At least two children preceded John, and at least three followed him, Henry, one year younger, being the closest of all. The mortality rate was high: an elder sister soon died. As the poet was to witness in his own offspring, about twice as many children were born as could be expected to grow up. At the time of Donne's birth the household comprised, besides his parents, his sisters Elizabeth and Anne, a cousin Alice, and three servants.

Besides the natural deaths, there were the unnatural deaths. When the boy was two, the shadows that stalked his family came closer: his granduncle "Sir Thomas the Parson" fell a victim to the state's increasingly harsh measures against papists. Stow's *Annals* tells of a rash of arrests on Palm Sunday, April 4, 1574. "There was also taken at the same instant in the Lady Brown's house in Cow Lane for saying mass one Thomas Heywood priest and one John Cooper priest, with the Lady Brown, and divers other were likewise taken, being hearers of the said mass. All which persons were for the same offences indicted, convicted, and had the law according to the statute in that case provided. There was also found in their several chapels divers Latin books, beads, images, palms, chalices, crosses, vestments, pixes, paxes, and such like." Cow Lane was just two streets from the Donne home, the whole neighborhood being strongly Roman Catholic. The execution, public, horrible in every detail, took place June 14.

Donne was not to have his father long. Just on the verge of appointment as Master of his company, John Donne the elder, "being sick in body," drew up his will January 16, 1576; it was proved by the widow February 8. A fortune of between 3000 and 4500 pounds went to the widow and children.

As Donne was scarcely four when his father died, he could not have retained many memories of him, but, no doubt with the aid of his mother's reminiscences, what he remembered was favorable, perhaps determinedly favorable. The Ironmongers' Company records are still closed to the investigator. Would they reveal a good deal more against the senior Donne as an unscrupulous businessman; not at all fastidious as to how his wealth was garnered? Did John the younger hear rumors to this effect? A satirist was to speak of his father's "chemic usury." Was John being autobiographical when he declared in a sermon, "Many a son, many a good heir, finds an ill air from his father; his father's life stinks in the nostrils of all the world, and he hears everywhere exclamations upon his father's usury, and extortion, and oppression: yet it becomes him by a better life and by all other means to rectify and redeem his father's fame." He kept faith, telling his mother what she doubtless had told him, dilating in a letter to her on "the happiness which God afforded to your first young time, which was the love and care of my most dear and provident father." There can be no financial doubt about the "provident." Donne left the equivalent of more than a quarter of a million dollars, ironmonger—or rather, steel magnate and entrepreneur in real estate—that he was.

A favorable attitude was rendered sentimentally easy by the late father's place being taken by a stepfather: within a half year (the law regarding property was such as to encourage the remarriage of widows) Elizabeth Donne had found another husband, also Romanist (it was a tight community, like huddled sheep), also well-to-do, and higher on the social scale—Dr. John Syminges, president of the Royal College of Physicians. He was a widower: they moved with a son of his, who was at least sixteen, to a comfortable home in Little Trinity Lane, two blocks from Bread Street.

There, privately tutored, within sight of the Thames, the boy who was to sail with Essex resided until, at twelve, he went to college. He saw ships from many lands riding anchor or unloading at the quays. Before he had mounted a single galleon he rode countless times on the river in a wherry or a barge, for that was the only convenient way to go up to Westminster—where, on the north bank, the mansions of the nobles followed one another in dazzling array—or down to Greenwich, where the Queen's favorite palace (she had been born there in the Virgin Chamber) stretched—or across to Southwark, one of the two theater districts. The Thames estuary was London's principal thoroughfare, its easy ebb and flow from the sea twice a day a purging contrast to the mud of the gutters and the ancient narrow streets and alleys. A prisoner of state could disembark right at his cell door at the Tower, where now all is dry, even as flats have been reclaimed that once brought money only to watermen. The river passed indistinguishably into the sea, beckoning out to another kind of full life. Donne's house was good middle-class, but no London home—not even such lordly mansions as Leicester House or York House—was far from crowded medieval slums, where rats slithered along rotting timbers, disappearing at the bark of stray dogs: professional rat-catchers and dog-catchers were hopelessly busy. What with home plagues and smells (the floors at Greenwich were strewn, for good reason, with rushes, and when the barn-like situation became too intolerable the Queen and her court moved out until a general cleaning could be accomplished) and rickety children, one might occasionally mix envy of a sailor with admiration for a sea dog. At the end of many an alley was, quite literally, a sail.

Of the stepfather of his childhood Donne makes no mention. He picked up medical lore from him and perhaps shared in certain professional experiences that contributed to the morbid strain, the preoccupation with disease and decay, that marks some of his most powerful writing, both in prose and verse. It may have been that, like so many sons, he took a dim view of his mother's remarrying. When his own wife died he assured his children that he would never "bring them under the subjection of a stepmother." After his mother, having outlived Dr. Syminges, married yet again, her grown son spoke rather condescendingly of his second stepfather; the nearest he came to mentioning the first was in a reminiscence to the effect that his nurse, contrary to common practice, was not allowed to whip him but only to report his fault to his mother. "My parents

would not give me over to a servant's correction." Which-
ever father this refers to, it is mainly a reference to his
mother, "from whom I had that education, which must
make my fortune."

In Walton's words, "His mother and those to whose
care he was committed were watchful to improve his knowledge and to that end appointed him tutors both in the
mathematics and in all the other liberal sciences to attend
him. But with these arts they were advised to instil into
him particular principles of the Romish Church; of which
those tutors professed (though secretly) themselves to be
members." He proved such a ready pupil that it was said
"that this age had brought forth another" Pico della
Mirandola, that Renaissance prodigy whose life had been
written in English by More (a book, by the way, that the
great-grandnephew loyally praised).

Blurring painful distinctions of churches, Donne sometimes (outside of controversial works) preferred to recall
his upbringing as simply Christian. "God wrapped me up
in his covenant, and derived me from Christian parents.
I sucked Christian blood, in my mother's womb, and
Christian milk at my nurse's breast. The first sound that
I heard in the world was the voice of Christians, and the
first character that I was taught to know was the cross of
Christ Jesus." But he was surrounded by family memories
of what it meant to belong to the minority group, to be,
in that time and that place, papists.

The Elizabethan settlement, or compromise, in religion
exacted outer conformity from lay Catholics. The Queen
did not attempt to meddle with their thoughts; she insisted
only that they attend the Anglican service on Sunday or,
as recusants—*refusers* to go to church—fill her coffers with
a fine, a fine that in the case of the gentry or nobility
could grow to large and ruinous proportions. It was often
difficult to know who was a Catholic, who might be celebrating mass secretly in some darkened chamber, or preparing to emigrate, or to aid an invader. Did William
Shakespeare have Catholic sympathies? His father was
charged for not attending services, as was Donne's mother;

the ghost in *Hamlet* comes from purgatory. Was the Earl
of Southampton, the dedicatee of *Venus and Adonis* and
The Rape of Lucrece, a Catholic? Pinning down a member
of this minority could be as vexing as being sure of the
identity of a Communist in the United States today, and
their loyalty was equally suspect. King Philip thought that
if the Armada could cover the landing of that able general,
the Duke of Parma, the Catholics in England—numbering,
it was rumored, half the population—would rally to his
standard. Mary Queen of Scots, whose execution had oiled
the ways of that armada, had had similar dreams. They
were mistaken, but who could be sure? Suspicion was rife.
Witch hunting went on—for witches and for papists, with
paid informers and a paid persecutor, the cruel Richard
Topcliffe, who had the Privy Council's license to torture
in his home those he called "lewd Popish beasts."

Seminary priests and Jesuits were in a worse category
than lay Catholics, the category of capital punishment.
They formed a secret army, waging fanatic war among the
heretics. They lived—were picked and trained to live—dangerously, the roughness with which they were treated, if
caught, being proportional to the government's fears of
the latest maneuvers of the continental Catholic powers.
In the summing up of A. L. Rowse in *The England of
Elizabeth*: "In this conflict for power, which grew desperate and flamed into open war in the last half of the reign,
here within the country was a Fifth Column, part of it
actual, conscious, and determined, part potential, part
passive victims, caught irremediably and tortured by the
ineluctable—often unendurable—conflict of allegiances."
Rome had more or less sanctioned the assassination of
the Queen. On the eve of the Spanish Armada she was
declared by Cardinal Allen "a most unjust usurper and
injurer of all nations, an infamous, depraved, accursed,
excommunicate heretic, the very shame of her sex and
princely name, the chief spectacle of sin and abomination
in this our age and the only poison, calamity and destruction of our noble church and country." The Privy Council
answered conspiracy and aggression with stern measures.

Of the three hundred Catholics who went to their deaths in the last thirty years of Elizabeth's reign—a figure that slowly equaled the three hundred burnings of Protestants in the last three years of Mary's reign—one of the first to suffer was, as we have seen, Donne's granduncle, the exiled John Heywood's brother, "Sir Thomas the Parson." What the statute provided for the priest that said the mass was horribly different from what it held for the hearers of it: to fill in the details from birth to martyrdom, we can take the typical career of Alexander Briant as sketched by the seventeenth-century antiquary Anthony Wood in his *Athenae Oxonienses*: "Alexander Briant received his first breath in Somersetshire, was admitted a student of Hart Hall about Lent term in 1571-2, aged 17 or more, where being trained up under a tutor sufficiently addicted to popery, left the university and went to Rheims, and afterwards to Douai: at the last of which places, taking the priesthood on him, he returned into his own country, anno 1579, and settling for a time in Somersetshire, converted the father of Robert Parsons the Jesuit to the Roman Catholic religion. On the 28th April 1581, he was taken in the nighttime in his lodging by one Norton, who took away 3 pounds in money from him, besides clothes, and conducting him to the Compter in London, where enduring great misery till the morrow after the Ascension, was removed to the Tower of London, and there, as 'tis reported, he was tormented with needles thrust under his nails, racked also otherwise in cruel sort ... At length being found guilty of High Treason at a sessions in London, he was hanged, drawn and quartered at Tyburn, on the first day of December in 1581, whereupon his quarters were hanged up for a time in public places."

With Briant, a youth "of singular beauty," died five other priests, one of whom was the saintly Edmund Campion, whose eloquence as an Oxford student had charmed Queen Elizabeth and whom the Queen had lately tried to save, interrogating him herself. But his answers were not satisfactory and he was turned over to the professional examiners, who tortured him so that on trial he could no longer raise his hand to take the oath. One of his companions had to pull the crippled hand out of his gown and hold it up for him. Campion, unlike Briant, was hanged but not "drawn"—that is, he was allowed to hang till dead instead of being cut down while still alive and disemboweled, intestines drawn out by the hangman and burned before his eyes.

Such, if he had had the call, might have been the fate of Donne himself, for he went to the same crypto-Catholic college that Briant did, and he had the sufferings of three uncles down three generations for prime inspiration: great-granduncle More and granduncle Heywood, martyrs both, and, currently in serious trouble, uncle Jasper Heywood, who had taken the place of the famous Father Parsons as the vice-prefect or superior of the English Jesuit mission. Jasper was in the Tower during Donne's first winter at college; of six priests taken he was the only one who was not executed: he was finally, after being allowed the comforting visits of his sister, put on a ship to France under pain of death if he ever set foot in England again.

The persecution struck still nearer, at Donne's younger brother Henry, but that lay in the future. Meanwhile, he and Henry, aged twelve and eleven, matriculated at Hart Hall, Oxford, on Friday the twenty-third of October, 1584. They were sent early to obtain what higher education they could, short of the full four-year course for the baccalaureate. The Oath of Supremacy was not imposed on freshmen under the age of sixteen; a good Catholic could never take a degree, for he would have had to subscribe to that and to the Thirty-Nine Articles (which are still the accepted summary of the doctrine of the Church of England and, in the United States, the Protestant Episcopal Church). This in fact was to be Donne's greatest outer sacrifice to the faith of his parents—that he never proceeded to a college degree (with the subsequent limitation of career opportunities). Under instructions, this teen-age boy never signed the loyalty oath. "I, John Donne, do utterly testify and declare in my conscience that the Queen's Highness is the only supreme governor of this realm, and of all other

Her Highness' Dominions and Countries, as well in all
spiritual or ecclesiastical things or causes, as temporal, and
that no foreign prince, person, prelate, state or potentate
hath or ought to have any jurisdiction, power, superiority,
pre-eminence, or authority, ecclesiastical or spiritual, within this realm . . . ." For similar scruples his great-granduncle
had lost his head.

The boy pursued the old medieval curriculum under
friendly enough auspices, the principality of Philip
Rondell, who, presiding at Hart Hall for fifty years,
"weathered out several changes of religion (though in his
heart he was a papist, but durst not show it)." Wood goes
on to observe that "many persons who were afterwards
noted in the Roman Church were educated under him."
Happily, that particular college had no chapel and therefore no compulsory services.

One thing that the boy received training in was disputation, sophistical or not. He was to show a talent for
it all his life, in verse as well as in prose. Without choice
he followed the trivium—grammar, rhetoric, and logic or
dialectic. Music and arithmetic were added from the
quadrivium to complete the regular undergraduate curriculum under the Elizabethan statutes.

At Hart Hall (which no longer exists—it became Hert-
ford College in the eighteenth century), Donne and Henry
Wotton struck up a friendship, the famous (to be) Sir
Henry Wotton, envoy, dilettante, provost of Eton, author
of the deathless lyric "You meaner beauties of the night"
in honor of King James's daughter, Elizabeth Queen of
Bohemia (to whom and for whom Donne also was to write).
Wotton was to become such a busy ambassador that the
two could not have seen much of each other in later life,
but they maintained an epistolary and literary friendship.
While they were at Oxford Wotton's four-year seniority
was not necessarily a bar to a mutual attraction. Wotton
was a sybarite and wit who would have appreciated—and
encouraged—precocity. The gifted amateur, he wrote little
but talked well. Sometimes he talked too much, as when
he got into serious trouble for defining an ambassador as

"an honest man, sent to lie abroad for the good of his country." His motto has been variously given as "Love joins all" or "Love conquers all." He left unfinished a book on education, which he was pleased to label "moral architecture." He lived to plan a life of Donne, which Walton had to do instead, by default. In the next generation he was to praise and give travel advice to the author of *Comus*.

Wotton's roommate was Richard Baker, who entered Hart Hall the same day as the Donnes. He it was, a minor chronicler, who looked back and reminisced "of my old acquaintance" as "a great visitor of ladies," etc., in the period when both were young men living in London. There were several future minor poets also at Oxford at this time, such as John Hoskyns and John Davies (of Hereford), who became part of Donne's circle of friends. Hoskyns was expelled from New College for his bitter satires. All these wits being older than John Donne, he must have followed rather than led, some of his first experiments in verse possibly being prompted by theirs. Oxford had also been, ever since the great humanist Juan Luis Vives had taught there, a center for the study of Spanish. A fellow student of Donne's at Hart Hall was James Mabbe, who was to publish a number of picaresque stories from that language. In this way we may expect that Donne got launched on another of his interests. His very first surviving portrait, taken at the end of his teens, has a Spanish motto.

After three years at Oxford Donne was, in 1587, "transplanted ... to Cambridge, where, that he might receive nourishment from both soils, he stayed till his seventeenth [or eighteenth] year: all which time he was a most laborious student, often changing his studies, but endeavoring to take no degree, for the reasons formerly mentioned." Walton is the sole authority—he has been doubted—for Donne's transfer to the sister university, where his college, judging by a remark in Fuller's *Church History of Britain*, was Trinity. There is nothing implausible or unprecedented about such a migration. If Donne had stayed another year at Oxford he would have had to face the issue of his degree. Instead he preferred, doubtless under family advice, to start all over again in a different intellectual atmosphere and see what he could absorb at Cambridge. He was still too young to be anything but a student.

He was to accuse himself of "the worst voluptuousness, which is an hydroptic, immoderate desire of human learning and languages." Whether or not this was his "worst voluptuousness," "often changing his studies" with characteristic restlessness, he became a specialist in several different fields—divinity, medieval and Renaissance philosophy, law—and, on his own, was to branch out from medicine and the old physics to other sciences in their latest development. In the Renaissance, learning was thought to help—not hinder—a poet. Some might manage a lyric—and evidently anyone could write a play—without having gone to college, despite "small Latin and less Greek," but mostly the poet was one who knew, and he would have betrayed his function if he hid what he knew. Donne had a penchant for seizing on the very latest and mixing it with the medieval, for a concoction that is still heady.

Needless to say, the great medieval subject was theology. "Theology was still the queen of the curriculum and logic her handmaiden," and this was true at Cambridge in a livelier way than at Oxford, for Cambridge had developed as the Protestant, if not the Puritan, stronghold. Donne saw enough dispute there between Anglicans and Calvinists to say a plague on both your houses, indeed all three: London, Geneva, and Rome: that is what he comes to in Satire III, which he wrote in his early twenties. But such a position, for one with his background, was not easily arrived at. His writings in middle life show him in accordance with the Nicene Creed, accepted by all the Churches: "I believe one Catholic and Apostolic Church."

The year 1588, when we may suppose Donne to have been in the midst of his studies at what was then definitely the more expansive and forward-looking of the two universities, was not only the year of the Armada but also the year of the Earl of Leicester's death. He had been the Queen's favorite of favorites ever since her accession (before that they had been fellow prisoners in the Tower), but already she was playing cards, if not other games, with his stepson and heir, the slender, auburn-haired twenty-one-year-old Robert Devereux, Earl of Essex. The transition was easy and natural for that fifty-five-year-old coquette from one Robert—"Robin" was the Queen's nickname for them—to the other. Leicester House, the great Gothic mansion overlooking the Thames, was renamed Essex House, and followers began flocking to the new favorite. Wotton was to return from extended residence in Europe to appointment as one of his secretaries.

The month of the scattering of the Armada, July (by English dating), when Donne would have been home for the long vacation, saw his stepfather, Dr. Syminges, die. The redoubtable widow began looking for a third husband. For a fresh start she moved to a new neighborhood, the parish of St. Saviour's in Southwark, a Catholic refuge known as "Little Rome." Before February 7, 1591, she was married to Richard Rainsford, about whom nothing is known.

Around 1590 her son returned to the capital. For posterity, though not necessarily for him, the important fact is that he then began (or continued) to write verse. He probably wrote most of his secular poems (including half the "verse letters") in the last decade of the sixteenth century—the satires, the "songs and sonnets," the elegies. But this could not be his profession, and he was not looking to a patron's bounty as a poet. His poems circulated in manuscript only. His was a diversion, one of the delightful accomplishments of a gentleman, in this golden age of verse-making.

Although a sizable sum awaited him when he came of age, he had to choose a future. What profession? The Church? Which one? Should he cross over to Douai and become a seminarian, following the dangerous profession of his uncles? Secret conversions, secret masses, with a good chance of the rack and a grisly death at Tyburn. What about medicine, in which his late stepfather had been so successful? What about the law?

Of the three professions, the law was the most non-committal. Donne characteristically chose it, as if he were taking refuge in a graduate school. Still not out of his teens, for professional training he now turned to "the third university"—the Inns of Court. By 1591 he was at Thavies Inn; on May 6, 1592, he was admitted a student at Lincoln's Inn. Oxford and Cambridge had provided for the civil and canon law, but what was needed in the world was the common law. This he pursued, with fluctuating diligence, until November, 1594. He was following the normal path of young men of means, equipping themselves possibly for the management of business or for greater usefulness to a patron as councilor or secretary.

At the outset we are offered a provocative thing, if we can take it at face value—a picture still earlier than the Newbattle Abbey one, a picture dated 1591, when this student of many disciplines was nineteen. It turned up as the frontispiece to the 1635 edition of his poems. An oval—maybe originally a medallion—it shows him grasping the hilt of his rapier. Was the aggressiveness of it—the very soldier's costume—another pose? Was he leaping to take, had he already taken, refuge from thought in action?

In later life he was to be bearded, or at least goateed, but this youth is clean-shaven except for a thin mustache. His wavy hair is swept behind his earringed ears. Much has been made, by Fausset and others, of the face so amply revealed, but the discovery of the Newbattle Abbey portrait now helps to the realization that this earlier picture is as false as we have always wanted to believe. It is coarse and ugly, the eyes leering and the nose bulbous: perhaps its faults are due entirely to its notoriously unskillful engraver, William Marshall (who was not the original portraitist but belonged to a later generation), who ten years afterward, with that much more experience, also botched the frontispiece to Milton's minor poems (and was satirized by the outraged poet in Greek iambics).

Pictures of authors work their way upon us, although it may be objected that they should not and that physiognomy is not a science. The First Folio frontispiece, based on the Stratford bust, has driven some to the conclusion that someone else must have written Shakespeare's plays. We should like to believe that Donne had a sensitive face; on the question of sensuality—so grossly answered in the affirmative in the Marshall engraving—we have other evidence. One could begin with Elegy XVIII, "Love's Progress," and then go on to the better-known XIX, "To his Mistress Going to Bed." (To an Elizabethan an "elegy" could be a funeral elegy *or* a love poem in couplets. Marlowe, when he translated them, called Ovid's *Amores* "Elegies.")

But the poems are best discussed in a group, later, since hardly any can be specifically dated. The main guidepost, a loose one, is Ben Jonson's remark to Drummond of Hawthornden that Donne wrote "all his best pieces ere he was twenty-five years old." Walton, who is never to be trusted about dates, pushed the age back to twenty, on the theory that the further back the better.

One of Donne's manucaptors, or sponsors, when he entered Lincoln's Inn was Christopher Brooke. Brooke, a versifier himself and the friend of half a dozen poets, had been with him at Cambridge. Donne was never to have a stauncher friend, as was to be proved in 1601-2. Christopher's younger brother, Samuel, having matriculated at Trinity College, Cambridge, Donne, veteran student, forwarded him advice:

O thou, which to search out the secret parts
Of the India or rather Paradise
  Of knowledge, hast with courage and advice
Lately launched into the vast sea of arts,
Disdain not in thy constant travelling
  To do as other voyagers, and make
  Some turns into less creeks, and wisely take
Fresh water at the Heliconian spring.
I sing not, siren-like, to tempt, for I
  Am harsh, nor as those schismatics with you,
  Which draw all wits of good hope to their crew;
But seeing in you bright sparks of poetry,

I, though I brought no fuel, had desire
With these articulate blasts to blow the fire.

Who were Samuel's "schismatic" associates? Protestants?
Puritans? Sectarians? Maybe the reference is to literary
heretics. At any rate we see how seriously Donne could
take poetry, and presumably did in his own student days
as a change from the muddier waters of Latin dialectic
and theology and the law.

Roger Ascham, author of *The Schoolmaster* and the
Queen's own tutor, complained that young gentlemen
were given too much liberty in England. He granted they
did well enough as boys from seven to seventeen, "but
from seventeen to seven-and-twenty (the most dangerous
time of all a man's life, and most slippery to stay well in)
they have commonly the rein of all license in their own
hand." This was definitely true of Donne, well before he
received his patrimony and began spending it. The amuse-
ments open to a student in London were manifold, the
envy and longing of the lads at the university. Donne
moved among a gay, as well as a keen-witted, crowd, "Of
study and play made strange hermaphrodites" ("Epithalamion Made at Lincoln's Inn," 30). The afternoons were
free for going to a play, at one of the public theaters
outside the Puritanical pale of the city walls. The nights
could be made free for almost anything. The budding
lawyers had their formal revels and feasts and amateur
play-acting in hall. The last we hear of Donne at
Lincoln's Inn is that he was elected Steward of Christmas
on November 26, 1594—and that, when the time came, he
was not there to serve. Francis Bacon's mother felt it
necessary to warn: "I trust that they will not mum,
masque, nor sinfully revel at Gray's Inn." But even the
future Lord Chancellor was once slightly young and
managed to have a good time in the midst of his ambitious pursuit of the law.

"What city in the world so populous, so merchantable,
more rich, more stored with women of most amiable
countenance and beauty, more civiler in their attire?" An

apothecary could not restrain himself from this wanton digression in a professional treatise published at this time. Jack Donne (who had a weakness for civil attire) was bearing the same testimony in his poems, and when he once said the opposite, at the beginning of Satire II, "Sir, though—I thank God for it—I do hate / Perfectly all this town—"—sounded foppishly insincere.

One must pluck the day, gather the rose, in a time of violent uncertainties. In the summer of 1593 Donne lost his brother to the government's continued vigilance against subversive Catholics. A proscribed secular priest named Harrington was found hiding in Henry's chambers, and Henry, for harboring an enemy of the state, was thrown into prison, where he died of gaol-fever or the plague.

How long, through how many more victims, was it to continue to be true that, as the Preface to John's *Pseudo-Martyr* declares, "no family (which is not of far greater extent and greater branches) hath endured and suffered more in their persons and fortunes, for obeying the teachers of Roman doctrine"? This was partly up to John himself. Would he definitely part company with those "men of suppressed and afflicted religion, accustomed to the despite of death and hungry of an imagined martyrdom" (Preface to *Biathanatos*), his own family?

The slitting of the thread of Henry's life at twenty occurred in the year that John came of age and the year that Cardinal Bellarmine issued at Lyons the last volume of his famous three-volume apology for the Roman Catholic faith, the Latin *Disputations concerning the Controversies of the Faith, against the Heretics of this Present Time,* a work that Donne would ponder and argue with. He had broken through the exclusively Roman Catholic circle of his minority forever (although that did not mean complete departure and he had not become officially an Anglican). It was not with Henry that he had resided in London. "Were we not weaned till then?" John's position was analogous to that of the young person today who goes to college and has the faith of his fathers shaken. Sophistication took place—had been taking place for several years, at the lower levels and at the highest.

Piety is not easy when one is young and in good health and has a large patrimony to spend in London or abroad. In Gosse's words, "the tumult of the senses and the enraged curiosity of life" had to be satisfied first. But we are not dealing with a commonplace reveler, who simply and unheroically turned in full-blooded revulsion from martyrdom, from the death and suffering that had followed his family so closely. Donne could not feel without thinking—that was his famous feature. Intellectual conviction had to go along with his other motives. It had to be a matter of demonstration that the Roman Catholic position, at least in regard to civil disobedience, was wrong, wholly wrong, and the suffering therefore perverse and unnecessary.

It took time for Donne to come fully around to the view that he could have subscribed to the Act of Supremacy after all and taken his degrees. *Pseudo-Martyr*, 1610, argues in favor of Roman Catholic allegiance to the English monarch to the extent of 400 pages. If a subject of Elizabeth, for example, could not forthrightly say that if the Pope sent an army to dethrone her he would fight on the side of the Queen, that subject was a traitor. Let there be no sentimentality about sedition, no Jesuitical evasions. Campion's words to his judges were just sophistry: "The only thing that we have now to say is that if our religion do make us traitors we are worthy to be condemned, but otherwise are, and have been, as true subjects as ever the Queen had." "But otherwise"! A good citizen witnessing the execution shouted the last word, "In your Catholicism all treason is contained!"

The great Sir Edward Coke, the law, all legal reasoning, law and order, patriotism, were on Donne's side, when he finally got there himself. But it was hard to reject all that blood. Hesitation enters one of his early sermons. "At many executions, half the company will call a man an heretic, and half, a martyr." Poor Henry a traitor? His brother came close enough to alluding to him in his

Easter sermon of 1627 when he taught that a wife must "not harbor in her house a person dangerous to the public state." Be it noted, however, that in the period we have reached, 1593-94, Donne slipped into Satire II, with affected detachment, his sympathy for the prosecuted. He said of poets, "their state / Is poor, disarmed, like papists, not worth hate."

Certainly it should have been hard to hate a papist who left his loyalty unambiguous and made his anguish clear, such as Robert Markham, who wrote as follows to his father and mother "upon his departure beyond the seas, for conscience's sake" in 1592:

> I assure you, by the duty I owe unto you, that I will never serve in France or in Flanders against Her Majesty: neither whatsoever beggary betide me will I ever serve the King of Spain, nor any of his agents, so long as he remaineth enemy to England: neither be guilty to any conspiracy against Her Majesty's person, but reveal it if ever any such matter chance to come to my hearing. I am, and will be, as good a subject to Her Majesty for allegiance as any is in England. But such is my present state at this time that every hour presenteth a hell unto me. On the days, I go like a man distract of senses for fear of death at this instant. In the night, I cannot sleep nor take any rest: when I pray, I am discomforted, for I pray without hope to be heard because I am not of that church which I believe to be His.

Such was the quandary. This is a Catholic son writing to Protestant parents. It would be fascinating to have a letter from Donne after he became a Protestant, explaining his conversion to his Catholic mother. What did he ever say to her on this point? And who thought who was guilty of what?

Roman Catholicism in England at this period seems to have been split into two groups—an aggressive and uncompromising one, led by violent Jesuits, and one prepared to compromise and be more Fabian in tactics. Those of the latter who even occasionally conformed by attending the services of the Church of England, in order to avoid the penalties denounced against recusants, were bluntly labeled "schismatics" by the former. The moderates, for their part, felt that the activities of the extremists only did harm to all concerned, caused useless suffering, deaths like that of Henry Donne. And the more passive group to which John Donne belonged was, when it had to choose, not unaffected by loyalty to England in opposition to a Spanish-dominated papacy.

On coming of age Donne received a patrimony of about 750 pounds. When he was fined for not serving as Steward of Christmas at Lincoln's Inn in 1594 it was probably because he had set out on his travels. By Walton's account he "stayed... first in Italy and then in Spain, where he made many useful observations of those countries, their laws and manner of government, and returned perfect in their languages. The time that he spent in Spain was at his first going into Italy designed for travelling to the Holy Land and for viewing Jerusalem and the sepulchre of our Saviour. But at his being in the furthest parts of Italy, the disappointment of company or of a safe convoy or the uncertainty of returns of money into those remote parts denied him that happiness."

A visit to Spain, the archenemy, called for an explanation, and this, that Donne really wanted to go to the Holy Land (in a 1633 poem Walton said he did go), is a satisfying one, such as we can always count on from this biographer, who was in most cases passing on what the renowned Dean of St. Paul's told him (or told a mutual friend, such as Henry King or Henry Wotton). The biography is unbalanced towards piety: it was originally composed as the preface to a collection of sermons. Walton was far more interested in the reverend preacher than in the errant youth whom he had never known and whom Donne himself was glad to have shed, putting off the body of that flesh. A visit to Spain would in itself be proof that Donne in 1595 was neither an Anglican nor, in the conventional way, a patriot. It did have the consequence that he was one of the few English poets in a position to be acquainted with Spanish literature. He wrote Buckingham in 1623, "I can thus make myself believe that I am where your Lordship is, in Spain, that in my poor library, where indeed I am, I can turn mine eye towards no shelf, in any profession, from the mistress of my youth, Poetry, to the wife of mine age, Divinity, but that I meet more authors of that nation than of any other."

Donne could scarcely have stayed abroad "some years," as Walton, with his foggy sense of chronology, hazards. He was back by July 20, 1595, when he was engaged "to instruct and bring up one Thomas Danby of the age of 15 years or thereabouts." Donne as tutor in the midst of his other activities? This newly discovered fact takes getting used to. Tutoring was one of the few paying occupations a gentleman might turn to; it might or might not lead to establishing oneself with the right people. For Donne it was just one of his multifarious experiments, soon given up.

Poetry was not the only "mistress" of his youth. A new portrait was commissioned to testify to that. He did not affect to be uninterested in images of himself, but this was part of a larger artistic bent. Lines 225 26 of Satire IV fit a Bosch now in the Prado; line 70 is a more certain but less distinguished reference to Romano. Donne collected medals and paintings that were not personal; a Titian owned by him passed into the collection of Charles I. But, ever conscious of mutability, he did want something to look at—or to be looked at—after a change in him that time or travel or war might make. Now, harking back to the first portrait—or combining both portraits, that of the warrior and that of the lover—he penned Elegy V, "His Picture," passing that souvenir on to his mistress for contrast:

> When, weather-beaten, I come back, my hand
> Perhaps with rude oars torn, or sunbeams tanned, . . .
> And powder's blue stains scattered on my skin.

This looks like a poem belonging to the first half of 1596, along with Elegy XX, "Love's War," with its line, "And Midas' joys our Spanish journeys give," prompted by Sir Walter Ralegh's 1595 voyage to Guiana in quest of the gold of El Dorado. "Love's War" comes to the conclusion:

> Thousands we see which travel not
> To wars, but stay, swords, arms, and shot
> To make at home. And shall not I do then
> More glorious service, staying to make men?

Robert Burns took the same stance: "In wars at home I'll shed my blood— / Life-giving wars o' Venus; / The deities that I adore / Are social peace and plenty. / I'm better pleased to mak' one more / Than be the death o' twenty."

But the one lover went to war, after all, proving his patriotism and using his Spanish. In June of 1596 Donne took part in the greatest foray in the decade, if not in the whole of the Queen's reign—the raid on Cadiz. That important harbor in the southwest had been raided by Drake the year before the Armada, but lately the "singeing of the King of Spain's beard" had been confined to grand-scale commerce-raiding, privateering, in an undeclared war that continued until James the timorous peace-maker came to the throne. The Queen, being a woman, had herself no zest for aggressive war, which was, among other things, expensive, but at last she had been persuaded that it was time for a "royal" enterprise, a national effort. It was an impressive conglomeration that kept its rendezvous in Plymouth harbor, upwards of 150 ships of various kinds—galleons, armed merchantmen, transports, flyboats, victualers, pinnaces, manned by 5000 sailors and carrying more than 6000 soldiers, including 1000 "gentlemen voluntaries." The latter were gaily "covered with feathers, gold and silver lace." Most did not know exactly where they were going—the orders were sealed. Donne "waited upon his lordship," the Earl of

Essex, who officially shared the command with the Lord Admiral Howard, who had been in charge in '88. Howard was now sixty, white-bearded, Essex twenty-eight: in the popular view, in the preparation of, during, and after the expedition the latter was the real commander, the young aggressive tactician, the risen star to which all eyes turned. Wotton had preceded Donne in hitching his wagon to this star, and probably it was Wotton who recommended his friend, mentioning his knowledge of Spanish.

The splendid fleet set out from Plymouth, to a favoring northwest wind, June 1, only to be driven back by a squall. The gentlemen voluntaries got their feathers wet. The second departure, June 3, was successful, and when they reached Cadiz on a Sunday morning two and a half weeks later they were a complete surprise. The Spaniards' church bells jangled the alarm at 2 A.M. The English found good hunting—four great galleons with eighteen galleys, protecting some twoscore merchantmen laden with rich cargoes—mostly the West India fleet. How the mouth of Ralegh, who commanded one squadron, must have watered at the prospect. He remembered his 1592 capture off the Azores of the carrack *Madre de Dios.* It held all the materials of paradise: finished jewels; spices—"pepper, cloves, maces, nutmegs, cinnamon, green ginger;" drugs—"benjamin, frankincense, galingale, mirabolans, zocotrine and camphor;" silks—"damasks, taffetas, sarcanets, altobassos, that is counterfeit cloth of gold, unwrought China silk, sleeved silks, white twisted silk, curled cypress;" a like variety of calicoes; also "canopies and coarse diaper towels," "carpets like those of Turkey," and "elephants' teeth, porcelain, vessels of China, coconuts, hides, ebony wood as black as jet, bedsteads of the same; cloth of the rinds of trees, very strange for the matter and artificial in workmanship." Long live piracy and the Queen! Ralegh had been cut out of his proper share in 1592, but now he ventured to hope again, struggling to regain the favor he had lost when he seduced one of Elizabeth's maids-of-honor, Elizabeth Throckmorton.

The original plan was to attempt the town first, but the surf was rising dangerously, and this veteran, his eye on the treasure ships, prevailed with his advice to attack the fleet, a project that caused Essex to toss his hat into the sea for joy. Meanwhile a poet who was going to pen epigrams about the action was looking down from his post on Essex's flagship, the *Due Repulse.*

The sea fight lasted for five or six hours. "Volleys of cannon and culverins came as thick as if it had been a skirmish of musketeers." But the Spaniards' gunnery was poor. The galleons and galleys had looked for some protection from the two cannon in the Puntal Fort, which were duly fired off, whereupon one burst, the other collapsed. The four galleons in their panicky maneuvers ran aground. Two, the *St. Philip* and the *St. Thomas*, were set on fire by their commanders. Burned and blackened men poured out from the portholes of the *St. Philip*, or clung to the ropes where great flames were licking the masts. To the crackling sound of burning wood were added explosions and screams.

Donne wrote of the Dantean scene:

> Out of a fired ship, which by no way
> But drowning could be rescued from the flame,
> Some men leaped forth, and ever as they came
> Near the foes' ships, did by their shot decay;
> So all were lost which in the ship were found:
> They in the sea being burnt, they in the burnt ship
> drowned.

This is small, dispassionate cleverness, but, according to the taste of the time, added to the author's reputation for wit. The opinion of the judicious Scotch poet Drummond of Hawthornden was, "I think if he would he might easily be the best epigrammatist we have found in English, of which I have not yet seen any come near the ancients." This might be adjudged an accolade not inferior to that of being one of the sixty gentlemen knighted by the two generals for conspicuous valor—but possibly the poet, a careerist, would greatly have preferred to have come home as—and be greeted by the ladies as—Sir John Donne.

Instead of next attending to the capture of the merchantmen, helpless in the harbor of Port Royal, Essex resolved to assault Cadiz. Resistance was slight there, the fortifications unfinished. The fleeing Spanish soldiers climbed over their walls by means of piles of debris left alongside; the English followed them and opened the gates. The town was taken and given over to plunder. The English casualties in both the sea and land fighting came to no more than two hundred. The most prominent loss was Sir John Wingfield, colonel of one of the regiments. A musket ball from one of the loopholes in the castle smashed his head as he was riding on a captured jennet. On Saturday the twenty-sixth of June he was buried in the cathedral of Santa Cruz with military honors, the muzzles and pikes of the honor guard pointing downward and the generals casting their handkerchiefs "wet from their eyes" into the grave. Donne commemorated him:

> Beyond th'old Pillars many have travellèd
> Towards the Sun's cradle, and his throne, and bed.
> A fitter Pillar our Earl did bestow
> In that late island, for he well did know
> Further than Wingfield no man dares to go.

Cadiz is on an island and was often called an island. Other epigrams attributable to this adventure under "our Earl" include "Fall of a Wall" and "Cadiz and Guiana"— to Ralegh.

During the occupation a theological argument got going, for those qualified to enter it, between victors and vanquished. How useful Donne's talents could have been here! The Spanish friars, who had run up and down in vain with their crucifixes trying to rally their people, now conquered one English gentleman. William Alabaster, whose devotional sonnets, recently collected, are crude precursors of Donne's, became a Romanist. Meanwhile the

Lord Admiral and the Duke of Medina-Sidonia, who had been opponents in 1588, dickered about ransom—but the latter gave orders, successfully carried out, for the merchant fleet to be fired. All this civilized exchange of views went on in a city that had been so thoroughly pillaged, according to the rules of war, that a Spaniard who in 1599 visited Lisbon during a pestilence that carried off 40,000 could think of but one comparison: "There was nothing like it but Cadiz after the sack."

But all those treasure-ships gone up in smoke! All thirty-six. The Spaniards had offered two million ducats in ransom for them, while the English had demanded four. Now nobody had any of the millions. Curled cypress and mirabolans gone in flames or rotting in the sea! Ralegh, whose leg had been splintered, had plenty to grumble about. "What the generals have gotten I know least; they protest it is little. For mine own part, I have gotten a lame leg, and a deformed. For the rest, either I spake too late, or it was otherwise resolved."

In an expedition that, glorious as it was, did not, after all, do what it should have done for the Queen's treasury, Faro in Portugal was also raided, where the main booty was literary—the library of the bishop of Algarve. Essex burned Faro to the ground as he had burned Cadiz, but the books were carefully stowed on board to become eventually part of the newly founded Bodleian Library at Oxford. "A number of them are still recognizable bound in black calf and marked with the coat of arms of their original possessor."

Back home the gallants who had taken part in the glorious enterprise (and many who had not) sported the full square beard of the commander who was now at the peak of favor. It became known as the Cadiz-beard or Cadz-beard, and is referred to in *Henry V*: "a beard of the general's cut" (III, vi, 80).

Essex was placed in sole charge of the next piece of defensive aggressiveness against Spain, in the summer of the following year. Again Donne attended him. This 1597 adventure, known as the Islands Voyage because its object was to raid the Azores, was much less successful and was dogged by bad weather from the very start. Out of the bad weather emerged two fine poems, "The Storm" and "The Calm," either of which is worth all of Donne's epigrams put together. Ben Jonson long remembered some lines from "The Calm." "The Storm" was addressed to Christopher Brooke.

Interestingly, Donne's first surviving prose letter (the ascription to him has been doubted, but we should be sorry to lose it) is of the same month, August, 1597, as "The Storm," which is listed as the first of the "Verse Letters to Several Personages." Both epistles were written in Plymouth. Both prove that the author had "Jonas" (Jonah) as well as the bad weather on his mind, but, covering rather different topics, they form a valuable complement to each other.

The background of the prose letter is that the fleet had sailed out of Plymouth July 10, and one squadron—Lord Thomas Howard's—had cruised in sight of Cape Finisterre (Donne implies a comparison with Moses on Mount Nebo), but all were driven back by the most dangerous of a series of storms. The objection to viewing the letter as Donne's (as certainly some of the letters in the Burley manuscript are) has been that its writer was apparently not with Essex's squadron, but with the squadron that separated from the others and got within sight of Spain. But it may be that Donne was on one of those ships that Essex sent to find—and that did find—Lord Howard's squadron, in which case he would have experienced twenty days of bad sea also. Or it may be that Walton was wrong in indicating that on both the Cadiz and the Islands Voyage Donne was attached personally to Essex .... The fit of puns in the antepenultimate sentence refers to Essex's return early in August from a visit to the court: the letter must have been written the seventh or eighth.

The first act of that play which I said I would go over the water to see is done, and yet the people hiss. How

it will end I know not, *ast ego vicissim risero* [but I shall
have mocked in turn]. It is true that Jonas was in a whale's
belly three days, but he came not voluntary as I did, nor
was troubled with the stink of 150 land soldiers as we; and
I was there 20 days of so very, very bad weather that even
some of the mariners have been drawn to think it were
not altogether amiss to pray, and myself heard one of them
say "God help us!"

For all our pains we have seen the land of promise,
Spain. Whether we shall enter or no, I guess not: I think
there is a blot in their tables, but perchance 'tis not on
our dice to hit it.

We are now again at Plymouth, quasi ply-mouth—for
we do nothing but eat, and scarce that: I think when we
came in the burghers took us for the Spanish fleet, for
they have either hid or conveyed all their money. Never
was extreme beggary so extremely brave, except when a
company of mummers had lost their box. I do not think
77 Kelleys [Edward Kelley was a notorious alchemist]
could distil £ 10 out of all the town. He that hath supped
and hath 2 or 3s is a king, for none hath a crown faith.
Lands, jerkins, knighthoods are reprobate pawns, and but
for the much gay clothes (which yet are much melted) I
should think we were in Utopia: all are so utterly coinless.
In one bad bare word, the want is so general that the
Lord General wants, and till this day we wanted the Lord
General. You will pardon me if I write nothing earnest.
Salute all whom thou lovest in my name and love me as
I would deserve.

Notable is the perennial opposition between the
young poet or artist and the bourgeoisie—"the burghers."
As a matter of fact, Sir Arthur Gorges in *A Larger Relation of the Said Island Voyage* paints a very different
picture of the behavior of the merchants of Plymouth.
"During all this time of our abode in Plymouth (which
was some six or seven weeks) we neither found either want
or dearth of any manner of victuals, either in the town,
where our mariners were daily resident, or in the country,
where the land army was quartered; nor yet that extreme

manner of enhancing the prices of all things used in London, and in other places of the realm, upon the extraordinary assembling of any such great troupes." But Sir Arthur was neither bohemian, nor young, nor (his first wife having been a great heiress) penniless. Donne was spending his sizable patrimony fast.

"The Storm" begins by announcing to Brooke, in the high Renaissance vein of "one soul in bodies twain" friendship,

> Thou which art I ('tis nothing to be so),
> Thou which art still thyself, by these shalt know
> Part of our passage.

Today, friends clever with words might still indulge in the practice of exchanging verse letters, but the verse would probably be light verse. The sheer reporting in "The Storm" and "The Calm" is superb. One does not encounter anything comparable until the eighteenth century— e.g., Swift's "A Description of a City Shower." Donne's extravagant comparisons illuminate, even as they pull away from, a center, a main object—to tell what it was truly like for a landlubber to be waked up in his berth by a violent storm:

> Thousands our noises were, yet we 'mongst all
> Could none by his right name but thunder call:
> Lightning was all our light, and it rained more
> Than if the sun had drunk the sea before.
> Some coffined in their cabins lie, equally
> Grieved that they are not dead, and yet must die;
> And as sin-burdened souls from graves will creep
> At the last day, some forth their cabins peep,
> And tremblingly ask what news, and do hear so,
> Like jealous husbands, what they would not know.
> Some sitting on the hatches, would seem there
> With hideous gazing, to fear away fear.
> Then note they the ship's sicknesses, the mast
> Shaked with this ague, and the hold and waist

> With a salt dropsy clogged, and all our tacklings
> Snapping, like too-high-stretchèd treble strings.
> And from our tottered sails, rags drop down so,
>   As from one hanged in chains a year ago.

This sufficiently dampened the zest for adventure of a goodly number of the young gallants, as Gorges relates: "this violent and dangerous tempest had so cooled and battered the courages of a great many of our young gentlemen (who seeing that the boisterous winds and merciless seas had neither affinity with London delicacy nor Court bravery) as that, discharging their high plumes and embroidered cassocks, they secretly retired themselves home, forgetting either to bid their friends farewell or to take leave of their general."

But Donne stayed on for the calm that followed the storms, this too before the expedition reached its final unprofitable goal, the Azores. Gorges, who was Ralegh's captain in the *Warspite*, describes such a calm. "Whilest we were before Saint Georges [San Jorge], we were very much becalmed for a day or two, and the weather extremely hot, insomuch as the wind could not bear the sails from the masts, but were fain to hull in the sea, to our great discontentment." "The Calm" commences with a characteristic example of crabbed syntax.

> Our storm is past, and that storm's tyrannous rage
> A stupid calm, but nothing it, doth 'suage.

The reader has to stop to realize that the construction is, "A stupid calm doth assuage that storm's tyrannous rage, but nothing doth assuage it—the calm." The thought is densely packed in. Donne's proportion of thoughts to words is high, whereas in a decorative poet like Spenser (allegory apart) it is low. A differentiation began to be made between what was called masculine style or "strong lines" and feminine. Carew declared that Donne "had drawn a line / Of masculine expression." Benlowes, a minor metaphysical, boasted: "The masculine and refined pleasures of the understanding transcend the feminine and sensual of the eye."

The couplet Ben Jonson remembered was, "No use of lanthorns; and in one place lay / Feathers and dust, to-day and yesterday." Lanterns in the Admiral's poop helped to keep a squadron together, but they were plaintively superfluous on this occasion.

The most interesting part of "The Calm" from a biographical standpoint is the review of motives:

> Whether a rotten state and hope of gain,
> Or to disuse me from the queasy pain
> Of being beloved and loving, or the thirst
> Of honor or fair death, out pushed me first,
> I lose my end.

The Islands Voyage, thanks to the mismanagement of Essex, brought no gain. They had not burnt the fleet at Ferrol, treasure ships in the Azores had easily eluded them, and only Ralegh, to his commander's envy, had shown military efficiency. The ships straggled home, scattered by another storm, in October, with little to show for four months of vacillating effort. Lacking "gain," not having succeeded in attaching himself to a patron who could make particular use of his talents, any thirst for honor still unsatisfied, Donne had only got respite "from the queasy pain of being beloved and loving"—a phrase that in itself constitutes a sufficient answer to any who contend that Donne's mistresses, like Herrick's, were imaginary.

But he no longer, if he ever did, found them wholesome. "It is the nature of nice and fastidious minds to know things only to be weary of them" (Paradox I). In his twenty-sixth year Donne was a rather old young man. A few months later in a verse letter to Wotton he spoke retrospectively of "my youth's giddiest days" as if they were a hundred years behind him. The flesh was weary, alas, and he had read all the books. He was neither a Catholic nor a Protestant, nor had he found a true woman, or a career.

We do not know from what restlessness or inner discontent he had broken off his law studies, traveled even to forbidden Spain, tried tutoring, tested his luck as a gentleman soldier, spent freely his money and his energies in sundry adventures. On the Islands Voyage he had made friends with two young men who were relatives of a possible patron. The Court beckoned dazzlingly. All wealth and power and glory seemed centered there. The high road to a career was through a patron. One might win an advantageous tutorship in a lord's household or become his executive secretary. Spenser, for instance, twenty years older, had managed to get near the Earl of Leicester, had dwelt "in some use of familiarity" at Leicester House with Sir Philip Sidney. Such had been his bright beginning, but now he was a civil servant in disagreeable and dangerous Ireland. He had come down from his hopes, having in some way offended "the great." It did not pay to be outspoken. A petitioner's life was difficult, as Spenser now told others.

> Full little knowest thou that hast not tried,
> What hell it is, in suing long to bide:
> To lose good days, that might be better spent;
> To waste long nights in pensive discontent;
> To speed today, to be put back tomorrow;
> To feed on hope, to pine with fear and sorrow;
> To have thy prince's grace, yet want her peer's;
> To have thy asking, yet wait many years;
> To fret thy soul with crosses and with cares;
> To eat thy heart through comfortless despairs;
> To fawn, to crouch, to wait, to ride, to run,
> To spend, to give, to want, to be undone.

There was the voice of experience. Maybe Donne already felt old enough—and had seen enough—to believe it, but, if so, there was nothing he could do about it: it was the way of the world, and would remain so for his lifetime.

By Jonson's reckoning his best poems were behind him. They circulated widely in manuscript, had given him an undoubted reputation as a wit. Jonson himself said three seemingly contradictory things of them on his 1619 visit to Drummond: "that Donne, for not keeping of accent, deserved hanging," "he esteemeth John Donne the first poet in the world in some things," and that "Donne himself, for not being understood, would perish."

The contradiction is only apparent, for what Jonson was pointing to in all three statements myriad other readers have found. The standard view (we shall soon see that it needs modification), from Carew to modern textbooks, stresses Donne's break with the past, the smooth, mellifluous, Petrarchan, classical-mythological, woman-pedestaled high-Renaissance past. "Instead of Spenser's melody, clarity, and abundance, there are harshness, subtlety, and economy; instead of Jonson's steadiness, reasonableness, and sense of form, there are intensity, forced ingenuity, and abruptness."

From medievalism Donne leapt to modernity. As he told the Countess of Huntingdon:

> I cannot feel the tempest of a frown;
> I may be raised by love, but not thrown down.
> Though I can pity those sigh twice a day,
> I hate that thing whispers itself away . . . .
> Who first looked sad, grieved, pined, and showed his pain,
>   Was he that first taught women to disdain.

In the words of the same author's "Essay of Valor," "only by our pale asking, we teach them to deny."

Since but a half dozen of Donne's poems were published in his lifetime, it is best to imagine a contemporary turning to one of the early posthumous editions, the title page of which read: *Poems, by J. D. with Elegies on the Author's Death.* A number of the elegies were by men destined to fame, Walton, Thomas Carew, Thomas Brown—evidently the first publication of the future knight, who was to be a metaphysical in prose—the too sensitive Lord Falkland, a virtual suicide on the battlefield of the Civil War, Henry King, who was to be author

of "The Exequy" and "The Surrender" and bishop of
Chichester. The second edition, 1635, unlike the first of
1633, had the poems in the now familiar grouping and
that Marshall carving of the author with the Spanish tag
ribboned on, "Antes muerto que mudado"—"Sooner dead
than changed"—a defiant motto that proved false.

Assume the reader is using the 1635 edition or any of
the subsequent seventeenth-century editions. Assume his
critical stance is similar to Carew's Elegy and assume he
is not acquainted with European metaphysical poetry, has
not read the realistic sonnets of Michelangelo, has even
forgotten the rough measures and knotty conceits of Sir
Thomas Wyatt (indeed both poets were subjected to
smoothing out by their early editors): he turns to the first
page of text under the heading "Songs and Sonets" (but,
characteristically, there were no sonnets, no Petrarchan
quatorzains; the term was being used loosely for short
poems), and the first title is "The Flea"! This sounds so
preposterous, so unpromising for a poem, that the reader
perhaps postpones it (as modern editors do) and goes on
to the first stanza of "The Good-Morrow":

> I wonder, by my troth, what thou and I
> Did till we loved? Were we not weaned till then,
> But sucked on country pleasures, childishly?
> Or snorted we in the Seven Sleepers' den?
> 'Twas so; but this, all pleasures fancies be.
> If ever any beauty I did see,
> Which I desired, and got, 'twas but a dream of thee.

This seemed a break with the usual. In the first place, it
was colloquial. "By my troth" has the effect of an oath,
an exclamation, like Suckling's (but he was a whole generation later) "Out upon it! I have loved / Three whole
days together" or "Why so pale and wan, fond lover? /
Prithee, why so pale?" And such ugly, non-poetic words
as "sucked" and "snorted," to say nothing of the contemptuous "weaned"! What was happening to aureate
poetic diction? Was no convention sacred? One might as

well use the word "garbage": come to think of it, that fin-de-siècle product, *Hamlet*, does (I, v, 57). (*The Second Anniversary*, 82, tops this: "What fragmentary rubbidge this world is.") Moreover, the mistress was no longer merely sighed for at a Platonic distance: she was "got."

The third stanza of this three-stanza poem furrowed the brows in a different way:

> My face in thine eye, thine in mine appears,
> And true plain hearts do in the faces rest;
> Where can we find two better hemispheres
> Without sharp north, without declining west?
> Whatever dies was not mixed equally;
> If our two loves be one, or thou and I
> Love so alike that none do slacken, none can die.

What was first remarkable was the intimacy. These lovers get so close that each can see the other in the pupils of the other's eyes. This is their mystique again and again: "the glasses of your eyes"; "Our eye-beams twisted, and did thread / Our eyes upon one double string"; "I fix mine eye on thine, and there / Pity my picture burning in thine eye." Then, following a reference in the second stanza to the Renaissance discoverers of new worlds, comes that strange but apt analogy of the eyes and faces—and then the lovers—as hemispheres. (It is as stunning as calling a mistress, at the moment of physically exploring her, "O my America! my new-found-land"—Elegy XIX.) Finally, a particular philosophic doctrine is employed: "Whatever dies was not mixed equally." Scholasticism and fresh young love meet; Aquinas is put to carnal use (it should have been Abelard!): "for corruption is found only where there is contrariety." No wonder Dryden was to complain that Donne "affects the metaphysics, not only in his satires, but in his amorous verses, where nature only should reign; and perplexes the minds of the fair sex with nice speculations of philosophy, when he should engage their hearts, and entertain them with the softnesses of love."

But Dryden's is the old mindless view of love poetry—and of women. Our imagined contemporary had not, of course, read Dryden. We do know of one early reader, an Anglican clergyman, who, surprised at such output from the late dean of St. Paul's ("J. D." could be identified from the accompanying elegies), decided he must be in the presence of allegories. "The Good-Morrow" he took as addressed to God!

All readers had before them, from the publisher, what was at once a warning and an advertisement.

The Printer to the Understanders

For this time I must speak only to you: at another, *Readers* may perchance serve my turn; and I think this a way very free from exception, in hope that very few will have a mind to confess themselves ignorant.

If you look for an Epistle, as you have before ordinary publications, I am sorry that I must deceive you; but you will not lay it to my charge when you shall consider that this is not ordinary, for if I should say it were the best in this kind that ever this kingdom hath seen, he that would doubt of it must go out of the kingdom to inform himself, for the best judgments, within it, take it for granted.

So, already, the chord of cultism was struck. This poet is "not ordinary," he is for the cognoscenti, "the best judgments," for "the understanders," not hoi polloi. One of the accompanying elegies issues the same challenge: "Indeed so far above its reader, good, / That we are thought wits when 'tis understood." No one would ever say that of the ballads that used to please, of the Renaissance lyrics, "When daisies pied and violets blue," or "Cupid and my Campaspe played." Or of (though its author also scorned hoi polloi) "Drink to me only with thine eyes," with its classical clarity, its intention to be old (based as it is on some prose letters of Philostratus), its allusion to Jove, its careful keeping of a distance between lover and beloved. Donne studiously avoided anything of the sort.

But the third piece in the collection was entitled "Song," and was indubitably that. It had the lilt of a song, and the music for it survives.

> Go and catch a falling star,
>   Get with child a mandrake root,
> Tell me where all past years are,
>   Or who cleft the devil's foot;
> Teach me to hear mermaids singing,
>   Or to keep off envy's stinging,
>   And find
>   What wind
> Serves to advance an honest mind.

Incantation, a charm, with the magic number of *seven* impossibilities. What far-flung references are compounded! The universe is ransacked. Folklore rather than mythology. "Get with child a mandrake root"—what a weird fancy. The mandrake root is x-shaped, and was supposed to shriek like the human being it somewhat resembled, when pulled from the ground: "Make me a mandrake, so I may groan here" ("Twicknam Garden").

The main first impression must be how "Song" differs in attitude from "The Good-Morrow." "The Good-Morrow" is a greeting after a night of love to a true love; "Song" goes to dizzying lengths of hyperbole to proclaim that no woman can be counted on to be true:

> If thou find'st one, let me know;
>   Such a pilgrimage were sweet.
> Yet do not; I would not go,
>   Though at next door we might meet.
> Though she were true when you met her,
>   And last till you write your letter,
>   Yet she
>   Will be
> False, ere I come, to two or three.

Tenderness, a personal-seeming idolatry, has been succeeded by cynicism. "Woman's Constancy," the fourth poem, is about woman's inconstancy: "Now thou hast loved me one whole day, / Tomorrow when thou leav'st, what wilt thou say?" There is the surprise ending: he will not argue, "For by tomorrow I may think so too." And tomorrow comes: "I can love both fair and brown . . . . I can love any, so she be not true" ("The Indifferent"). The same writer attitudinized in prose in what were called, when they were published, *Juvenilia: or Certain Paradoxes and Problems*, of which the first is "A Defence of Woman's Inconstancy." "That women are inconstant, I with any man confess, but that inconstancy is a bad quality, I against any man will maintain." Sophomoric impudence! The eternal Elizabethan "boy"—rampant in Shakespeare and Nashe! One of the lyrics is called "The Paradox"—naturally. The young men at Oxford and Cambridge were trained, not to write "sincerely," but to argue well on either side, or both sides, of a controversial topic assigned them. Milton as a student almost met with the misfortune of having to defend ignorance, but he was switched to the other side just in time. Of course this practice was still truer—or falser—for budding lawyers. The second Paradox argues "That Women ought to Paint," the sixth, "That it is Possible to Find some Virtue in some Women," and the last, "That the Gifts of the Body are Better than those of the Mind." The seventh of the Problems inquires, "Why are the Fairest, Falsest?" and works out an analogy with gold—e.g., "all snatch at them, but the worst possess them," concluding that, like coins, women need the alloy of baser metal, which falseness is.

Thus it is not surprising to find that some of the poems are precise arguments or demonstrations—"A Lecture upon the Shadow," "The Flea" (which turns out to be an argument for seduction). Donne writes on all sides of the question of love. His is not a little mind hobbled by the hobgoblin of consistency. He is the poet of change. "Change is the nursery / Of music, joy, life, and eternity."

He is the poet of quick action and reaction rather than stasis; this is shown in the very structure of his English, which has more verbs in proportion to adjectives and nouns than most poets—far more than Milton, who liked to come to a conclusion and rest in it. With Donne ideas, like similes, were functional. If he said in "The Good-Morrow" "true plain hearts do in the faces rest," he took it back in "Twicknam Garden": "Alas, hearts do not in eyes shine." He changes direction in the midst of a single poem, his endings being as striking as his beginnings. His beginnings are striking indeed, pulling one at once into a dramatic situation: "Busy old fool, unruly Sun"; "For God's sake hold your tongue, and let me love"; "I am two fools, I know"; "Send home my long-strayed eyes to me." Poetically he worshiped women, and he trod upon them, and in between he covered them: there is that punning ending of "To his Mistress Going to Bed," a paean to undressing: "What need'st thou have more covering than a man." Women were the instruments of his lust, and of his revenge, and of his almost theological love. Some of the most memorable poems were metaphysical in the etymological sense—they went beyond the physical. "The Ecstasy," which has been so much analyzed and disputed in the twentieth century, is the key poem here—that word which means, literally, standing outside the body. (The second Paradox calls kissing "the strange and mystical union of souls.") There was ever the play of opposites, or what had been thought to be opposites—the concrete and the abstract, the flesh and the spirit, the beginning and the end, earth and heaven, the momentary and the eternal, mortality and immortality, the false love and the true. How much *was* play? Who can be sure of what was in jest and what was in earnest?

And what range, including forty-six different verse forms—forty-two of his own invention! And what density! A single lyric, "A Valediction: of the Book," contains references to the Sibyl, Pindar, Lucan, Homer, theology, cipher writing, Platonic philosophy, lawyers, statesmen, the Bible, alchemy, and astronomy (celestial navigation).

What is more, the references are, for the most part, teasingly obscure. It does no good to know Pindar, Lucan, and Homer well: one must identify the unnamed women· placed vis-à-vis these poets in the first stanza: Corinna, Polla Argentaria, and whoever it is "whose book (they say) Homer did find and name." This involves having in mind the right passage in Aelian or Pausanias, Apollinaris Sidonius, and possibly the *Myriobiblon* of Photius, which helpfully abstracts a work by Ptolemy Hephaestion of Alexandria.

Finally, in his unsophisticated review, our first reader could not but be struck by the conceits, the lines and similes that leapt out at him. "A bracelet of bright hair about the bone"; "I like a spied spy shook"; "the rags of time"; "That subtile knot which makes us man"; "a naked thinking heart." The spinal column is "the sinewy thread my brain lets fall / Through every part." Two separated lovers are like the circle-drawing compass, the fixed foot,' the leaning foot, joined in the center. Who but Donne, or who before Donne, would have thought of this comparison for uselessness: "a sun-dial in a grave"? (More than one seventeenth-century reader quoted it.) He can be vividly ugly: "And like a bunch of ragged carrots stand / The short swoll'n fingers of thy gouty hand." With him the springs of Helicon ceased to be rose water.

To sum up, Donne's greatest accomplishment in the turbulent last decade of the sixteenth century was to write about love realistically in a new style.

But what ever is wholly new? Recent research has put him into a European Baroque or Mannerist movement of which an omnivorous multilinguist such as Drummond of Hawthornden would have been aware. Thus a 1963 issue of *Seventeenth-Century News*, reviewing H. M. Priest's *Renaissance and Baroque Lyrics: An Anthology of Translations from the Italian, French, and Spanish*, remarks: "Certainly those old-fashioned instructors who are still teaching Donne as a highly rebellious and original poet will profit from Priest's sound insistence that in Continental poetry there are striking parallels 'for every trait or concept identified' with the Metaphysicals in England; and, in the main, they preceded Donne. Tension, distortion, imbalance, straining for novelty and the spectacular; deliberate use of rough meters, vehement expressions, imprecations, and exhortations; dramatic patterns of speech; wrenched sentence order and staccato effects; contorted phrasing and compressed thought; figures of substitution such as synecdoche; ingenuity and striving for the unexpected—all these are revealed in the poems in this volume in work prior to, and contemporary with, Donne." This does not abolish Donne's personal originality as a combiner of elements and traits that, though they can be found elsewhere, have never had the same impact before or since.

Also it is too easy to be superficial about such a poem as "The Good-Morrow." The Aristotelian turns out, on closer examination, to be a Platonist. We commence with the traditional bedroom setting of the *aube*—two lovers awakening side by side at dawn. But it is "good-morrow to our waking *souls*." The poem is on the discovery of what true, total love is like, in contrast to a previous merely sensual love. Something new has been fused, and the difference—in the language of modern science—is comparable to the difference between a physical mixture and a chemical compound. A physical mixture breaks up, as had happened with the speaker and his carnal loves before; the new entity does not break up or die. A number of the poems begin with a false lead: they appear to be merely about sexual love, but when carefully read prove to have a higher love in mind. Sometimes, also, the movement is downward, bodyward, as in "The Ecstasy."

Donne's cynicism could be attributed to his personal feelings, or his school training in debate, or his reading of Catullus, Horace, Ovid, or his playgoing. One is reminded of the reparteeing lovers in Shakespeare. Tillyard said that Donne led "the Elizabethan drama he loved into the Elizabethan lyric he despised." What has been called "colloquial" or "natural speech rhythm" might more properly be called simply "dramatic."

Donne's lesser accomplishment at this time was his satires, a form of social criticism he practiced in verse along with Everard Guilpin, who imitated, and, as we shall see, satirized him, Joseph Hall, who shared patrons with him and became a bishop, and John Marston, who also entered the church. One may appropriately quote Hall, "It is not for everyone to relish a true and natural satire, being of itself, besides the native and inbred bitterness and tartness of particulars, both hard of conceit and harsh of style."

Jonson must have had Donne's satires especially in mind when he said he should be hanged for not keeping of accent. Satire IV is verse largely by courtesy of the printer. (Pope rewrote it.) In his lyrics Donne saw to it that the rhythms of speech and certain emphases he wanted took precedence over metrical smoothness. But the Satires, including some of the Elegies that might as well be called satires (such as XI and XIV), are laboriously "hard of conceit and harsh of style," apparently because Juvenal—whose text is so corrupt—and Persius were thought to be. We do get pictures of London life and London types—the social butterfly, lawyers, the affectedly religious, the court-loving traveler, the briber. The frocked guide to Henry VIII's chapel is still there:

> "At Westminster,"
> Said I, "The man that keeps the Abbey tombs,
> And for his price doth with whoever comes,
> Of all our Harries and our Edwards talk,
> From king to king and all their kin can walk:
> Your ears shall hear naught but kings, your eyes meet
> Kings only."

The most interesting for its content is Satire III, which looks at the different denominations with detachment and presents the author's hovering attitude towards truth:

> On a huge hill,
> Cragged and steep, Truth stands, and he that will

Reach her, about must and about must go,
And what the hill's suddenness resists, win so.

The next words are remarkably prophetic:

Yet strive so that before age, death's twilight,
Thy soul rest, for none can work in that night.

But Donne was twenty-five. He knew—the saint was
his favorite church father—Augustine's prayer, "Give me
chastity and continency, only not yet!"

A revealing, if exaggerated, picture comes to us at this
time from a satirist. Everard Guilpin was an old acquaintance from Cambridge and Inns of Court days. Donne
wrote him, perhaps as far back as 1593, one of the
pleasantest of his verse letters, begging for Parnassian
fruits from him as a native of Suffolk then living in the
suburb of Highgate: "Bless us with Suffolk's sweets, and
as it is / Thy garden, make thy hive and warehouse this."

But by the time Donne had returned from the Essex
expeditions there was an alienation, and it was not
"Suffolk's sweets" that Guilpin delivered in his
Skialetheia—"The Shadow of Truth," printed early in
1598.

With them in rank La volto Publius,
Who's grown a reveller ridiculous.
And for his dad with chemic usury
Turned iron to sterling, dross to land and fee,
And got so by old horse-shoes, that the fool
Entered himself into the dancing-school;
Thinks scorn to speak: especially now since
H'hath been a player to a Christmas prince.
When these and such like do themselves estrange,
I never muse at their fantastic change:
Because they are phantasma's butterflies,
Inconstant, but yet witless Mercuries.
I know some of their humorous near of kin,
Which scorn to speak to one which hath not been

In one of these last voyages: or to one
Which having been there, yet (though he hath none)
Hath not a Cades-beard: though I dare swear
That many a beardless chin hath marchèd where
They durst not for their beards come, though they dare
Come where they will not leave their beards one hair.
But I do wonder what estrangeth thee,
New cast in mold of deep philosophy,
Thee whom that Queen hath taught to moderate
Thy mounting thought, not to be elevate
With puffingst fortunes, though (for aught I know)
Thy fortunes are none such to puff thee so.

It is surprising how much Guilpin remembers of Donne's
long-dead father, the ironmonger who indeed did well in
real estate. As for the old acquaintance, he now seems
foppish and snobbish: the dandiacal impression given by
Baker is confirmed. He had money, but is probably
running out. His study of philosophy has done him little
good. "H(e) hath been a player to a Christmas prince"
tells us that Donne did some amateur acting—perhaps at
the Christmas show of 1597—98 at Lincoln's Inn, where
he had once been appointed Steward of Christmas. (One
of the aphorisms in Donne's "News from the Very Country"
is "That only Christmas Lords know their ends.") Maybe
he had taken a female part. "La volto Publius"—the
"turned about" Publius—points to a feminine role.
Guilpin does not choose his sobriquets at random. He
satirizes the populace-courting Essex as "Felix," "Happy,"
because of a belief that the family name Devereux meant
that—"devenir heureux" or simply "heureux." The most
prominent Roman with the praenomen Publius was
Publius Clodius Pulcher, a dissolute young patrician
(Cicero's enemy, Caesar's friend) who, disguised as a
female musician, attended the Bona Dea mysteries meant
only for women. Guilpin has split Donne into several
characters (the satirist's safeguard against accusations).

To what extent may Donne's poems, especially the
love poems, be employed to document what Walton

modestly called his "irregular youth"? That incomplete angler would be the last person to supply incriminating details, if he was possessed of any, and no one else has done so—unless the poet himself. Biographers abhor a vacuum. Sir Edmund Gosse, followed by Fausset, decided that "there is hardly a piece of his genuine verse which, cryptic though it may seem, cannot be prevailed upon to deliver up some secret of his life and character." The major result of such coaxing of the oracle is the tracing of a "deplorable but eventful liaison" that began "in the summer of 1596." "We can reconstruct the story almost without danger of a mistake." (!) (The one poem Gosse did *not* ponder is "The Curse": "Whoever guesses, thinks, or dreams he knows / Who is my mistress, wither by this curse.") With wonderful confidence, by picking and choosing from poems the very chronology of which is impossible of determination, the 1899 biographer works out the whole adulterous affair to his own undoubted satisfaction, from the first kindling sight of the rich, deformed man's not very intelligent spouse until the lover's "volcanic passion sinks back into its crater" with splutterings of hate "now quickly subsiding into a heap of the ashes of indifference and satiety."

A test case is Elegy I, entitled "Jealousy," commencing "Fond woman, which would'st have thy husband die." How literally should it be taken? The husband is seen, possibly, as a hunchback, like Sir Robert Cecil, whom the Queen appointed Secretary instead of Essex's candidate while Essex and Donne were on the Cadiz voyage.

> We must not, as we used, flout openly,
> In scoffing riddles, his deformity;
> Nor at his board together being sat,
> With words, nor touch, scarce looks, adulterate.
> Nor when he, swoll'n and pampered with great fare,
> Sits down and snorts, caged in his basket-chair,
> Must we usurp his own bed any more,
> Nor kiss and play in his house, as before.

From this passage Gosse derives the information, "The husband was a deformed man, and was stationary all day in a basket-chair." But this may not even be a correct reading of the words. "Deformity" may mean only ugliness, as it does in the next elegy, on a hideous mistress: it is easy enough for any husband (this one may be old, or have warts, or a crooked nose) to seem ugly to the lover and the unfaithful wife. Nor is it a necessary, or even a plausible, assumption that the husband was some sort of cripple helplessly "stationary all day in a basket-chair." What has happened to the husband is that, having eaten and drunk heavily, he has fallen asleep. "Snorts"—that ugly word again—means snores. Except for the first couplet above, the lines bear a suspicious resemblance to some quoted by Grierson from Ovid's *Amores*. The last three of these offer the advice to the wife: "While he is drinking, secretly refill his cup if you can. If we can get him to lie thoroughly prostrate from sleep and wine, the situation and place will tell us what to do." So not only do we have our supposedly autobiographical, triangle-entangled author failing to particularize on the "deformity," and never mentioning it in any other poem, but we catch him imitating Ovid and, as Gosse himself notes, Propertius, in the elegies, each one of which, like the lyrics, tells a different story, with apparently different characters. This would give Donne seventy-five mistresses; do we prefer the opposite extravagance of fancying that we discern one well?

The actual figure for this dandiacal "great visitor of ladies" lies somewhere in between, doubtless. All that we can say is that Donne had enough amatory experience to be able to write his poems. He had enough to be able to assert, "Love's not so pure and abstract as they use / To say, which have no mistress but their Muse." Joan Bennett steers a proper medium: "His *Songs and Sonets* and the *Elegies* may be dramatic or they may be subjective, more probably they are a mixture of the two, for experience and detachment are equally essential to a poet. Donne had enough experience to realize love's many moods, from the most brutally cynical to the most idealistic, and enough dramatic power to escape from the limits of anecdote into the expanses of poetry. That he scorned, hated, lusted after, loved, worshipped, there can be little doubt for anyone who has read his poetry; and his biography confirms it." This critic points out, perhaps a little too triumphantly, that "Break of Day" is actually put into the mouth of a woman. This (not counting "Self-Love") is the only one of the Songs and Sonnets and the Elegies that is, and is the exception from which one can infer either that Donne was egocentric or that he found male personae more natural or interesting to assume. Gosse might say that the poet heard these words when he rose from a woman's side one morning, pleading business. Our overall conclusion should be that the most successful of the poems have the ring of authenticity, that we are hearing the many-mooded voice of experience, but that, unfortunately for the biographer, it is a hopeless task to extract from such nebulous, volatile, and mercurial matter lost facts, specific episodes, faceless and nameless mistresses.

One final excess must be dealt with—the excess of insisting that Donne had no youthful excesses, of crediting him with no mistresses at all. This is an attractive stance to the sophisticated and to English professors. The former, who of course are aware of the assault by the "new criticism" on "the personal heresy," know that the connection between literature and life can be so tenuous as to be untraceable. The latter—quite apart from whether they are ivory-towered and old and dry—are glad to play down with skepticism what their adolescent students are all too prone to play up—the carnality of poets. It is altogether wholesome to take every opportunity to point out that genius—the best genius—not only modifies for purposes of art the raw material of life; it can even perform the miracle of creation *ex nihilo*: imagine perfectly what others can report on only from experience. Besides, a mere longing can create an extremely erotic poem: it, especially, can. Both the sophisticated and the English professors, having seen enough of vulgarity, get themselves into the esthetic position of wishing all authors to be nameless, dateless, and lifeless—that is, biography-less, since the alleged facts are so often put to such crude use, in the classroom and elsewhere. T. S. Eliot, for instance, in a 1931 essay reacts against Gosse by wondering if Donne did not pretend to have been wilder than he ever was. "It is pleasant in youth to think that one is a gay dog, and it is pleasant in age to think that one *was* a gay dog." This makes of the Dean of St. Paul's a sort of Justice Shallow. "We have heard the chimes at midnight." This goes against the grain of that painfully repentant figure, whom the thought of sin made sick, who, far from being inclined to boast of his youthful rakishness, felt such embarrassment as led him "in later years to disguise the footprints of his earlier indiscretions." These last are the words of Grierson, who yields to none as a close student of the writer in question.

Donne, looking back in a 1625 letter, said of his verses: "I did best when I had least truth for my subjects." Is this defensive—as defensive, say, as the disclaimers always prefixed to *romans à clef*? Is it the lover of paradoxes again—anything for a paradox? Is it virtuous contempt for those by-gone "subjects"? Is it the man of imagination warning against literal interpretations? Such are the complexities of the case, it could be a mixture of all four.

We must give due attention to Walton. That prim man does not tell us much, but he drops a sufficiency in the way of hints. First, on two separate occasions he quotes the oral words of Donne: "Some irregularities of my life have been so visible to some men, . . . though I have, I thank God, . . . by the assistance of His grace banished them my affections." "I cannot plead innocency of life, especially of my youth." We are given a glimpse of Donne's early habits: "in his irregular youth to neglect the visible practice of" Christianity; "in the most unsettled days of his youth, his bed was not able to detain him beyond the hour of four in a morning; and it was no common business that drew him out of his chamber till past ten. All which time was employed in study, though he took great liberty after it." There are also some hints that the poems owe a good deal to "nature," and this perhaps is to be taken in conjunction with the summing up: "He was by nature highly passionate, but more apt to reluct at the excesses of it." "Highly passionate" may have more than one meaning, all at the opposite pole from phlegmatic. But the really decisive touch in the midst of many ambiguities comes (this is typical of Walton) as part of a commendation: "Now the English Church had gained a second St. Au(gu)stine, for, I think, none was so like him before his conversion." Anyone who has so much as dipped into the *Confessions* will have no trouble recalling what "the *infirmities*" of "*his* youth" (the words are still Walton's, italics supplied) were. A 1958 book describes Augustine as "obsessed with the ravages which unbridled sexuality produces in human beings." Moreover, as we shall see but as Walton does not tell us, Donne was accused by his father-in-law of having a rakish past—and was unable to issue (we have his letter) an unequivocal denial at a time when his whole future was at stake. Then, if ever, was the golden opportunity to rise in virtuous indignation and scotch all rumors once and for all, the rumors that Walton feebly ventilates.

Finally, there is the ventilating that Donne himself does in his sermons. This vast body of evidence should become better known, now that the sermons are back in print again for the first time in a hundred years. Addressing old classmates, old playmates, when he returned, as official chaplain, to that scene of his youthful gaiety, Lincoln's Inn, he realized that hypocrisy before *that* audience would be worse than useless. They knew or had heard too much about him. He took the course of painful openness, bursting out: "I preach but the sense of God's indignation upon mine own soul, in a conscience of mine own sins, I impute nothing to another that I confess not of myself, I call none of you to confession to me—I do but confess myself to God, and you. I rack no man's memory, what he did last year, last week, last night—I only gather into my memory and pour out in the presence of my God and His Church the sinful history of mine own youth." Thus Theodore Gill in 1958 felt justified in saying: "Far more than in his poems, the variety and thoroughness of Donne's youthful profligacy comes through in his sermons." Whether or not this is putting it too strongly, there is one exceedingly suspicious recurrence in the sermons, namely warning against the danger and the sin of remembering one's past sin with delight: "first we rock it by tossing and tumbling it in our fancies and imaginations." (This is what Pepys did with servant girls: he tossed and tumbled them.) Donne comes back to this caveat so often, so obsessively, as to make it sound like a personal problem. What insidiously pleasurable memories can he be referring to but the sins of the flesh? The one All Saints' Day sermon spells it out: "*The spirit of fornication*, that is, some remembrance of the wantonness of my youth."

Having received more than enough of education and having proved his genius, the worldly but tormented young man of twenty-five had the good fortune to find a satisfactory patron. At last he was on the first rung of the ladder of a career. But that same "highly passionate" nature of his (the *sine qua non* of his genius) was to fling him abruptly down.

He passed as frivolous in his pursuit of "the sport": "Let me love none, no, but the sport." It was like hunting.

> I spring a mistress, swear, write, sigh, and weep:
> And the game killed, or lost, go talk and sleep.

Thus he shrugged his shoulders.

He must be judged as the Elizabethan that he unsurpassably was. In the words of John Hayward, "His unabashed delight in describing sensual pleasure may shock the prudish, but will not surprise those who recognize in this gratification of the senses an essential quality of Renaissance man." In an expansive age Jack Donne did not practice self-denial; he strenuously reacted against abnegation. He flung himself into a variety of typical experiences. As a distinguished historian, G. M. Trevelyan, observes, "The Elizabethan English were in love with life, not with some theoretic shadow of life." This meant that they were both amorous and materialistic. Even gentle Shakespeare was no exception. He was keenly interested in making money, and when he had done so he bought the largest house in Stratford, with a sixty-foot frontage and three stories and five gables and ten fireplaces and a bay window facing the garden, to which in due course he retired to live at his ease. As for his sportiveness, John Manningham, a young templar, tells of an assignation that the playwright overheard the actor Richard Burbage make with a citizen's wife (compare Elegy XIV) at the time that Burbage was starring as Richard III. Shakespeare got to the apartment first, and when Burbage arrived and said that Richard III was at the door, Shakespeare sent down word that William the Conqueror came before Richard the Third. The story is worthy of Jack Donne; but the point is that it is worthy of Shakespeare, or of any other wit of the time. For future comparison, be it noted that the man from Stratford, having married and had three children by his wife, was content to leave her and go up to London and live there without her for twenty years.

It remained to be seen how Donne would behave if he married. Meanwhile he passed as frivolous, arrogant, sensual, irresponsible, self-centered, and ambitious. Like most extremely clever youths, he easily proved annoying to those less clever than he, that is, just about everybody: he still does. A modern English professor has berated him in print as "one of the most egregious and offensive young coxcombs that even the Elizabethan age produced." It remained to be seen what other qualities the whirligig of time would bring to the surface.

2 / *The Secret Marriage*

It was Donne's sophistication that he could write about matters that were of large concern to him as if they were not. (Presumably the obverse was also part of his genius— that he could make fictitious situations seem personal.) The reader, knowing his Satires are early, probably the earliest of the Elizabethan ventures in this genre, would expect Donne to leave the Catholic predicament out (because it touched him so nearly) or to sneak in transparently sympathetic references. But if in II he dropped the remark (a remark that could be interpreted as kind— or contemptuous) that "papists" were "not worth hate," in III he makes the accusation of mere antiquarianism: Mirreus seeks Religion "at Rome—there, because he doth know / That she was there a thousand years ago." In IV the recusancy fine is mentioned: "Glaze, which did go / To 'a mass in jest, catched, was fain to disburse / The hundred marks, which is the statute's curse." No one can say that this is other than dramatic: that is, the fine is a curse from Glaze's point of view, since he now has to pay it. Into V, on the corruptibility of judges, enters the pursuivant (also lightly mentioned in IV), the official police raider:

                    Would it not anger
            A Stoic, a coward, yea a martyr,
            To see a pursuivant come in, and call
            All his clothes copes; books, primers; and all
            His plate chalices, and mistake them away,
            And ask a fee for coming?

Here is the agent of death (death for an uncle and death
for a brother) being put to purely literary use, for the
purpose of an analogy. Donne maintains Olympian
detachment, losing himself and the reader in the exaggerated side issue of unlawful attachment of goods. Similarly,
the poet writes to Wotton in 1597 or 1598 of the "Court's
hot ambitions," as if he himself were looking on from the
cool moon. Actually he was in the thick of striving. It was
the age of ambition, and he was of it, not just in it, to
the length and depth of his talent. He had spent, and now
it was necessary to earn, and be recognized.

How to catch the eye of a patron? Go on an expedition with his son and stepson. This is what Donne did
when he sailed to the Azores. He made friends with the
well-connected Thomas Egerton and Francis Wooley. The
former conducted himself so well that Essex knighted him
for gallantry. He was the elder son—and Francis Wooley
was the stepson—of Sir Thomas Egerton, who presently
"taking notice of" Donne's "learning, languages, and other
abilities, and much affecting his person and behavior,"
made him his "chief secretary."

Egerton was an alumnus and benefactor of Lincoln's
Inn, where Donne had studied for two and a half years;
Donne had been entered there less than a month when
Queen Elizabeth appointed Egerton her Attorney-General.
He had been Solicitor-General since 1581: the story goes
that the Queen, having heard him plead against the
Crown, decided the only recourse was to have him on her
side: "In my troth he shall never plead against me again."
He was knighted after his 1592 advancement, and gained
appointment as Master of the Rolls in 1594. On May 6,
1596, this brilliant lawyer in his mid-fifties rose still higher

to be Lord Keeper of the Great Seal and a member of the
Privy Council. Lord Keeper was the highest honorary
position a lawyer could attain: it involved the charge of
Her Majesty's seal, which, the size of a barrow-wheel, was
borne before him in a brocaded purse on his way to and
from court. The Lord Keeper had pride of place in pro-
cessions and ceremonies over everyone except the Archbishop of Canterbury. No action in the courts could
commence without a writ issuing under the Great Seal. On
being affixed to public edicts and documents, it made them
official. In simultaneous possession of more than one
lucrative post, installed in the Lord Keeper's official residence, York House in the Strand, Sir Thomas had need
for—and could well afford—a conscientious secretary.

He was no friend to papists, however. He had taken
part in the trial of Mary Queen of Scots, had prosecuted
Campion and the weak-willed Earl of Arundel (whom we
shall find Donne mentioning), and when Lord Chancellor
under James was to treat both Catholics and Puritans
with conspicuous severity. We must conclude that in 1597
Donne, if he had not yet entered the Anglican fold (and
it is very possible that he had), was aggressively nothing,
was regarded as "safe" and unembarrassing in his religion,
or his astute employer would never have taken him into
his household. "Nor did his Lordship in this time of
Master Donne's attendance upon him account him to be
so much his servant as to forget he was his friend; and to
testify it, did always use him with much courtesy, appoint-
ing him a place at his own table, to which he esteemed his
company and discourse to be a great ornament."

Besides being a good companion, a good courtier,
Donne handled his master's correspondence, copied letters
in his neat legible script, helped compose them, made
translations, aided official business with his presence and,
when asked, his advice. It was an important post, a most
promising beginning. Donne gave full satisfaction.

Satire V shows him basking. First he refers to
Elizabeth: "Greatest and fairest empress"; then to
Egerton: "You, Sir, whose righteousness she loves, whom

I, / By having leave to serve, am most richly / For service paid."

Meanwhile he had his eye on a girl, Wooley's cousin. Wooley was the son of the Lord Keeper's second—and current—wife, Elizabeth, née More, the widow of Sir John Wooley. Her favorite niece was Anne More, who lived intermittently at York House, for her mother was dead. Her father was Sir George More of Loseley in Surrey, an irascible man appropriately destined to be Lieutenant of the Tower. Sir George found his sister's residence a convenient place to stay when he was in Westminster and was glad enough, while his aged father was alive and thus head of the household at Loseley, to lend his third daughter in virtual adoption. In 1598 she was fourteen. But that was not too young for interest in those accelerated days. Juliet was fourteen: if you cared for high-flown romantic poetry you could go over to Shoreditch and see her, played by a boy. Donne, contemplating Anne More, was thinking of doing some poems in a different vein from his cynical ones.

The years 1598-1600 were the years of Essex's decline, sad years for such wise friends of the Earl as the Lord Keeper and a former Lord Keeper's son, Francis Bacon, both of whom purveyed prudent advice in vain. The reckless favorite's vanity, knowing no limits, at last affected his loyalty; he was heading for a traitor's end. But first it was necessary to his paranoid destiny that he further demonstrate his ineffectualness in the field. He failed where better Englishmen than he had failed before him—in the bogs and woods of Ireland. He wasted time—six months in all—and he wasted men. A victim jointly of inept leadership and the Irish rebels was young Thomas Egerton, who gave final proof of his gallantry by getting killed in August, 1599.

To such a loss Donne refers in a verse epistle to Wotton, in Ireland as Essex's secretary. His own military adventuring safely over, the poet, who took friendship and letter-writing seriously, complains about lack of written word, worries "lest your waking mind should be a prey /

To lethargies." This he presents as the unforgivable sin. "Better cheap / I pardon death (who though he do not reap, / Yet gleans he many of our friends away)." Wotton replied with equal stoutness, "Sir, It is worth my wondering that you can complain of my seldom writing, when your own letters come so fearfully as if they tread all the way upon a bog. I have received from you a few, and almost every one hath a commission to speak of divers of their fellows, like you know whom in the old comedy that asks for the rest of his servants. But you make no mention of any of mine, yet it is not long since I ventured much of my experience unto you in a long piece of paper, and perhaps not of my credit; it is that which I sent you by A. B., whereof till you advertise me I shall live in fits or agues." Such were the worries of attempting to exchange letters in those days: it took luck, or the most careful arrangement, for them to arrive. And a loss of choicest news—or expressions—was serious: carbon copies were as unknown as post offices.

The same metaphor of such a death as young Egerton's as a gleaning occurs in a prose letter of Donne's, likewise written to a friend in Ireland in the summer of 1599. Fortune "hath gleaned lately many of my dearest friends, as though it were fault enough to love me." The friend addressed was a new one—Wotton had been the intermediary—who had sent over a "kind letter" that won warm wishes for the young campaigner's return. "I would be sorry you should stay long in the loathsomeness of Ireland, for death and misery is in fashion there, and much worn by the best men, whom I fear lest you should too much imitate and do as they do, die." The conclusion is in the best tradition of Elizabethan "courtesie": "Sir, amongst all your oldest friends you have none more gladder of your love than I, and this youth of my friendship hath such strength that I hope it shall grow to have experience with yours. And so, full of a thankful desire to see you, I rest."

Essex, instead of conquering and capturing the arch-rebel Tyrone in Ulster, made a truce with him. Wotton served as one of the negotiators. Then, the end of September, the lord general, against his monarch's express command, quit Ireland, sneaked home with a few of his followers as armed guard. The first news the Queen had of this came when he surprised her in her bedchamber, with her hair about her face. She weathered this crisis with remarkable self-command, sending him away in his muddy clothes. After conferring with her Council she had him put under house arrest.

His gaoler was the Lord Keeper, the house of his enforced residence from October 1, 1599, to March 20, 1600, was York House. There, in that huge mansion in Westminster, Donne had a chance to become better acquainted with that enigmatic, hubristic figure, who, charming but overwrought and indecisive, may have served as the model for Hamlet. Indeed Shakespeare, if the Earl of Southampton was still his patron, belonged to the Essex faction, and may have bidden him a cryptic farewell in the last seventy lines of that 1601 play. He had gone out of his way to mention him and his popularity in the Prologue to the fifth act of *Henry V*, written in that summer of hope, 1599, when all eyes were turned to the "loving likelihood" of "the general of our gracious empress . . . from Ireland coming, / Bringing rebellion broachèd on his sword." O what a falling off was there!

As for Wotton, he had no intention of seeing the rest of the tragedy played out with himself too near. It was time to dissociate himself, "knowing treason to be so comprehensive." He went off to the country, and ultimately abroad. Another secretary of the Earl's was hanged.

The two friends continued to correspond with an elaborate formality that makes hollow reading today. They exchanged compliments and self-deprecations, according to the manner of the time. One missive[1] from Donne to Wotton contains no news, although Donne and Essex had been under the same roof for some weeks. It just pirou-

[1]See Letter I, Appendix.

ettes. Another[2] is a rarity in Donne's production as being something of a news-letter and shrewdly sizes up the imprisoned Essex's illness as in part psychogenic: "he conspires with it."

We have the mixed blessing of some two hundred letters attributed to Donne, far more than survive from any of his literary contemporaries. What would we give for even one from Shakespeare or Marlowe! But we might be disappointed, finding it no more interesting than—or even different from—a dedication. Donne's two hundred, by and large, are disappointing. Most of them, whatever else they are, are ornate exercises in etiquette: sometimes they are nothing else. The heading of one in the Sir Tobie Mathews collection fits all: "A Kind of Labored Compliment to a Friend of His." It is his poems that are colloquial. Literary, the letters are not concerned with literature. Contemporary poets are never mentioned. Arrogant in his originality, this poet had as his only friend among his peers that rugged individualist Ben Jonson. Rarely does Donne make even a passing allusion to his own literary productions.

For this reason two letters of around 1600 are of exceptional interest. Each ends by discussing a famous Italian author; what is better, each begins by saying something about Donne as an author. The first,[3] on the Paradoxes, with its allusion in the next-to-last paragraph to that ribald satirist Aretino, indicates that Donne is conscious enough of the boldness of some of his own verses. His attitude continued to be one of discreet tolerance: such things are neither to be published nor extinguished, but to circulate, the product of "a free spirit," among his friends. Actually, wider circulation was attained, even by the Paradoxes and Problems: it was no intimate friend who quoted one of the former in his diary in 1603. Donne went on with his writing of the latter, at least, well into the first decade of the new century, frivolous activity or

[2]See Letter II, Appendix.
[3]Letter III, Appendix.

not. Thirteen escaped into print in a Latin version published in Holland in 1616.

The second letter,[4] with its slight at "the manners of other popes," does not come, one would think, from a papist. On the other hand, more markedly than in the Satires, there is sympathy for the prosecuted or persecuted Catholic, in this case Philip Howard, Earl of Arundel, who died in 1595 after ten years in the Tower. Donne may have known him, difficult as that would have been. He says in Chapter III of *Pseudo-Martyr*, "For so at a consultation of Jesuits in the Tower in the late Queen's time, I saw it resolved that in a petition to be exhibited to her she might not be styled sacred." This fits *An Humble Supplication to Her Majesty* by Robert Southwell, the Jesuit poet and propagandist, who served as Arundel's chaplain and lived in Arundel House in the Strand—until he was executed.

The "Petruccio" reference to Arundel reveals that the "great frequenter of plays" had seen *The Taming of the Shrew* (not available in print), even as it would have been his duty as well as his pleasure to be in attendance with the Lord Keeper in the amphitheatrical great Hall of Whitehall when, January 6, 1600, *Twelfth Night* had its lavish premiere. The Queen was determinedly gay that Christmas season.

During this dark period of the Earl of Essex's downfall, Donne gave sufficient signs of where his sympathies lay. A courtier himself, he is critical of the court; like a Roman moralist he deplores his place and time. One phrase is "the corruption of these times." One letter begins, "In this sickly dotage of the world where virtue languisheth in a banishment." Is "virtue" the Earl? "It is as dangerous to have virtue in this world as it will be to have wanted it in the next." Another letter ends, "at Court, where you shall find me (a miracle in that place) your honest friend." This is partly the satirist again: "I know it a fault to commend a thing so much out of

[4] IV, Appendix.

fashion as honesty." But a particular situation lies behind the letters of this period, a situation in which the friends of Essex can scarcely avoid critical thoughts of the Queen, the aged moon whose cold light no longer shone on her erstwhile favorite. Expression of such thoughts had of course to be guarded, since an epistle could so easily fall into the wrong hands. "The courts and seats of princes are the hearts of all realms, which, taking form from their humors, are more or less corrupted as they confine or enlarge their own wills: when I speak of the wills of princes I speak of very unlimited things.... Thus it must be till we get above the moon, whose motions, as some have ingeniously erred, do make us variable." Clever, this, on the surface an allusion to astrology: but unmistakable to the recipient as a reference to a willful and fickle monarch. No need to supplement it with another letter expressing the hope "that we may sometimes together privately speak of the course of these worldly things which are governed with so much instability." Once Shakespeare also dared a topical allusion to the instability of England's "mortal moon." It was all very well for Falstaff to pun, "Let us be Diana's foresters, gentlemen of the shade, minions of the moon; and let men say we be men of good government, being governed, as the sea is, by our noble and chaste mistress the moon, under whose countenance we steal." But Prince Hal's reply is something else again, a palpable hit: "Thou sayest well, and it holds well too; for the fortune of us that are the moon's men doth ebb and flow like the sea, being governed, as the sea is, by the moon."

Even if Donne had had no sympathy for his former commander, whose health had ebbed with his fortune, it would have been the part of courtesy, or the office of friendship—his "second religion"—to show, in letters to Wotton, an interest in the Earl's fate. The Earl is "your Lord." However, there is every reason to believe that the sympathy was deeply genuine and darkened for Donne, as for many others, the last years of the Queen's reign. Feet of clay or not, this still young idol (like Philip Sidney, whose widow he married, he never reached thirty-four) had been the dashing representative of England's glory for a decade.

Meanwhile Donne's present Lord, the Lord Keeper, was doing his duty, both as gaoler and as prosecutor. Friendship was one thing, but the authority of the Queen, the State, had to be upheld. (Could Donne deny this? He did not do so with Catholic nonjurors.) In the Star Chamber on November 29, 1599, Egerton was the first to speak. He set forth with great lucidity the charges against Essex, ending with that of insubordination. Other Privy Councillors added details. But official decision was postponed. On March 20, 1600, Essex, whose long confinement at York House had become a nuisance from which Egerton had more than once pleaded to be relieved, was allowed to return to his own house, which was nearby. But he was still not allowed out: Sir Richard Berkley was given all the keys. Eventually he was permitted to walk in the garden. Censure was rendered at York House on June 5. The Lord Keeper opened the case for the Crown; Francis Bacon completed it. Bacon, who had been patronized by Essex, did not, as Queen's Counsel, have anything like Egerton's official obligation to be active against him. But his speech, which began by mentioning their friendship, proved to be an extremely effective indictment and added two deadly points that had not been made before, points which hovered over treason.

Bacon, called by Alexander Pope "the wisest, brightest, meanest of mankind," was right insofar as he pointed the finger at Essex's dangerous tendencies. Although clemency prevailed with the Queen, and the Earl, after having been kept dangling for eleven months, was set at liberty on August 26, he was not much happier. He was forbidden the court. He was in debt for 16,000 pounds, and his lucrative farm of sweet wines was a grant that was expiring and that the Queen might not renew. She in fact did not. An Earl without a proper income was ruined more than ordinary men. Essex was ready to listen to desperate counsels. Cuffe, his secretary, whispered them. It was a pity that the sensible Wotton was not at the other ear.

In every way except the religious way, the year 1601, the first year of the new century, was the most eventful year of Donne's life. It was the year of Essex's rebellion and execution. It was the year of the strange long poem *Metempsychosis: The Progress of the Soul*. It was the year that "John Dunn, Esquier," presumably the poet, served in Parliament, what was destined to be the last of Elizabeth's parliaments. And it was the year of what Walton denominates "the remarkable error of his life"— his marriage.

No one knows for certain what Essex had in mind that Sunday of February 8 when he trooped through the City with his followers, shouting, "For the Queen! For the Queen! A plot is laid for my life." The previous afternoon the players at the Globe had been paid forty shillings to present *Richard the Second*—with its deposition scene. Locked up in Essex House that Sunday morning was a deputation that had come from the Queen, headed by the Lord Keeper. At first they had had trouble being admitted. "The gates of the house were shut upon the dignified envoys, but, after some stay," as Gosse recreates the scene, "they were let in by the wicket, although all their servants were kept out. It was an exciting crisis, and Donne, shut outside, would, as his master entered, see for a moment the whole courtyard full and buzzing like a wasp's nest with malcontents, while Essex himself, half demented, was shouting and gesticulating in the midst of his creatures. Further into the adventure, one of the most picturesque in our social history, we must not proceed, since whoever was present when the Queen's envoys were guarded with cocked muskets in Essex's inner apartments, Donne certainly was not. But to him who had waited upon Essex, and experienced in the easy life of travel the fascination of his character, all these events must have been among the most poignant which he had to encounter; and their culmination on the scaffold, when Essex was executed on the twenty-fifth of February, an epoch in the life of Donne."

Donne reacted by writing *The Progress of the Soul*, a satiric poem, "poema satyricon," dated August 16, 1601. The prefatory Epistle is heavily sarcastic. The author wonders "if any colors can deliver a mind so plain, and flat, and through-light [transparent] as mine." He stands on his originality, as in that letter beginning, "I am no great voyager in other men's works." Now "when I begin this book, I have no purpose to come into any man's debt." The book, the epic, never got beyond the first canto, 520 lines, but it stands out not only for its length, though nobody before the twentieth century is on record as praising it with the important exceptions of De Quincey and Browning.

Jonson told Drummond: "The conceit of Donne's Transformation or Metempsychosis was that he sought the soul of that apple which Eve pulled, and thereafter made it the soul of a bitch, then of a she-wolf, and so of a woman. His general purpose was to have brought in all the bodies of the heretics from the soul of Cain, and at last left it in the body of Calvin. Of this he never wrote but one sheet, and now, since he was made Doctor, repenteth highly and seeketh to destroy all his poems." But Calvin is never mentioned in the poem, though Luther is. It is the great reigning Queen, arch-heretic, the persecutor of Catholics and of Essex, whom Donne had in mind as the errant soul's final host, as the seventh stanza—which draws on the moon figure again—proves:

> For the great soul which here amongst us now
> Doth dwell, and moves that hand and tongue and brow
> Which, as the moon the sea, moves us; to hear
> Whose story with long patience you will long
> (For 'tis the crown and last strain of my song),
> This soul to whom Luther and Mahomet were
> Prisons of flesh, this soul which oft did tear,
> And mend, the wrecks of th'Empire and late Rome,
> And lived when every great change did come,
> Had first in Paradise a low but fatal room.

"Crown" is doubtless a pun. So perhaps is the poem's title. The Queen was on one of her ceremonious "progresses"— those expensive visitations of hers—in July and August. In any case the vein of misogyny in the poem is deep and persistent, right up to the penultimate stanza, when the soul becomes the embryo of Cain's sister and wife, Themech: "she knew treachery, / Rapine, deceit, and lust, and ills enow / To be a woman." It all hovers in the neighborhood of attacking the woman-ruler. There could be no other personal basis for it in the year that the poet gave unmistakable proof that he was deeply in love. As Grierson notes, "Women and courtiers are the chief subject of Donne's sardonic satire in this poem, as of Shakespeare's in *Hamlet*"—also, in all probability, a product of the summer of 1601. Jonson got nearer the poem's goal in *Cynthia's Revels*, acted this year, than in his conversation eighteen years later with Drummond. In the first scene Cupid speaks of "some black and envious slanders hourly breathed against" Cynthia, the moon-goddess, "for her divine justice on Actaeon." Essex is "Actaeon" because of that notorious incursion into the Queen's bedchamber on his return from Ireland.

Before entering its first human being, the soul that began in the forbidden apple in paradise (where also the tree of Calvary legendarily grew) successively lodges in a mandrake, sparrow, fish, whale, mouse, elephant, wolf, dog, and ape. This is in evolutionary illustration of the philosophy expounded in the preface, "that the Pythagorean doctrine doth not only carry one soul from man to man, nor man to beast, but indifferently to plants also: and therefore you must not grudge to find the same soul in an emperor, in a post-horse, and in a mucheron [mushroom], since no unreadiness in the soul, but an indisposition in the organs, works this. And therefore though this soul could not move when it was a melon, yet it may remember, and now tell me, at what lascivious banquet it was served. And though it could not speak when it was a spider, yet it can remember, and now tell me, who used it for poison to attain dignity."

The sparrow is presented with a wonderful raw realism:

> Outcrept a sparrow, this soul's moving inn,
> On whose raw arms stiff feathers now begin,
> As children's teeth through gums, to break with pain;
> His flesh is jelly yet, and his bones' threads
> All a new downy mantle overspreads.
> A mouth he opes, which would as much contain
> As his late house, and the first hour speaks plain,
> And chirps aloud for meat . . . .

The only rival to this naturalistic natural history is the "unnatural natural history"—which the Elizabethans doted on—of the elephant. (After all, if Aristotle said that the elephant had no knees, it must be so.)

> Nature's great masterpiece, an elephant,
> The only harmless great thing, the giant
> Of beasts, who thought no more had gone to make one
> > wise
> But to be just and thankful, loth to offend
> (Yet nature hath given him no knees to bend),
> Himself he up-props, on himself relies,
> And foe to none, suspects no enemies:
> Still sleeping stood; vexed not his fantasy
> Black dreams; like an unbent bow, carelessly
> > His sinewy proboscis did remissly lie.

This is about all that Donne as an epic poet has in common with Milton—the elephant's "lithe proboscis" (*Paradise Lost*, IV, 347).

The ape gets some of Donne's best prurience. That anthropoid, gazing on "Adam's fifth daughter Siphatecia," becomes the first lecher:

> He reached at things too high, but open way
> There was, and he knew not she would say nay;
> His toys prevail not—likelier means he tries.

He gazeth on her face with tear-shot eyes,
And up lifts subtly with his russet paw
Her kidskin apron without fear or awe
    Of Nature: Nature hath no gaol, though she hath
        law.
  First she was silly and knew not what he meant.
That virtue, by his touches, chafed and spent,
Succeeds an itchy warmth that melts her quite;
She knew not first, now cares not what he doth,
And willing half and more, more than half loth,
She neither pulls nor pushes, but outright
Now cries, and now repents; when Tethlemite,
Her brother, entered, and a great stone threw
After the ape, who, thus prevented, flew.
    This house thus battered down, the soul possessed
        a new.

There is no reason why the poem (inscribed "Infinitati sacrum"—"sacred to infinity"!)—that is to say, the soul—could not have gone on indefinitely, except, as Gosse remarks, "at this rate of progress it would have taken millions of verses to bring us safely down to Queen Elizabeth."

One manuscript lacks the concluding stanza, indicating, as we should have surmised anyway, that that, "sullen," arrogant, impudently far from simple view of human nature and history was just tacked on, anything to write "finis" to a monstrosity.

Whoe'er thou beest that read'st this sullen writ,
Which just so much courts thee as thou dost it,
Let me arrest thy thoughts; wonder with me
Why plowing, building, ruling and the rest,
Or most of those arts, whence our lives are blest,
By cursed Cain's race invented be,
And blest Seth vexed us with astronomy.
There's nothing simply good, nor ill alone;
Of every quality comparison
    The only measure is, and judge, opinion.

Skepticism was in the air, the baroque doubt. "There is nothing good or bad but thinking makes it so." Nashe anticipated both Donne and Shakespeare. "So that our opinion . . . gives the name of good or ill to everything." Still earlier was the great skeptic Montaigne with his essay, "That the Taste of Good and Evil depends, for a good part, upon the Opinion we have of them."

On the other hand, the first six stanzas, before the narrative commences, are remarkable in a most earnest, searching way—the first three as invocation, IV-VI as self-revelation. V, employing the Latin term "lustres" for a five-year period, takes stock of past and future with supernatural insight:

> To my six lustres almost now outwore,
> Except Thy book owe me so many more,
> Except my legend be free from the lets
> Of steep ambition, sleepy poverty,
> Spirit-quenching sickness, dull captivity,
> Distracting business, and from beauty's nets,
> And all that calls from this, and to others whets,
> O let me not launch out, but let me save
> Th' expense of brain and spirit, that my grave,
>   His right and due, a whole unwasted man may have.

What a far cry—a *cri de coeur*—from the last stanza. The last stanza was by Jack Donne. This gets ready for Dean Donne. The writer is at the midway point in his life, the middle of the journey—and seems to know it. God's book was indeed to give him exactly thirty years more. He remembers his past, that half of his life lived in the sixteenth century. He remembers it with so little satisfaction that he could not stand another thirty years of it: he would rather die then and there. As it happens, he foretells his future in the new century, what Whitehead identifies as the first modern century. It was relentlessly to contain the "lets"—the hindrances—of "steep ambition, sleepy poverty, spirit-quenching sickness, dull captivity" (the last including jail), quite enough to induce a death wish.

The next lines can only be compared with the divine poems to come. He was a man—and it was an age—that took to the metaphor of sailing, by second nature: "For though through many straits and lands I roam, / I launch at paradise, and I sail towards home." As he would elaborate in a sermon, "The world is a sea in many respects and assimilations." Three lines of stanza VIII will be reused in a sacred sonnet, "La Corona," 2.

Thus *The Progress of the Soul* is a work of manifold interest, being partly secular and even political in its anchorage, partly spiritual. As satire it does not prove, as some have said, that Donne was a full-fledged Roman Catholic at this time. It is much clearer on what he is against than what he is for.

In the mood of bitterness over Essex's fate the false friend, Bacon, was not forgotten. He had taken a prominent part in the treason case, as at the Earl's former trial. Twice when Essex in defending himself digressed in the fever of his emotions, the astute Queen's Counsel rose to bring the examination coolly back to the fatal point. Donne gave Bacon two entries in his satiric *Catalogus Librorum Aulicorum* (The Courtier's Library) comprising thirty-four imaginary books ascribed to real authors. There are many hits at contemporaries in this Latin boutade, including Topcliffe, the notorious informer and persecutor of Catholics, and Foxe, the author of the Protestant *Book of Martyrs* (under Mary)—the truthful statements in which voluminous work could, Donne indicates, be inscribed on a penny! No. 27 is "The Brazen Head of Francis Bacon: concerning Robert the First, King of England." Roger Bacon, the thirteenth-century philosopher and friar, legendarily had an oracular brazen head, which is now reassigned: the implication being that Francis Bacon, when he figured the Earl's intentions, of course could not be wrong. Actually it was Coke who made the dramatic charge to "my Lord of Essex, that now stands all in black". "He of his earldom shall be Robert the Last, that of a kingdom thought to be Robert the First." The next title, No. 28, is even bitterer: "The Advocates'

Onion, or the Art of Weeping at Trials." Bacon was ever insistent on the regret with which he stabbed his patron in the front. Harvey declared "he had . . . the eye of a viper." For centuries he has been popularly labeled a hypocrite: his conduct towards Essex has been a black mark against his name more than his later admission of receiving bribes as a judge. Clearly he placed his loyalty to the Queen above his loyalty to Essex, as he should have and as he had warned the Earl he would. But was he, a genius of forty still low on the "winding stair" of advancement, motivated in any degree by the obvious fact that the Essex side of the bread no longer had any butter on it? Donne felt he knew crocodile tears—or onion tears—when he saw them.

It is impossible to measure the degree of irony, maybe two-edged irony, with which it is said of the citizen in Elegy XIV (to be dated 1609), "A Tale of a Citizen and his Wife," that that worthy "gave no praise / To any but my Lord of Essex' days; / Called those the age of action." Nostalgia became easy under the unheroic James, but it was also felt in the last years of the old Queen, as this and other shadows fell on the glory of Gloriana. Disillusion and dissatisfaction were widespread. They registered in the Queen's last parliament, which assembled October 27, 1601, was dissolved December 19. Donne sat with other friends, among them Robert Cotton, Francis Wooley, and also his future father-in-law. It is fairly certain that this "John Dunn" (the name was variously spelled, as with Shakespeare) was the poet, for he was elected for Brackley, Northamptonshire, which was in the control of Egerton. Egerton in fact became Viscount Brackley shortly before he died in 1617; the title then passed to his surviving son John, in whose honor the masque of *Comus* was written in 1634.

Cheyney sums up the 1601 parliament as follows: "It was more outspoken and headstrong than usual. The privy councillors had the greatest difficulty in guiding the course of debate and securing legislation, and they did not themselves work well together. Indeed it was to the future rather than to the past or even to the present that this parliament looked." The Queen on making what turned out to be her last public appearance before the representatives of her people "was less gracious than she might have been, and the members of parliament were somewhat lacking in their usual shows of loyalty and personal respect." Bacon was sufficiently subservient, supporting the Queen's prerogative and her system of monopolies. The latter came under such attack that the worst were revoked, and other grants were laid open to the courts of common law. When a "lawyer in a debate on the subsidies expressed absurdly high royalist doctrine, that the queen might take all the lands and goods of all her people if she liked, 'all the House hemmed and laughed and talked.' " In November the Lord Keeper met with a rebuff from the Speaker of the House. Events that Donne did not live to see cast their shadows before. He himself comes down to us as silent, as became a novice in politics—took no part in the debates of these few weeks.

He had more than politics on his mind. By the time this short parliament came to an end he was married.

For many months the Lord Keeper's secretary, no novice certainly at attracting the opposite sex, had had numberless opportunities to get better acquainted with the young Anne More. "He ... fell into such a liking as, with her approbation, increased into a love." She is thought to have inspired "The Ecstasy"—which balances so delicately the spiritual and the physical. Her innocence must have been not the least of her charms.

In January, 1600, the second Lady Egerton died. Normally Anne would have gone home to her father. But it was agreeable to her and to him that she should stay on at York House. For nine months she was there unchaperoned, the only lady (aged sixteen) of the household. On March 20 Essex and his train left. What conditions, spring and summer and early fall for the ripening of love!

This luck could not be expected to last forever. The Lord Keeper decided to marry a third time. On Octo-

ber 20 he took as his bride Alice, née Spencer (a distant
relative of the poet), the widow of the fifth Earl of Derby,
the future matriarch before whom Milton's *Arcades* was to
be presented. Also at this time Sir George More's father
died. The two events made it necessary for Anne to leave
London to preside over her father's household, as he had
not married again. At the sad parting of Anne and John,
"some faithful promises . . . were so interchangeably
passed, as never to be violated by either party."

There must have been correspondence for a year,
nothing of which, alas, was preserved. It is not easy to find
an Elizabethan love letter outside of fiction and poetry and
the drama. It would be thrilling to have one from Donne
—not least for another chance to compare his prose and
verse. It would help to have anything at all from Anne,
who stays unreachably in the background throughout her
not very long life. This was the custom.

The two had been warned by friends that they were
being imprudent. Walton warns them again. "The friends
of both parties used much diligence and many arguments
to kill or cool their affections to each other. But in vain;
for love is a flattering mischief that hath denied aged and
wise men a foresight of those evils that too often prove
to be the children of that blind father, a passion, that
carries us to commit errors with as much ease as whirl-
winds remove feathers and begets in us an unwearied
industry to the attainment of what we desire. And such
an industry did, notwithstanding much watchfulness
against it, bring them secretly together—I forbear to tell
the manner how—and at last to a marriage too, without
the allowance of those friends whose approbation always
was and ever will be necessary to make even a virtuous
love become lawful."

The principal "friend" whose "approbation" was
needed was the girl's father, in whom was vested both by
canon law and civil law—as the young templar well knew
—the power of consent, to say nothing of the power of the
purse, the dowry, the dot. Grierson in his *Cambridge
History of English Literature* article of 1910 casts an

unsound aspersion: "It may be that, in Donne's complex nature, love was blended with ambitious hopes of securing his position and strengthening his claims on Sir Thomas Egerton." This is surely unfair to a case of romantic love that no longer had anything to do with Sir Thomas Egerton, whose third wife was not the lady's aunt. Grierson seems to correct himself two years later when he speaks simply of "a runaway match for love." Romantic lovers always feel that they are a law unto themselves. Let society do its worst. And for a wretched while society did.

During the sitting of parliament in the fall of 1601 Anne More came to town with her father, who was a member. She and Donne were able to see each other, privately, two or three times. Three weeks before Christmas they went through with a secret wedding, only three persons besides themselves being present. Christopher Brooke, the friend to whom "The Storm" had been addressed, "gave"—in Gosse's dry words—"away the bride, a gift which he was certainly in no way competent to bestow." Brooke's young brother, Samuel, a fledgling clergyman, performed the ceremony, the validity of which, it developed, Sir George More had every intention of challenging.

They did not at this time cohabit: this would be Sir George's grounds for asking for annulment. But meanwhile he was blissfully ignorant of what had been going on. His daughter was back at Loseley with him, virgin and unaffianced, so far as he knew. Who would tell him the truth? Hints were dropped that merely made him uneasy. The Earl of Northumberland was chosen to serve as intermediary, to break the news and bear an apologetic letter from the groom. This Henry Percy, this Hotspur, was an impulsive busybody suspected of being a crypto-Catholic and a warlock. He had been friends with Essex until they quarreled in 1597. Now he belonged to the Ralegh faction, but Donne may have met him through Essex or through a friend, George Gerrard. He loved intrigue.

The letter that Northumberland carried to More at the beginning of February, 1602, is, for Donne, blunt:

Sir,

If a very respective fear of your displeasure, and a doubt that my lord (whom I know, out of your worthiness, to love you much) would be so compassionate with you as to add his anger to yours, did not so much increase my sickness as that I cannot stir, I had taken the boldness to have done the office of this letter by waiting upon you myself to have given you truth and clearness of this matter between your daughter and me, and to show you plainly the limits of our fault, by which I know your wisdom will proportion the punishment.

So long since as her being at York House this had foundation, and so much then of promise and contract built upon it as, without violence to conscience, might not be shaken.

At her lying in town this Parliament I found means to see her twice or thrice. We both knew the obligations that lay upon us, and we adventured equally; and about three weeks before Christmas we married. And as at the doing there were not used above five persons, of which I protest to you by my salvation there was not one that had any dependence or relation to you, so in all the passage of it did I forbear to use any such person, who by furtherance of it might violate any trust or duty towards you.

The reasons why I did not fore-acquaint you with it (to deal with the same plainness I have used) were these: I knew my present estate less than fit for her. I knew (yet I knew not why) that I stood not right in your opinion. I knew that to have given intimation of it had been to impossibilitate the whole matter. And then, having these honest purposes in our hearts and these fetters in our consciences, methinks we should be pardoned if our fault be but this, that we did not, by fore-revealing of it, consent to our hindrance and torment.

Sir, I acknowledge my fault to be so great, as I dare scarce offer any other prayer to you in mine own behalf than this, to believe this truth—that I neither had dishonest end nor means. But for her, whom I tender much more than my fortunes or life (else I would, I might neither joy in this life nor enjoy the next), I humbly beg of you that she may not, to her danger, feel the terror of your sudden anger.

I know this letter shall find you full of passion; but I know no passion can alter your reason and wisdom, to which I adventure to commend these particulars;—that it is irremediably done; that if you incense my lord, you destroy her and me; that it is easy to give us happiness, and that my endeavours and industry, if it please you to prosper them, may soon make me somewhat worthier of her.

If any take the advantage of your displeasure against me, and fill you with ill thoughts of me, my comfort is that you know that faith and thanks are due to them only that speak when their informations might do good, which now it cannot work towards any party. For my excuse I can say nothing, except I knew what were said to you.

Sir, I have truly told you this matter, and I humbly beseech you so to deal in it as the persuasions of Nature, Reason, Wisdom, and Christianity shall inform you; and to accept the vows of one whom you may now raise or scatter—which are, that as my love is directed unchangeably upon her, so all my labours shall concur to her contentment, and to show my humble obedience to yourself.

Yours in all duty and humbleness,

J. Donne.

From my lodging by the Savoy,
    2nd February 1602.
    To the Right Worshipful Sir George More, Kt.

Although he has not yet been dismissed from, Donne has withdrawn from York House to await the storm. In his brideless and spendthrift solitude the trouble he is in—the morning-after realization of rashness—has left him prostrate. He begins by admitting the psychosomatic aspects of his "sickness": many illnesses of this ambiguous

sort are to visit him in the coming years. He was the best
living clinical illustration of what it meant to be "sicklied
o'er with the pale cast of thought."

He slices up into four the reason he did not "fore-
acquaint" the father with their plans, but no matter how
he slices it it remains one reason, blatant in its bareness:
he knew Sir George would have stopped the marriage. It
is scarcely the height of tact to tell one's father-in-law that
he is a man of passion who explodes easily. There is little
in the letter but correct prophecy. It might have been
wiser to have taken a hopeful line. The Greeks when they
wished to propitiate the Furies did not call them the
Furies: they called them the Eumenides, the "well-
disposed."

Sir George reacted precisely as Donne feared. The
news that Northumberland bore was "so immeasurably
unwelcome and so transported him, that as though his
passion of anger and inconsideration might exceed theirs
of love and error" he secured from the reluctant Lord
Keeper Donne's dismissal from service. Egerton, no foe of
marriage, hated to lose his secretary just because of an
elopement. He reminded Sir George "that errors might
be overpunished, and desired therefore to forbear till
second considerations might clear some scruples." But
More was a relentless fury. The Lord Keeper yielded, but
not without saying, "He parted with a friend, and such a
secretary as was fitter to serve a king than a subject."

Walton tells, "Immediately after his dismission from
his service, he sent a sad letter to his wife to acquaint her
with it; and after the subscription of his name writ, 'John
Donne, Anne Donne, Undone,'—and God knows it proved
too true."

The father's vengeance against his son-in-law did not
stop here. Within a week he had him committed to the
Fleet for conspiracy to violate the common and the civil
law. He also had thrown into two other prisons, on the
same charge, the faithful friends and brothers, Christopher
Brooke, who had given the bride away, and the luckless
young cleric who had officiated, Samuel Brooke. This

made Donne sicker. It is a minor miracle that he survived this series of blows and, for even a brief while, this unhealthy environment that had carried off his brother. He had nothing to sustain him but a degree of youth (but thirty was not so young in those days as it is now) and the thought of his wife and such hope as the following epistle contains.

To the Right Wor. Sir Geo. More, Kt.

Sir,

The inward accusations in my conscience, that I have offended you beyond any ability of redeeming it by me, and the feeling of my Lord's heavy displeasure following it, forceth me to write, though I know my fault make my letters very ungracious to you.

Almighty God, whom I call to witness that all my grief is that I have in this manner offended you and Him, direct you to believe that which out of an humble and afflicted heart I now write to you. And since we have no means to move God, when He will not hear our prayers, to hear them, but by praying, I humbly beseech you to allow by His gracious example my penitence so good entertainment, as it may have a belief and a pity.

Of nothing in this one fault that I hear said to me can I disculp myself, but of the contemptuous and despiteful purpose towards you, which I hear is surmised against me. But for my dutiful regard to my late Lady, for my religion, and for my life, I refer myself to them that may have observed them. I humbly beseech you to take off these weights, and to put my fault into the balance alone, as it was done without the addition of these ill reports, and though then it will be too heavy for me, yet then it will less grieve you to pardon it.

How little and how short the comfort and pleasure of destroying is, I know your wisdom and religion informs you. And though perchance you intend not utter destruction, yet the way through which I fall towards it is so headlong, that, being thus pushed, I shall soon be at

bottom, for it pleaseth God, from whom I acknowledge the
punishment to be just, to accompany my other ills with so
much sickness as I have no refuge but that of mercy, which
I beg of Him, my Lord, and you, which I hope you will
not repent to have afforded me, since all my endeavours
and the whole course of my life shall be bent to make
myself worthy of your favor and her love, whose peace of
conscience and quiet I know must be much wounded and
violenced if your displeasure sever us.

I can present nothing to your thoughts which you
knew not before, but my submission, my repentance, and
my hearty desire to do anything satisfactory to your just
displeasure. Of which I beseech you to make a charitable
use and construction. From the Fleet, 11th Feb. 1602.—
Yours in all faithful duty and obedience,

J. Donne.

The parental power in those times, combined with the
ability to cut off patronage or employment, was awesome,
and could only be compared to God's, as the petition
repeatedly intimates. Indeed the words, "And though perchance you intend not utter destruction, yet the way
through which I fall towards it is so headlong, that, being
thus pushed, I shall soon be at bottom, for it pleaseth
God . . ."—such an etching of ruin and omnipotence
heralds a famous passage in a 1667 poem:

> Him the Almighty Power
> Hurled headlong flaming from th' ethereal sky,
> With hideous ruin and combustion down
> To bottomless perdition, there to dwell
> In adamantine chains and penal fire,
> Who durst defy th'Omnipotent.

The only advantage was that there was more than one
god. More, on receipt of this communication, referred
him to Egerton, who was in turn prayed to in the following
manner:

To excuse my offence, or so much to resist the just punishment for it, as to move your Lordship to withdraw it, I thought till now were to aggravate my fault. But since it hath pleased God to join with you in punishing thereof with increasing my sickness, and that He gives me now audience by prayer, it emboldeneth me also to address my humble request to your Lordship, that you would admit into your favorable consideration how far my intentions were from doing dishonor to your Lordship's house, and how unable I am to escape utter and present destruction, if your Lordship judge only the effect and deed.

My services never had so much worth in them as to deserve the favor wherewith they were paid; but they had always so much honesty as that only this hath stained them. Your justice hath been merciful in making me know my offence, and it hath much profited me that I am dejected. Since then I am so entirely yours, that even your disfavors have wrought good upon me. I humbly beseech you that all my good may proceed from your Lordship, and that since Sir George More, whom I leave no humble way unsought to regain, refers all to your Lordship, you would be pleased to lessen that correction which your just wisdom hath destined for me, and so to pity my sickness and other misery as shall best agree with your honorable disposition.

Almighty God accompany all your Lordship's purposes, and bless you and yours with many good days. Fleet, 12. Febr. 1602.—Your Lordship's most dejected and poor servant.

John Donne.

To the Right Honorable my very good
L. and Master Sr. Thomas Egerton, Knight,
L. Keeper of the Great Seal of England.

Probably out of fear for his health and survival Donne was transferred from the Fleet to his lodgings in the Strand. There he poured out his thanksgiving.

To Sir Thomas Egerton

Only in that coin, wherein they that delight to do benefits and good turns for the work's sake love to be paid, am I rich, which is thankfulness, which I humbly and abundantly present to your Lordship, beseeching you to give such way and entertainment to this virtue of mercy, which is always in you, and always awake, that it may so soften you, that as it hath wrought for me the best of blessings, which is this way to health, so it may give my mind her chief comfort, which is your pardon for my bold and presumptuous offence.

Almighty God be always so with you in this world, as you may be sure to be with Him in the next. 13th Feb. 1602.

Your Lordship's poor and repentant servant,

J. Donne.

His stay in the Fleet had not been, after all, more than three or four days. The same day he wrote a revealing letter to his father-in-law.

Sir,

From you, to whom next to God I shall owe my health, by enjoying by your mediation this mild change of imprisonment, I desire to derive all my good fortune and content in this world; and therefore, with my most unfeigned thanks, present to you my humble petition that you would be pleased to hope that, as that fault which was laid to me of having deceived some gentlewomen before, and that of loving a corrupt religion, are vanished and smoked away (as I assure myself, out of their weakness they are), and that as the devil in the article of our death takes the advantage of our weakness and fear, to aggravate our sins to our conscience, so some uncharitable malice hath presented my debts double at least.

How many of the imputations laid upon me would fall off, if I might shake and purge myself in your presence! But if that were done, of this offence committed to you I cannot acquit myself, of which yet I hope that God (to whom for that I heartily direct many prayers) will inform you to make that use, that as of evil manners good laws grow, so out of disobedience and boldness you will take occasion to show mercy and tenderness. And when it shall please God to soften your heart so much towards us as to pardon us, I beseech you also to undertake that charitable office of being my mediator to my Lord, whom as upon your just complaint you found full of justice, I doubt not but you shall also find full of mercy, for so is the Almighty pattern of Justice and Mercy equally full of both.

My conscience, and such affection as in my conscience becomes an honest man, emboldeneth me to make one request more, which is, that by some kind and comfortable message you would be pleased to give some ease of the afflictions which I know your daughter in her mind suffers, and that (if it be not against your other purposes) I may with your leave write to her, for without your leave I will never attempt anything concerning her. God so have mercy upon me, as I am unchangeably resolved to bend all my courses to make me fit for her, which if God and my Lord and you be pleased to strengthen, I hope neither my debts, which I can easily order, nor anything else shall interrupt. Almighty God keep you in His favor, and restore me to His and yours.

From my chamber, whither by your favor I am come, 13th Feb. 1602.

J. Donne.

Now it comes out. In his first letter Donne had said, "I knew (yet I knew not why) that I stood not right in your opinion." Was the parenthesis disingenuous? Had he really not the smallest inkling of a conventional man's grounds for objecting to him as a son-in-law? Anyway he has heard now. There were whisperers at Sir George's ear. They told him that the man his daughter had got too close to was a Romanist and a rake. He has "deceived some gentlewomen before." Of course that was to be expected from one with his upbringing. Whatever his outer compromises, his politic shifts, he loves "a corrupt religion." His mother, whom he probably still visits, is a papist in Southwark.

The best that Donne can reply is that the rumors are exaggerated.

He was addressing a man who had given vent to his convictions in the Parliament of 1586, "that only Popery is the chief and principal root of all the late horrible and wicked treacheries." The Member from Surrey had gone on to urge that the Queen take care to trust about her person "such only as may be well known to profess the true and sincere religion and also to be every way true and faithful subjects." What then would he want for his daughter?

Donne's two friends were still in their prisons. Christopher Brooke was detained in the Marshalsea for at least a fortnight longer. Donne was under house arrest, as Essex had been two years before, but he spared no effort "until he had procured an enlargement for his two imprisoned friends." They worked for each other. Christopher Brooke, overdue to practice his profession as a lawyer on the York Circuit, pleaded for himself to the Lord Keeper on February 25 but added a touching word in behalf of the friend who had caused him all this trouble. "Pardon me a word for Mr. Donne, my Lord. Were it not now best that everyone whom he any way concerns should become his favorer or his friend, who wants, my good Lord, but fortune's hands and tongue to rear him up, and set him out?"

In a bid for new employment Donne wrote to Robert Cotton, the antiquarian, February 20. He also set out to wring a further concession from Egerton.

The honorable favor that your Lordship hath afforded me in allowing me the liberty of mine own chamber, hath given me leave so much to respect and love myself that now I can desire to be well. And therefore for health, not pleasure (of which your Lordship's displeasure hath dulled in me all taste and apprehension), I humbly beseech your Lordship so much more to slacken my fetters that, as I am by your Lordship's favor mine own keeper and surety, so I may be mine own physician and apothecary, which your

Lordship shall work, if you grant me liberty to take the air about this town. The whole world is a strait imprisonment to me whilst I am barred your Lordship's sight; but this favor may lengthen and better my life, which I desire to preserve only in hope to redeem by my sorrow and desire to do your Lordship service, my offence past.

Almighty God dwell ever in your Lordship's heart and fill it with good desires, and grant them.

Your Lordship's poorest servant,

J. Donne.

By February 23, this note having been successful, his spirits rose. The Lord Keeper might take him back, after all. Was he not honest, if he did say so himself? He can write in the following jaunty vein.

Sir,

Of myself (who, if honesty were precious, were worth the talking of) let me say a little. The Commissioners by imprisoning the witnesses and excommunicating all us, have implicitly justified our marriage. Sir George will, as I hear, keep her till I send for her: and let her remain there yet, his good nature and her sorrow will work something. I have liberty to ride abroad, and feel not much of an imprisonment. For my return to my Lord, and Sir George's pacification, you know my means, and therefore my hopes.

This was to Sir Henry Goodyer, who became his favorite—for years his weekly—correspondent. This courtier and spendthrift and proprietor of Polesworth in Shakespeare's county of Warwick had been knighted by Essex in Dublin in 1599.

The two deities—one of whom, Sir George, was softening now—had to be invoked.

To Sir George More

Sir,

If I could fear that in so much worthiness as is in you there were no mercy, or if these weights oppressed only my shoulders and my fortunes and not my conscience and hers whose good is dearer to me by much than my life, I should not thus trouble you with my letters; but when I see that this storm hath shaked me at root in my Lord's favor, where I was well planted and have just reason to fear that those ill-reports which malice hath raised of me may have troubled hers, I can leave no honest way untried to remedy these miseries, nor find any way more honest than this, out of an humble and repentant heart, for the fault done to you, to beg both your pardon and assistance in my suit to my Lord.

I should wrong you as much again as I did if I should think you sought to destroy me; but though I be not headlongly destroyed, I languish and rust dangerously. From seeking preferments abroad, my love and conscience restrains me; from hoping for them here, my Lord's disgracings cut me off. My imprisonments, and theirs whose love to me brought them to it, hath already cost me £ 40. And the love of my friends, though it be not utterly grounded upon my fortunes, yet I know suffers somewhat in these long and uncertain disgraces of mine.

I therefore humbly beseech you to have so charitable a pity of what I have, and do, and must suffer, as to take to yourself the comfort of having saved from such destruction as your just anger might have laid upon him, a sorrowful and honest man. I was bold in my last letter to beg leave of you that I might write to your daughter. Though I understand thereupon, that after the Thursday you were not displeased that I should, yet I have not, nor will not without your knowledge, do it. But now I beseech you that I may, since I protest before God it is the greatest of my afflictions not to do it. In all the world is not more true sorrow than in my heart, nor more understanding of true repentance than in yours. And therefore God, whose pardon in such cases is never denied, gives me leave to hope that you will favorably consider my necessities.

To His merciful guiding and protection I commend you and cease to trouble you. March 1602.

Yours in all humbleness and dutiful obedience,

J. Donne.

To Sir Thomas Egerton

That offence, which was to God in this matter, His mercy hath assured my conscience is pardoned.

The Commissioners who minister His anger and mercy incline also to remit it.

Sir George More, of whose learning and wisdom I have good knowledge, and therefore good hope of his moderation, hath said before his last going that he was so far from being any cause or mover of my punishment or disgrace, that if it fitted his reputation he would be a suitor to your Lordship for my restoring. All these irons are knocked off, yet I perish in as heavy fetters as ever whilst I languish under your Lordship's anger.

How soon my history is despatched! I was carefully and honestly bred; enjoyed an indifferent fortune; I had (and I had understanding enough to value it) the sweetness and security of a freedom and independency, without marking out to my hopes any place of profit. I had a desire to be your Lordship's servant, by the favor which your good son's love to me obtained. I was four years your Lordship's secretary, not dishonest nor greedy. The sickness of which I died is that I began in your Lordship's house this love. Where I shall be buried I know not. It is late for me (but yet necessity, as it hath continually an autumn and a withering, so it hath ever a spring, and must put forth) to begin that course which some years past I purposed to travel,* though I could now do it, not much disadvantageously. But I have some bridle upon me now more than then by my marriage of this gentlewoman, in providing for whom I can and will show myself very honest, though not so fortunate.

To seek preferment here with any but your Lordship were a madness. Every great man to whom I shall address any such suit will silently dispute the case, and say, "Would my Lord Keeper so disgraciously have imprisoned him and flung him away if he had not done some other great fault

---

*"Referring to his earlier intention of adopting the profession of the law" (Jessopp).

of which we hear not?" So that to the burden of my true weaknesses I shall have this addition of a very prejudicial suspicion that I am worse than I hope your Lordship doth think me, or would that the world should think. I have therefore no way before me, but must turn back to your Lordship, who knows that redemption was no less work than creation.

I know my fault so well, and so well acknowledge it, that I protest I have not so much as inwardly grudged or startled at the punishment. I know your Lordship's disposition so well, as though in course of justice it be of proof against clamors of offenders, yet it is not strong enough to resist itself, and I know itself naturally inclines it to pity. I know mine own necessity, out of which I humbly beg that your Lordship will so much entender your heart towards me, as to give me leave to come into your presence. Affliction, misery, and destruction are not there; and everywhere else where I am they are. 1 Martii 1602.

Your Lordship's most poor and most penitent servant,

J. Donne.

Possibly the third Lady Egerton, that patroness of poets, put in a good word. Donne had no doubt made his usual headway with her and her three daughters. (He admits in a poem to having praised one of the latter.) And there was poor Anne to be pitied! At any rate Sir George relented, especially as he saw that the commissioners at the court of the Archbishop of Canterbury were going to declare the marriage valid. This they formally did on April 27. Walton may be hazily referring to these proceedings when he says, "his wife was (to her extreme sorrow) detained from him, and...he...was forced to make good his title, and to get possession of her by a long and restless suit in law, which proved troublesome and sadly-chargeable to him, whose youth and travel and needless bounty had brought his estate into a narrow compass." It is not likely that it became necessary to sue the father-in-law. That choleric gentleman, on the contrary, assumed the embarrassing position of begging the Lord Keeper to rescind the dismissal that he had himself importuned for. But the scandal was too public by now to pretend that it had never existed. The Lord Keeper replied with dignity and crushing finality, "That though he was unfeignedly sorry for what he had done, yet it was inconsistent with his place and credit to discharge and readmit servants at the request of passionate petitioners."

The wife was permitted to join her husband. "It was not long before Sir George appeared to be so far reconciled as to wish their happiness and not to deny them his parental blessing, but yet refused to contribute any means that might conduce to their livelihood." No dowry.

"Mr. Donne's estate was the greatest part spent in many and chargeable travels, books, and dear-bought experience; he out of all employment that might yield a support for himself and wife, who had been curiously and plentifully educated; both their natures generous and accustomed to confer and not to receive courtesies; these and other considerations, but chiefly that his wife was to bear a part in his sufferings, surrounded him with many sad thoughts and some apparent apprehensions of want."

Was he looking back to that sad time when, in a Candlemas Day sermon, he warned against overweening self-congratulation?

> Let no man say, I could not miss a fortune, for I have studied all my youth. How many men have studied more nights than he hath done hours, and studied themselves blind, and mad in the mathematics, and yet withers in beggary in a corner? Let him never add, but I studied in a useful and gainful profession. How many have done so too, and yet never compassed the favor of a judge? And how many that have had all that, have struck upon a rock, even at full sea, and perished there?

To resume another metaphor, not only had he slipped off the first rung of the ladder down to the bottom, but he would have to search for another ladder, a different use for his talents. But he possessed a true and faithful wife.

"All measure, and all language I should pass, / Should I tell what a miracle she was." She would not have understood his more intricate or his cynical poems. She was not a reader. "When I begin to apprehend that, even to myself, who can relieve myself upon books, solitariness was a little burdenous, I believe it would be much more so to my wife, if she were left alone." For her he wrote gentler lyrics, such as "Sweetest love, I do not go, / For weariness of thee" and "A Valediction Forbidding Mourning." She had heard of his libertine past, but that was thoroughly behind him. "Twice or thrice had I loved thee, / Before I knew thy face or name." In the *Essays in Divinity* he paused to thank God for having delivered him "from the Egypt of lust by confining my affections." His future would be wholesomely monogamous, to the grave and beyond. He passed on to, at most, Platonic friendships with countesses.

One aspect of their married life can be summarized by stating that in fifteen years Anne Donne bore her husband twelve children. Then, not surprisingly, she died. The father outlived them both. So almost as if to balance this, did Donne's mother, a papist to the last. She predeceased her son by two months.

3 / Struggle

Anne's cousin, Sir Francis Wooley, invited the hapless Donnes to stay with him. He had just come of age and into an estate at Pyrford in Surrey, on the Wey, a place, with a large deer-park, grand enough for the Queen to have visited it twice. From 1602 to the end of 1604 the Donnes were in dependence here. Here their first children were born, Constance in 1603, John (who was to be his father's editor) the following year.

On March 24, 1603, the Queen died, without encomia from Shakespeare or Donne. Fourteen years later, in an anniversary sermon, the latter paid a qualified tribute. "In the death of that Queen, unmatchable, inimitable in her sex,... we were all under one common flood and depth of tears.... She knew the world would talk of her after her death, and therefore she did such things all her life were worthy to be talked of. Of her gracious successor, and our gracious sovereign, we may say,... It would have troubled any king but him to have come in succession and in comparison with such a queen."

Sir George More, a country neighbor of Wooley's, had the honor of entertaining James I at Loseley that summer of 1603. The King and Anne his Queen, following an ill-attended coronation in plague-stricken London July 25, made a tour of the southern counties. August 12 may have been the day Donne met a monarch who was to exert a personal influence on him which was not that of the remote moon-goddess. James had a taste for theology, as Elizabeth did not, and Donne was to be drawn, not unwillingly, into the religious controversies of the new reign.

As happens to those who have made a love-match, he was subjected to worldly-wise criticism. He dramatized his situation in "The Canonization":

> For God's sake hold your tongue and let me love!
>   Or chide my palsy or my gout,
>   My five grey hairs or ruined fortune flout;
> With wealth your state, your mind with arts improve,
>   Take you a course, get you a place,
>   Observe his Honor or his Grace,
> Or the King's real or his stampèd face
> Contémplate, what you will approve,
>   So you will let me love.

That reference to "ruined fortune" was no joke. The reference to "the king's . . . face" (on coins) shows that the poem postdates Elizabeth's reign and thus Donne's marriage.

He was desperate for a suitable occupation and depressed without one. The country was exile for him. He felt out of things: he was. Friends tried to rouse him, in person and by letter. "Your friends [in London] are sorry that you make yourself so great a stranger, but you best know your own occasions." "I trust it shall be no offence to interrupt your melancholy, in which soever of the fair walks it shall possess you, with this remembrance of my good wishes."

When his friend Sir Henry Goodyer lost his wife, Donne could not get out of himself long enough to write a decent note of condolence:

Sir,-

  I live so far removed that even the ill news of your great loss (which is ever swiftest and loudest) found me

not till now. Your letter speaks it not plain enough; but
I am so accustomed to the worst, that I am sure it is so
in this. I am almost glad that I knew her so little, for I
would have no more additions to sorrow. If I should comfort you, it were an alms acceptable in no other title than
when poor give to poor, for I am more needy of it than
you . . . .

The wounded self-exposure also took the form of verse.

> Men say, and truly, that they better be
>   Which be envied than pitied: therefore I,
>   Because I wish thee best, do thee envy:
> O wouldst thou, by like reason, pity me!
> But care not for me: I, that ever was
> In Nature's and in Fortune's gifts (alas,
>   Before thy grace got in the Muses' school)
> A monster and a beggar, am now a fool.

He saw men like his father-in-law spending freely and
getting re-elected to Parliament—with charm and talents
nonexistent compared to his. Sir George had not yet overcome his unhappy compulsion to be a pompous bore.
"And surely, saving that Sir George More is your father
(in law and not in conscience), he speaks as ill as ever he
did, saving that he speaks not so much."

After some thirty months of isolation Donne developed wanderlust. On February 16, 1605, he received permission to go abroad with Sir Walter Chute. During the
interval—his wife was expecting again—it would be advisable to settle his family nearer London. What friend or
relative would next provide charity or hospitality? George
Donne was born May 9 in the suburb of Camberwell. One
of Mrs. Donne's sisters, Jane, Lady Grymes, had a house
here. But, with the father's return from, among other
places, Paris, the Donnes were able, in 1606, to leave their
borrowed nest for one of their own, however lightly
feathered, in Mitcham, not far off (where the lord of the
manor was another brother-in-law, Sir Nicholas Throck-

morton Carew). For John at last had found employment.
He had become that most abject but persisting creature—
a research assistant.

The man he assisted had started slowly but was now
gaining momentum, Thomas Morton, the future bishop
of Durham. The new reign saw the outbreak of a paper
war between Anglicans, Puritans, and Catholics. The latter
two categories were sometimes lumped together as trouble-
makers. Thus one 1605 tract, by Ormerod, professes the
"Discovery of Puritan-Papism." Morton had won the
respect of the Jesuits, was already noted "for his dexterity
and acuteness in disputing with the Romish Recusants."
James had proposed leniency, preferring that the "uniformity which we desire may be wrought by clemency and
by weight of reason, and not by rigor of law." He saw the
Church of England as the via media (so Donne would see
it, too), and himself as the mediator, the peacemaker, between warring religions, abroad as well as at home. He
made peace with Spain. But Spain insolently demanded
that his son Charles be educated as a Catholic. There was
a 1604 Parliament that insisted on rigor against Catholics.
There was the Gunpowder Plot of November 5, 1605.
Leniency vanished. But argument went on. Morton passed
from oral debate to learned pamphlets. The material for
the latter was largely supplied by Donne, in the years
1605 to 1607.

He began commuting between Mitcham and a
lodging in the Strand. He acquired books that would help
him in these polemics. Significantly, most of the two
hundred books that survive with signs of his ownership
were published before his own first publication, the 1610
Pseudo-Martyr.

He provided ammunition for such fusillades of
Morton's as *Apologia Catholica*, in Latin, and, in English,
*A Full Satisfaction concerning a Double Romish Iniquity:
Heinous Rebellion and more than Heathenish Equivoca-
tion.* The former had a sequel, and there was also a
quarto on the Gunpowder Plot entitled *An Exact Dis-*

covery of Romish Doctrine in the Case of Conspiracy and Rebellion. There were answers, from Parsons, among others. The opposition was never convinced, only silenced by death or stricter press regulation.

Donne's position was ambiguous, as a former Catholic, as an amateur among professionals, and as an anonymous contributor to another man's books. Gosse sums him up at this time as "a kind of Goethe, but without a Weimar. One of the most learned of living Englishmen in the law, he was not a lawyer; a profound theologian, he was not in orders; with a throng of exalted relations and friends, he possessed no post at Court." For a while he was as busy as a mole, but like a mole he remained underground and could not have felt very exalted.

Of course he was paid, in one form or another. Morton's 1669 biographer relates an instance of Donne's "ripe and sudden wit." Morton "gave him a good quantity of gold (then a useful token), saying, 'Here, Mr. Donne, take this. Gold is restorative.' He presently answered, 'Sir, I doubt I shall never restore it back again.' And I am assured that he never did." The same medicinal pun occurs in one of the poems (Elegy XI, 112).

But there was not enough gold to keep him well and in spirits, despite the Chaucerian doctrine, "For gold in physic is a cordial." Both his dwellings, at Mitcham and in the city, were cold and damp and cramped. A sketch of the little manor house at Mitcham was reproduced by Jessopp. It was known as "Donne's House" until the middle of the nineteenth century, when it was torn down. Edmund Campion's nineteenth-century biographer, Richard Simpson, lived there as a child, and, Gosse declares, "was told that certain of the trees there had been planted by Donne." This does not sound like Donne, and it is not what Jessopp, Gosse's authority, says. Rather, Simpson "was taught to believe that some of the trees then standing had been planted during Donne's tenancy." There tend to be romantic stories about poets and trees, but they ought not to be exaggerated. Christ's College, Cambridge, displays "the Milton mulberry tree" that, according to legend, was planted by his own hand. But now we cannot see Donne's Oxford college, nor even his London cathedral, which was rebuilt by Wren. The cottage where Donne spent some melancholy years looks picturesque, with, as someone has said, "two pointed gables at one end sticking up like a rabbit's ears." But what was it like inside? He exposes it with one word—"thin"—"that incommodity of a little thin house."

At Mitcham the only relaxation seems to have been in connection with the begetting of children. Francis Donne arrived at the beginning of January, 1607, as the following note informed Goodyer:

> Sir,-
>
> Though you escape my lifting up of your latch by removing, you cannot my letters; yet of this letter I do not much accuse myself, for I serve your commandment in it, for it is only to convey to you this paper opposed to those, with which you trusted me. It is (I cannot say the weightiest, but truly) the saddest lucubration and night's passage that ever I had. For it exercised those hours, which, with extreme danger of her, whom I should hardly have abstained from recompensing for her company in this world, with accompanying her out of it, increased my poor family with a son. Though her anguish, and my fears and hopes, seem divers and wild distractions from this small business of your papers, yet because they all narrowed themselves, and met in *Via regia*, [the King's highway], which is the consideration of ourselves and God, I thought it time not unfit for this dispatch. Thus much more than needed I have told you, whilst my fire was lighting at Tricombs [at] ten o'clock.
>
> —Yours ever entirely,
>
> J. Donne.

Francis was one of the children that did not live long. Also, the time was coming when Anne, worn out, began to have miscarriages.

There was correspondence with Ben Jonson, the only prominent writer so favored. These two, each with his

literary arrogance, appreciated—and gave advice to—each
other. If the advice was not invariably taken, as when
Donne intervened in one of Jonson's frequent quarrels, it
was at least declined with gratitude. "You cannot but
believe how dear and reverend your friendship is to me
(though all testimony on my part hath been too short to
express me) and therefore would I meet it with all
obedience. My mind is not yet so deafened by injuries but
it hath an ear for counsel. Yet in this point, that you
presently dissuade, I wonder how I am misunderstood....
Well, my modesty shall sit down, and...I will yet thank
you...." Each paid honest tribute to the other. As
Jonson said in one of the three poems he wrote on Donne,
"Rare poems ask rare friends." *Volpone* appeared in
quarto early in 1607 with some Latin lines of Donne's
prefixed. The epigram ends with an appropriate reference
to the modern viciousness that exceeds the ancient. Both
writers took a personal and endless satisfaction in belabor-
ing their times.

But Jonson (who was himself for twelve years a
Catholic and got into trouble with the authorities on that
account) could earn a living with plays and masques. He
did not need to find a patron. If worst came to worst he
could always go back to his old craft of laying bricks. But
when Morton stopped writing, Donne was out of employment again. This happened in 1607. With Donne's aid
Morton's reputation as a confounder of Catholics had
grown enough for him to be marked for further advancement. He had become James's chaplain-in-ordinary. The
Archbishop of Canterbury looked favorably upon him. On
June 22 he was preferred to the Deanery of Gloucester.

On this occasion he did not forget his assistant's "due
deserts of learning."

> He sent to Mr. Donne and entreated to borrow an hour
> of his time for a conference the next day. After their
> meeting, there was not many minutes passed before he
> spake to Mr. Donne to this purpose: "Mr. Donne, the
> occasion of sending for you is to propose to you what I

have often revolved in my own thought since I last saw
you. Which nevertheless I will not declare but upon this
condition, that you shall not return me a present answer
but forbear three days and bestow some part of that time
in fasting and prayer; and after a serious consideration of
what I shall propose, then return to me with your answer.
Deny me not, Mr. Donne; for it is the effect of a true
love, which I would gladly pay as a debt due for yours to
me."

This request being granted, the doctor expressed himself thus:

"Mr. Donne, I know your education and abilities; I
know your expectation of a state-employment; and I know
your fitness for it; and I know too the many delays and
contingencies that attend court-promises; and let me tell
you that my love begot by our long friendship and your
merits hath prompted me to such an inquisition after your
present temporal estate as makes me no stranger to your
necessities; which I know to be such as your generous spirit
could not bear, if it were not supported with a pious
patience. You know I have formerly persuaded you to
waive your court-hopes and enter into holy orders; which
I now again persuade you to embrace with this reason
added to my former request. The King hath yesterday made
me Dean of Gloucester, and I am also possessed of a
benefice the profits of which are equal to those of my
deanery; I will think my deanery enough for my maintenance—who am and resolve to die a single man—and will
quit my benefice and estate you in it—which the patron
is willing I shall do—if God shall incline your heart to
embrace this motion. Remember, Mr. Donne, no man's
education or parts make him too good for this employment,
which is to be an ambassador for the God of glory, that
God who by a vile death opened the gates of life to mankind. Make me no present answer, but remember your
promise, and return to me the third day with your resolution."

At the hearing of this, Mr. Donne's faint breath and
perplexed countenance gave a visible testimony of an

inward conflict; but he performed his promise and departed without returning an answer till the third day, and then his answer was to this effect:

"My most worthy and most dear friend, since I saw you I have been faithful to my promise and have also meditated much of your great kindness, which hath been such as would exceed even my gratitude; but that it cannot do; and more I cannot return you; and I do that with an heart full of humility and thanks, though I may not accept of your offer. But, Sir, my refusal is not for that I think myself too good for that calling for which kings, if they think so, are not good enough; nor for that my education and learning, though not eminent, may not, being assisted with God's grace and humility, render me in some measure fit for it. But I dare make so dear a friend as you are my confessor; some irregularities of my life have been so visible to some men that though I have, I thank God, made my peace with Him by penitential resolutions against them and by the assistance of His grace banished them my affections, yet this, which God knows to be so, is not so visible to man as to free me from their censures and it may be that sacred calling from a dishonor. And besides, whereas it is determined by the best of casuists that God's glory should be the first end and a maintenance the second motive to embrace that calling, and though each man may propose to himself both together; yet the first may not be put last without a violation of conscience, which he that searches the heart will judge. And truly my present condition is such that if I ask my own conscience whether it be reconcilable to that rule, it is at this time so perplexed about it that I can neither give myself nor you an answer. You know, Sir, who says, 'Happy is that man whose conscience doth not accuse him for that thing which he does.' To these I might add other reasons that dissuade me; but I crave your favor that I may forbear to express them and thankfully decline your offer."

Walton received this account from Bishop Morton himself, still alive at ninety-four. Whether it embodies Donne's exact words or not, it does picture a man of con-

science who will not enter the Church just for "maintenance," sorely as maintenance was needed. There had
to be a calling, and Donne was still listening for
a more worldly music. Two weeks before, knowing
his employment with Morton was at an end, he had
written to Goodyer, "one of the gentlemen of His
Majesty's Privy Chamber," about a post in the household of Queen Anne. Morton's was, in Walton's words, "a
most generous offer . . . for the moderating of his worldly
cares"—but it was not along the worldly lines that he
expected, and he would keep trying for "state-employment." Within two years, in fact, he would be desperate
enough to want to go to Virginia! And before that,
Ireland! But nothing worked. The King was determined
that he should advance only as a priest.

A seed had been planted. There was "inward conflict." It would grow.

He began writing religious poetry, which he sent to
Mrs. Magdalen Herbert. He sent her seven linked sonnets
entitled "La Corona," besides a dedicatory sonnet com-
paring her to St. Mary Magdalen. This group he was
careful to send out on St. Mary Magdalen's day, "this good
day," in July of 1607—or so Walton, affixing perhaps too
early a date, would have us believe. "La Corona," besides
meaning The Crown, can denote in Spanish seven decades
of the rosary offered to the Virgin. Sonnets 2-7 meditate
on six of the fifteen mysteries of the rosary—"Annuncia-
tion," "Nativity," "Temple," "Crucifying," "Resurrection," and "Ascension." The first sonnet sets the mood:

> Deign at my hands this crown of prayer and praise,
> Weaved in my low devout melancholy.

K. W. Gransden is doubtless right in seeing the series as
"an attempt to find in a religious exercise some respite
from an unsatisfactory and depressing everyday existence:
that is, they were prompted more by a deep interest in
theology than by that personal need for, and effort
towards, salvation which characterizes the more celebrated

Holy Sonnets." As Burton's *Anatomy of Melancholy* was soon to show, there was such a thing as religious melancholy, and Donne was not the only seventeenth-century genius to turn to versifying at a time of personal trouble. But he showed his genius better than Milton did when Milton mechanically translated some psalms at two low points in his life, or than Bacon did in 1625 when, sick and in disgrace, he put out his *Translation of Certain Psalms into English Verse.* Donne's work is original and it is poetry. For him there was no conflict between his "muse's white sincerity" and "wit, whose one spark could make good things of bad." He deftly exploits the Christian paradoxes, as in the sestet of the sonnet on the Virgin:

> Ere by the spheres time was created, thou
> Wast in his mind, who is thy Son, and Brother;
> Whom thou conceiv'st, conceived; yea thou art now
> Thy Maker's maker, and thy Father's mother;
> Thou 'hast light in dark; and shutst in little room
> *Immensity cloistered in thy dear womb.*

There is no more daring conceit in all his poetry than the line in "Ascension": "O strong Ram, which hast battered heaven for me." That the Lamb of God should be pictured as a battering ram! We are able to appreciate better the onset of the future Holy Sonnet XIV, "Batter my heart, three-personed God."

If the wit leaps out, so does the death wish:

> The ends crown our works, but thou crown'st our ends,
> For, at our end, begins our endless rest;
> The first last end, now zealously possessed,
> With a strong sober thirst my soul attends.

The Christian was supposed to scorn the present life, this wicked and sinful world, and long for the next. It would be logical for him to wonder if he might hasten his own demise, thereby attaining salvation sooner. If he was miserable now, why should he wait for heaven and go on blackening his soul with sin, including the sin of despair? Was not suicide justifiable as the ultimate form of *de contemptu mundi?* Looking back over the history of the Church it could be said, paradoxically, that "certainly the desire of martyrdom, though the body perish, is a self-preservation, because thereby, out of our election, our best part is advanced. For Heaven, which we gain so, is certainly good; life, but probably and possibly."

This is one of the arguments in a book that Donne took to constructing at this depressed time, *Biathanatos.* The Greek word means "death by force." The subtitle explains the treatise's aim: "A Declaration of that Paradox or Thesis, that Self-Homicide is not so naturally Sin that it may never be otherwise; wherein the Nature and the extent of all these Laws which seem to be violated by this Act are diligently surveyed." The first words of the Preface show that this curious tract, first published by Donne's son during the Civil War, did not originate as an impersonal exercise:

Beza, a man as eminent and illustrious in the full glory and noon of learning as others were in the dawning and morning, when any, the least spark, was notorious, confesseth of himself that only for the anguish of a scurf, which overran his head, he had once drowned himself from the Miller's bridge in Paris, if his uncle by chance had not then come that way. I have often such a sickly inclination. And, whether it be because I had my first breeding and conversation with men of suppressed and afflicted religion, accustomed to the despite of death and hungry of an imagined martyrdom; or that the common Enemy find that door worst locked against him in me; or that there be a perplexity and flexibility in the doctrine itself; or because my conscience ever assures me that no rebellious grudging at God's gifts nor other sinful concurrence accompanies these thoughts in me, or that a brave scorn, or that a faint cowardliness beget it, whensoever any affliction assails me methinks I have the keys of my prison in mine own hand,

and no remedy presents itself so soon to my heart as mine own sword. Often meditation of this hath won me to a charitable interpretation of their action who die so: and provoked me a little to watch and exagitate their reasons, which pronounce so peremptory judgments upon them.

But the work as a whole is impersonal, with little attractiveness of style. It belongs to the history of casuistry, a by-gone art. He had once made up a short Paradox, "That All Things Kill Themselves," postulating self destruction as a universal principle: "To affect—yea to effect—their own death, all living things are importuned, not by Nature only, which perfects them, but by Art and Education, which perfects her." Now he would stuff two hundred margins with citations from almost that many authors, not counting the Bible, which gets a formal going over in the third, concluding part, "Of the Law of God." The case of Samson (returned to in Donne's last sermon) was particularly intriguing, since the last words of this "man so exemplar" were plainly suicidal: "Let me die with the Philistines." Even a death wish in Christ himself is hinted at.

In 1619 the author wrote a self-conscious letter[1] about this manuscript on sending it to Sir Robert Ker. We learn from it that he himself started the careful separation between Jack Donne and Dr. Donne or Dean Donne. Another copy of the manuscript was sent to Mrs. Herbert's oldest son, who gave it to the Bodleian in 1642, where it still is. The author was witty in that letter, too. "It shall not therefore kill itself, that is, not bury itself. For if it should do so, those reasons by which that act should be defended or excused were also lost with it." Jokes are an outlet for nervousness. Of course the work was a very unorthodox production for a clergyman, as questionable, in its utterly different way, as the love poems.

But the scholarly dryness of *Biathanatos* would save it from corrupting the young, whatever passion lies coiled in

[1] XII, Appendix.

its springs. It is a lawyer's brief, anticipating such modern books, which are not lawyers' briefs, as Freud's *Beyond the Pleasure Principle* (1922) and Dr. Karl Menninger's *Man Against Himself* (1938) and Norman O. Brown's *Life Against Death* (1959). De Quincey wrote an essay on whether animals commit suicide. Donne found that in bees and pelicans self-destruction is part of the life cycle. How he would have rejoiced in the North American salmon forcing its suicidal way up to the heads of rivers to spawn —or the Scandinavian lemmings with their heedless propensity to drown! There were numerous suicides in classical antiquity to savor. As for Christianity, after it "had quenched those respects of fame, ease, shame, and such, how quickly naturally man snatched and embraced a new way of profusing his life by martyrdom!" "From such an inordinate desire, too obedient to nature, proceeded the fury of some Christians who, when sentence was pronounced against others, standing by, cried out, 'We also are Christians.' " The mania could still be found in England among those whom Donne would soon label pseudo-martyrs: "if this desire of dying be not agreeable to the nature of man, but against it, yet it seems that it is not against the nature of a Jesuit."

The very severity of the enactments against attempted suicide only proves "that everywhere men are inclinable to it," there being "a watchful solicitude in every state, by all means to avert men from this natural love of ease, by which their strength in numbers would have been very much impaired." Consider what permissions there are: "I may give another my board in a shipwreck, and so drown .... I may hasten my arrival to heaven, by consuming penances." Blinking at nothing "to allow Truth her natural and comely boldness," this historian and psychologist came close to discovering masochism, in the course of finding the death wish everywhere, not to speak of a side journey into euthanasia, where the great-granduncle led the way: "Sir Thomas More (a man of the most tender and delicate conscience that the world saw since Saint Augustine), not likely to write anything in jest mischievously interpretable, says that in Utopia the priests and magistrates did use to exhort men afflicted with incurable diseases, to kill themselves, and that they were obeyed as the interpreters of God's will."

So much for what "in all ages, in all places, upon all occasions, men of all conditions have" been "inclined to do." Donne has traveled far from his earlier Paradox "That Only Cowards Dare Die." The bravest and most saintly men have known the death instinct and have dared to respond to it. The author has worked out permission for himself. In like vein is his gloomily analytical letter to Goodyer of September, 1608,[2] on the plight of one who has not fitted in, who is not among those that have been "so incorporated into the body of the world that they contribute something to the sustentation of the whole."

Poverty, insecurity, and illness put their triple blight on the growing family at Mitcham, a home that began to be referred to as either "my hospital" or "my dungeon." Maybe writing *Biathanatos* was the only thing that saved Donne from suicide at this time, even as compiling *The Anatomy of Melancholy* helped Robert Burton with his own melancholy. "I write of melancholy, by being busy to avoid melancholy." May we not substitute, "I write of suicide, by being busy to avoid suicide." Donne issued despondent letters "from the fireside in my parlor, and in the noise of three gamesome children, and by the side of her whom because I have transplanted into a wretched fortune I must labor to disguise that from her by all such honest devices as giving her my company and discourse. Therefore I steal from her all the time which I give this letter, and it is therefore that I take so short a list and gallop so fast over it. I have not been out of my house since I received your pacquet. As I have much quenched my senses, and disused my body from pleasure, and so tried how I can endure to be mine own grave, so I try now how I can suffer a prison." To think that the writer

[2]V, Appendix.

of these lines was once an outwardly gay blade who trumpeted the motto, "Sooner dead than changed"!

But Donne put on many masks, and it is possible that *Biathanatos* was one of them. It is possible that the harmony with his letters may be false. It is possible that on account of its subject, its heap of citations, its somber logic, what the title page denominates a "paradox" has been taken too seriously. The latest suggestion has it that *Biathanatos* is "a somewhat half-hearted, somewhat unsuccessful satire on scholastic and casuistical learning." It poses a problem for which there is no solution. The opening sentence is disingenuous—and if that does not hold up, what does? A follow-up of the reference reveals that Beza was a child, not "a man . . . eminent and illustrious," when a companion tempted him to jump from the bridge. Moreover Beza the child was suffering frightful and continuous pain. He was not a philosopher who had judiciously considered the moral and theological issue. Was Donne just shadow-boxing for 218 pages?

Yet the shadows, at least, were real, and so was Donne's pain. That paroxysmal fever known as the ague caught him and pinned him down, as he wrote Goodyer. "I cannot obey you if you go tomorrow to Parson's Green; your company, that place, and my promise are strong inducements; but an ague flouts them all, of which I have had two such threatenings that I provide against it by a little physic. This is one fetter; but I have a pair; for I attend Sir George More's answer in a little business, of which I can have no account till his return, so I am fastened here till after Sunday." Obviously Sir George was still a great power, greater for not having opened—but forever dangling the hope that he might yet open—his purse strings. The spring—the season when, by modern statistics, most suicides occur—only deepened the gloom of this correspondent. "Because I am in a place and season where I see everything bud forth, I must do so too, and vent some of my meditations to you; the rather because all other buds being yet without taste or virtue, my letters may be like them. The pleasantness of the season displeases me. Everything refreshes, and I wither, and I grow older and not better, my strength diminishes, and my load grows . . . ." But the other seasons were just as bad. "This letter hath more merit than one of more diligence, for I wrote it in my bed, and with much pain. I have occasion to sit late some nights in my study, . . . and now I find that that room hath a wholesome emblematic use; for having under it a vault, I make that promise me, that I shall die reading, since my book and a grave are so near. But it hath another unwholesomeness, that by raw vapours rising from thence (for I can impute it to nothing else), I have contracted a sickness which I cannot name nor describe. For it hath so much of a continual cramp, that it wrests the sinews, so much of a tetane, that it withdraws and pulls the mouth, and so much of the gout (which they whose counsel I use, say it is) that it is not like to be cured . . . Sir, you would pity me if you saw me write, and therefore will pardon me if I write no more: my pain hath drawn my head so much awry, and holds it so, that mine eye cannot follow mine hand." Even before these ailments came, he had written, impatiently, "I would every day provide for my soul's last convoy, though I know not when I shall die, and perchance I shall never die."

His compliments had a self-pitying sincerity, now. He was "not of the best stuff for friendship, which men of warm and durable fortunes only are." "I hope you have both pleasure and business: only to me, who have neither . . . ."

But it was good to have friends, distinguished friends, to complain to, to exchange news, compliments, or poems with, to nurse still some hope of being advanced by their influence. Magdalen Herbert, some seven years Donne's senior, was the mother of ten, two of whom turned out to be geniuses. Her eldest son became Lord Herbert of Cherbury, an intellectual poet of Donne's school, famous also for Latin treatises that made him the father of deism and for his vainglorious, swashbuckling autobiography in which he confides that among other marks of the divine favor a sweet odor attended him at all times: when he opened his robes it was almost overpowering. He freely acknowledged that he was so handsome that one married lady carried his picture "hid ... under her breasts," taking it out at night to pore over it by candle: he caught her at this secret adoration, which led to a duel with her husband. The other genius was George Herbert, the first of Donne's outstanding followers in religious poetry, who, consumptive, outlived his master by only two years. Donne and Mrs. Herbert had met while the latter was residing at Oxford supervising the education there of her oldest son. Perhaps the poet had gone down on an errand for Sir George More, who had won the young man's wardship by the payment of 800 pounds to his guardian, Sir Francis Newport, Mrs. Herbert being a widow until her second marriage in 1608 to a rich knight less than half her age. Presumably, it was at this time, when she was in her evidently new-flowering middle forties, that she received the mixed compliment of Elegy IX, "The Autumnal."

It begins most quotably:

> No spring nor summer beauty hath such grace
> As I have seen in one autumnal face.

"Of all fair things the autumn too is fair" was a Greek saying remembered by Bacon in his essay "Of Beauty." We are promised a poem that will glow with an appreciation for the graces of middle age. But soon Donne has buried everything but his cleverness in Mrs. Herbert's wrinkles:

> Call not these wrinkles *graves*; if graves they were,
> They were Love's graves, for else he is nowhere.
> Yet lies not Love dead here, but here doth sit
> Vowed to this trench like an anachorit;
> And here till hers, which must be his death, come,
> He doth not dig a grave, but build a tomb.

A wrinkle easily becomes a trench, with just a bit of digging. There follows, by a natural horticultural development, a typical recondite reference to "Xerxes' strange Lydian love, the platan tree," then a ghastly distinction:

> But name not winter faces, whose skin's slack,
>   Lank as an unthrift's purse, but a soul's sack;
> Whose eyes seek light within, for all here's shade;
>   Whose mouths are holes, rather worn out than made;
> Whose every tooth to a several place is gone,
>   To vex their souls at resurrection:
> Name not these living death's-heads unto me,
>   For these, not ancient, but antique be.

Such was the egregious taste—or the taste for egregiousness—that can so often be found in the metaphysical poets and that Dr. Johnson deplored. Have the decency not to live too long, Mrs. Herbert. Meanwhile treasure such compliments as I in my incredible ingenuity (and obsession with decay) have bestowed upon you. For all the difference between that time's way of thinking and ours, we may presume to imagine that the poem was not found to be an unalloyed compliment, whatever the recovered serenity of its ending,

>   may still
> My love descend, and journey down the hill.
> Not panting after growing beauties; so
>   I shall ebb out with them who homeward go.

At least we know how Queen Elizabeth would have taken it. When the bishop of St. David's in 1596 was so presumptuous—so inexcusably homiletic—as to dilate in a sermon on her age, her wrinkles, and the approach of death, the Queen was highly displeased, and that was the end of Anthony Rudd's chance of further preferment. Essex might never have been executed if he had not struck at the core of her womanhood with the contemptuous words, on someone's mentioning "Her Majesty's conditions": "Her conditions! Her conditions are as crooked as her carcass!" Jonson told Drummond, "Queen Elizabeth never saw herself after she became old in a true glass; they painted her, and sometimes would vermilion her nose." Of course there is an honesty in Donne's poem—he does not peddle biological escapism. But there is a perversity, too. It has been suggested that the aim was "a philosophical paradox on the golden mean."

Another good friend and recipient of poems was the Countess of Huntingdon. Thomas Morton had been patronized by the third Earl. The nephew, Henry Hastings, the fifth Earl of Huntingdon, married Elizabeth, the third daughter of that Countess of Derby who became Egerton's third wife. Thus Donne, while in Egerton's employ, had known this stepdaughter of the Lord Keeper's before her marriage in 1603. In the words of Jessopp, "Lady Huntingdon grew to be one of the leaders of fashion at the court of James I, and her salons were frequented by men of letters and conversationalists, who always found a cordial welcome." She was on occasion to help Donne with his debts, as did his other Countess, her first cousin, the brilliant Lucy Russell, Countess of Bedford.

Lucy's marriage dated back to 1594, and she had been a lady-in-waiting to Queen Elizabeth. She grew in favor under James and Anne, and appeared in masques by Jonson and Daniel between 1603 and 1610. She provided the inspiration for "Twicknam Garden," if not "A Nocturnal Upon St. Lucy's Day," and was addressed seven of the Verse Letters. Donne saw a good deal of her in 1608, the year he named a daughter after her, she coming to Mitcham to stand as godmother. This "friend of the muses" aspired to verse herself; Grierson attributes to her an Elegy on Mistress Boulstred beginning, like one of the Holy Sonnets, "Death be not proud." Goodyer was attached to her household; she was the more active in her piety and graciousness for her husband's being paralyzed. She drew Donne to ecstatic freedom from misogyny:

> for you are here
> The first good angel, since the world's frame stood,
> That ever did in woman's shape appear.

Another verse letter starts, "Madam, You have refined me, and to worthiest things." She was ever, as by the salutation of a prose letter, "Happiest and Worthiest Lady," or, as if Dante and Beatrice were alive again, "the best Lady," "the good Lady." He even wrote elegies on her friends and relatives, whom he did not know well or at all. But this he was soon to do at phenomenal length for a girl he had never seen.

We have abundant evidence that Donne was good company, even during his years of greatest discouragement. True, he could plunge into letters that, anticipating the future, sounded like sermons. He apologized for this. "But I must not give you a homily for a letter." "I mean to write a letter, and I am fallen into a discourse." But it was a thoughtful age, and he gave his highly intelligent friends no more than they wanted. "My meditations are neither too wide nor too deep for you, except only that my way of expressing them may be extended beyond your patience and pardon." He was moody, but his moods were interesting. "Sometimes when I find myself transported with jollity and love of company, I hang leads at my heels, and reduce to my thoughts my fortunes, my years, the duties of a man, of a friend, of a husband, of a father, and all the incumbencies of a family; when sadness dejects me, either I countermine it with another sadness, or I kindle squibs about me again, and fly into sportfulness and company." A squib was a fizzing firecracker, and secondarily a lampoon. He used the word about this time of the sun, no less: "The Sun is spent, and now his flasks / Send forth light squibs, no constant rays" ("A Nocturnal," 34). Closer is the contrast in "The Litany": "Dead clods of sadness, or light squibs of mirth" (128).

It was in the fall of 1608 that Donne applied for a post in Ireland. "To come a little nearer myself," he told Goodyer in his weekly letter, "Sir Geoffrey Fenton, one of his Majesty's secretaries in Ireland, is dead; and I have made some offer for the place, in preservation whereof, as I have had occasion to employ all my friends, so I have not found in them all (except Bedford) more haste and words (for when those two are together, there is much comfort even in the least) than in the L[ord] Hay. In good faith he promised so roundly, so abundantly, so profusely, as I suspected him, but performed whatever he undertook (and my requests were the measures of his undertakings) so readily and truly, that his compliments became obligations, and having spoke like a courtier, did like a friend." James Hay was one of those good-looking young Scots that the King liked to have around him. Beginning as Gentleman of the Bedchamber, he rose to be Lord Hay, Viscount Doncaster, and Earl of Carlisle. In February, 1607, the King had paid his debts, when all the City knew that money was low in the Exchequer. Now Hay was being good-natured in his turn, but Donne had not yet acquired the odor of sanctity. "I have been told, that when your Lordship did me that extreme favour of presenting my name, his Majesty remembered me by the worst part of my history, which was my disorderly proceedings, seven years since, in my nonage. As your Lordship's earnestness and alacrity in doing good, and almost unthriftiness in multiplying and heaping your favours, gave me scarce leisure to consider how great your first favour of promising was, because you overtook it presently with a greater, which was the performing it; so I humbly beseech your Lordship to add another to these, not to be too apprehensive of any suspicion, that there lies upon me any dishonourable stain, or can make my King have any prejudice against me, for that intemperate and hasty act of mine: for the Lord Chancellor and his brother-in-law, Sir G. M., whose daughter I married, would both be likely, and will be ready to declare it, for his Majesty's satisfaction, or your Lordship's, that their displeasure, commenced so long since, should be thought to continue still, or interrupt any of my fortunes." What Donne said was true, of course. Egerton, now Lord Chancellor Ellesmere, had never ceased to respect his former secretary: as for the latter, he was soon to present his first published book, with a personal letter, "to make it a testimony of my gratitude towards your Lordship and an acknowledgment that those poor sparks of understanding or judgment which are in me were derived and kindled from you, and owe themselves to you." As for Sir George, he was soon going to open his purse strings at last. But in the narrow involuted rounds of the Court, scandal was slow to· evaporate, as would have been natural in open, airier places. These people had the leisure, the malice, and the ambition to remember—and regurgitate—gossip.

The talk in February, 1609, was, "News is here none at all, but that John Donne seeks to be Secretary at Virginia." It is piquant to think of Donne in the company of Captain John Smith (who was to die the same year he did and to whose 1624 *History of Virginia* he contributed commendatory verses) and Pocahontas. But this was another will-o'-the wisp. No one would have him as secretary anywhere. "Since therefore I am but mine own secretary (and what's that?), I were excusable if I writ nothing, since I am so." He traveled no further than Twickenham garden, where he and the Countess of Bedford showed each other their verses.

The great ladies now around him did not tempt him (him the worried family man nearing forty) in the old ways, or rather, the young ways. If carnal love had given him poetry, now sickness or religion did, especially the two in combination. "Since my imprisonment in my bed, I have made a meditation in verse, which I call a Litany; the word you know imports no other than supplication, but all Churches have one form of supplication by that name."

This, the longest of the religious poems, arose, like *Biathanatos,* out of deep depression:

> Father of Heaven, and him, by whom
> It, and us for it, and all else, for us
>   Thou madest, and govern'st ever, come
> And re-create me, now grown ruinous:
>   My heart is by dejection clay,
>   And by self-murder red.
> From this red earth, O Father, purge away

All vicious tinctures, that new fashioned
I may rise up from death before I'm dead.

Melancholy, the cold and dry humor, corresponds to clay.
Just as there is preoccupation here with the sin of Adam,
so the etymology of "Adam" is played on—"red earth"—
the ground from which man was formed. As one of the
Sermons would put it, "We are made but men ... and
man ... is but Adam: and Adam is but earth, but red
earth, earth dyed red in blood, ... the blood of our own
souls." In the new direction in which he turns, Donne has
lost none of his agility. The Virgin Mary is "that she-
cherubin." The Twelve Apostles are "Thy illustrious
Zodiac." A man to whom ingenuity came so easily has to
pray to be saved from it: "When we are moved to seem
religious / Only to vent wit, Lord deliver us." He has to
steer, too, between the Scylla of excess passion and the
Charybdis of no feeling at all, supplicating "That our
affections kill us not, nor die." What a modern light to
beam forth suddenly from this baroque, more Catholic
than Anglican, church! Self-awareness shows the difficulty
of all paths. "From thirst, or scorn, of fame deliver us."

There came to the Donnes financial easement at last,
"Sir George conditioning by bond to pay to Mr. Donne
£ 800 at a certain day as a portion with his wife or £ 20
quarterly for their maintenance as the interest for it till
the said portion was paid." Walton says that this rendering
up of Mrs. Donne's dower—some seven years late—was
achieved through the intervention of Sir Francis Wooley,
"a little before" that stanch friend's death in 1610. Eighty
pounds a year—10 per cent interest on the promised
portion—was a very fair sum to be able to count on. The
health of the Donnes improved, thanks, no doubt, to a
better diet. John, able now to outfit himself as a gentleman
had to, began turning up in London.

He also became a published author. "About this time
there grew many disputes that concerned the oath of
supremacy and allegiance in which the King had appeared
and engaged himself by his public writings now extant.

And His Majesty discoursing with Mr. Donne concerning many of the reasons which are usually urged against the taking of those oaths, apprehended such a validity and clearness in his stating the questions and his answers to them that His Majesty commanded him to bestow some time in drawing the arguments into a method and then to write his answers to them and having done that not to send but be his own messenger and bring them to him. To this he presently and diligently applied himself and within six weeks brought them to him under his own handwriting as they be now printed, the book bearing the name of *Pseudo-Martyr*, printed *anno* 1610."

That the book was written by royal command, and within six weeks, are both doubtful assertions. Donne seems to contravene Walton on the first point in his dedicatory address to the King: "Of my boldness in this address, I most humbly beseech your Majesty to admit this excuse, that having observed how much your Majesty had vouchsafed to descend to a conversation with your Subjects by way of your books, I also conceived an ambition of ascending to your presence by the same way . . . ." This is the courtier who is not so close to the King as he would like to be, or is going to be. Nor was this four-hundred-page mound of learning shaped in six weeks: Donne himself speaks of having circulated a table of contents "many months." But Walton, though exaggerating, as usual, has some truth in his statements: the work was done "by your Majesty's permission," and given "a hasty despatch that it might cost no man much time, either in expecting before it came, or in reading, when it was come." It has numerous misprints.

The dedication had Donne's name on it, the title page not: "Pseudo-Martyr, wherein Out of Certain Propositions and Gradations this Conclusion is evicted, that Those which are of the Roman Religion in this Kingdom may and ought to take the Oath of Allegiance." King James received a copy on the evening of January 24, 1610. Egerton was given one, as previously mentioned. The copy presented to Rowland Woodward—a courtier who was addressed several of the Verse Letters—is extant with a Spanish tag neatly topping the title page meaning, "Of games the best is with the leaf." However, this promise of light reading is not fulfilled, and it is understandable that this has been the one work of Donne's that has never been reprinted.

In assisting Morton, Donne had accumulated material that he saw he could put to use. Moreover he did not think much of a book that had lately come out on the Anglican side: so that conviction that has led to the making of so many books took root in him: he could do a better book himself. The author who unintentionally inspired him was William Barlow, who had been bishop of Lincoln since 1608. Barlow had already come in for attention in "The Courtier's Library" for his sycophantic sermon, delivered according to Cecil's instructions, on the Sunday after Essex's execution, defending that judicial murder. In 1609 Barlow answered an attack by Parsons the Jesuit on James I's work, *An Apology for the Oath of Allegiance* (1607). Goodyer received from Donne a lengthy comment on Barlow's *An Answer to a Catholic Englishman.* The climax of the criticism is, "I will adventure to say to you, without inserting one unnecessary word, that the book is full of falsifications in words and in sense, and of falsehoods in matter of fact, and of inconsequent and unscholarlike arguings, and of relinquishing the King, in many points of defence, and of contradiction of himself, and of dangerous and suspected doctrine in divinity, and of silly ridiculous triflings, and of extreme flatteries, and of neglecting better and more obvious answers, and of letting slip some enormous advantages which the other gave and he spies not."

So Donne in his own tract was determinedly moderate and scholarly and, for the most part, free of coruscation that might have been interesting but unfair. Except for some self-references at the beginning, which also had their relevance, he kept to the heavily documented point, a rather legal one. Did Ben Jonson ever get through *Pseudo-*

Martyr, the friend who said, "These fencers in religion I like not"?

The subject of *Pseudo-Martyr* was not wholly unrelated to that of *Biathanatos,* as the "Advertisement to the Reader" brings out:

> And for myself, because I have already received some light that some of the Roman profession, having only seen the heads and grounds handled in this book, have traduced me as an impious and profane undervaluer of martyrdom, I most humbly beseech him (till the reading of the book may guide his reason) to believe that I have a just and Christianly estimation and reverence of that devout and acceptable sacrifice of our lives for the glory of our blessed Saviour. For, as my fortune hath never been so flattering nor abundant as should make this present life sweet and precious to me, as I am a moral man: so, as I am a Christian, I have been ever kept awake in a meditation of martyrdom by being derived from such a stock and race as, I believe, no family (which is not of far larger extent and greater branches) hath endured and suffered more in their persons and fortunes, for obeying the teachers of Roman doctrine, than it hath done. I did not therefore enter into this as a carnal or over-indulgent favorer of this life, but out of such reasons as may arise to his knowledge who shall be pleased to read the whole work.

"Pseudo-martyr" was a term that had been applied by a continuator of Holinshed's *Chronicles* in 1587 to Campion: "What trust is to be given to the words of such pseudo-martyrs?" Those Englishmen, Donne now reasoned, who followed their Jesuit masters down the road of recusancy and sedition were not true martyrs but rebels and suicides. They were entitled to no honor whatsoever, and their hope of receiving a heavenly crown was delusive. "To offer our lives for defence of the Catholic faith hath ever been a religious custom; but to call every pretence of the Pope, Catholic faith, and to bleed to death for it, is a sickness and a medicine, which the Primitive Church never understood."

I call to witness against you those whose testimony God himself hath accepted. Speak then and testify, O you glorious and triumphant Army of Martyrs, who enjoy now a permanent triumph in heaven, which knew the voice of your shepherd and stayed till he called, and went then with all alacrity: Is there any man received into your blessed Legion by title of such a death as sedition, scandal, or any human respect occasioned? Oh no, for they which are in possession of that laurel are such as have washed their garments, not in their own blood only (for so they might still remain red and stained), but in the *blood of the Lamb which changes them to white.*

As in *Biathanatos,* Donne detects a widespread human tendency towards wanton suffering, the martyr complex. He had known his own vacillations, the latest recorded in "The Litany": "Oh, to some / Not to be martyrs is a martyrdom." He recognizes in the Jesuits a lust for self-destruction.

This, then, with its implications of successful struggle against the past, is the most interesting general feature of a tract that has been gathering dust in rare book rooms these three and a half centuries. The prefatory part is the only ostensibly personal part. "A Preface to the Priests and Jesuits, and to their Disciples in this Kingdom" states: "And if they will be content to impute to me all human infirmities, they shall need to feign nothing: I am, I confess, obnoxious enough. My natural impatience not to dig painfully in deep, and stony, and sullen learnings; my indulgence to my freedom and liberty, as in all other indifferent things, so in my studies also, not to betroth or enthrall myself to any one science which should possess or denominate me; my easiness to afford a sweet and gentle interpretation to all professors of Christian religion, if they shake not the foundation, wherein I have in my ordinary communication and familiar writings often expressed and declared myself—hath opened me enough to their malice, and put me into their danger, and given them advantage to impute to me whatsoever such degrees of laziness, of liberty, of irresolution, can produce." So much for Donne's public view of himself. He is not shy of what his critics would certainly consider "natural impatience" with canon law, papal pretensions, wrestlings with texts, and "this comical-tragical doctrine of purgatory" of which "all discourse . . . seems to me to be but the mythology of the Roman Church, and a moral application of pious and useful fables."

In two places *Pseudo-Martyr* is not without anecdotal interest. By way of pointing to the absurd extremes of literal obedience practiced by monks and friars, Donne tells of two youths whom their Abbot sent with a load of figs to an eremite, whom they never succeeded in finding because they got lost in the desert, whereupon they starved to death rather than touch the figs meant for another. A hundred pages later Donne has fun with the naïvete of the Gloss to the Decretals of Gratian: "And when Lanfred, a young lusty bishop and a great huntsman, was defamed also for immoderate familiarity with his own daughter, the Gloss says, 'It was not for any evil, for they were too near in blood, but because he kissed her so much openly and put his hand in her bosom.'" The same gloss offers also a charitable definition of a *meretrix*, a harlot: she is not one until "she hath lain with 23,000 men." (Donne was so fascinated by this figure, as well he might be, that he repeated it in his next book.)

Once only does Donne raise his voice, in a resounding indictment of the Jesuits (Uncle Jasper? Uncle Ellis?) for "kindling and blowing, begetting and nourishing jealousies in Princes, and contempts in subjects, dissension in families, wrangling in schools, and mutinies in armies, ruins of noble houses, corruption of blood, confiscation of states, torturing of bodies, and anxious entangling and perplexing of consciences."

In an age that doted on controversy, he was bound to be answered sooner or later. Thomas Fitzherbert blasted at him, three years later, in 1613, charging him with having "disgorged all the venom of his satirical vein against Catholic religion." This pamphleteer's objection to

"M. Donne's Lucianical and atheistical" humor gives the impression that Fitzherbert had meanwhile read Donne's 1611 publication, *Ignatius his Conclave*. This work, in quite a different vein from *Pseudo-Martyr*, is so lively that one twentieth-century publisher dropped it in putting out a popular edition of Donne's prose and verse, although the same publisher's more expensive edition, the basis for the cheaper edition, contained it. The masses must be protected from offense—and Donne was certainly out, this time, to make infernal fun of the Jesuits, his former teachers, his bygone relatives. He reacted with a vengeance: none so zealous as he who has lately changed sides.

The satire, which fills but forty or fifty pages in a modern edition, ran through three editions in 1611, two in Latin and one in English, all without the author's name, which was added in 1634. The advantages of writing in Latin were two. The book could be read on the Continent. Being confined to an audience of scholars, it could also be more scurrilous. The contrast with *Pseudo-Martyr* is acknowledged in "The Printer to the Reader": "The Author was unwilling to have this book published, thinking it unfit, both for the matter which in itself is weighty and serious, and for that gravity which himself had proposed and observed in another book formerly published, to descend to this kind of writing. But I on the other side mustered my forces against him, and produced reasons and examples."

Ignatius his Conclave, or His Inthronisation in a Late Election in Hell: wherein Many Things are Mingled by Way of Satire, concerning the Disposition of Jesuits, the Creation of a New Hell, the Establishing of a Church in the Moon has a double interest reflected in its form. It carries on the old controversy of whether there can be any sanction for a Catholic conspiracy against—or even assassination of—a monarch regarded as heretical or resistant to the temporal sovereignty of the papacy. In May, 1610, Henry IV of France was slain by Ravaillac; his predecessor, Henry III, suffered the same fate at the hands of a Dominican. In 1605 there had been the Gunpowder Plot against James. The fears and suspicions that had marked Elizabeth's reign were rampant again. A Spanish Jesuit, Juan de Mariana, had given his blessing, in a book first published in 1598, to what he called tyrannicide: "if the Prince overstep the limits of his authority, he may rightfully be restrained by force, warred upon and deposed and killed"; "tyrannicide is justified in anyone by any means, except poison: and even poison may be used so long as the tyrant is not made to kill himself with it." After Henry IV's murder Mariana's book was proscribed by the Parliament of Paris and the Sorbonne: thus there was laid the basis for a conflict that Donne took pleasure in setting forth on his title page: "All Dedicated to the two Adversary Angels, which are protectors of the Papal Consistory, and of the College of Sorbonne." Why should he not let himself go, for a change? "He chooses and desires that his other book should testify his ingenuity and candor, and his disposition to labor for the reconciling of all parts. This book must teach what human infirmity is, and how hard a matter it is for a man much conversant in the books and acts of Jesuits so thoroughly to cast off the Jesuits as that he contract nothing of their natural drosses, which are petulancy and lightness."

In a dream vision or "ecstasy" the author "saw all the rooms in Hell open to my sight," and particularly "a secret place where there were not many, beside Lucifer himself, to which only they had title which had so attempted any innovation in this life that they gave an affront to all antiquity." Hovering jealously by Lucifer's chair is Ignatius Loyola, the founder of the Society of Jesus (who had been beatified by Pope Paul V in 1609). He speaks against six innovators who come in succession knocking for admission. "Knowing well that many thousands of his family aspired to that place, he opposed himself against all others. He was content they should be damned, but not that they should govern." The named applicants who try to win a place close to Lucifer are Copernicus, Paracelsus ("Philippus Aureolus Theophrastus Paracelsus Bombast of Hohenheim") the alchemist, Machiavelli, Aretino, Columbus, and Philip Nerius, the founder of the Congregation Oratorii. Machiavelli is given the main speech, making allegations at unwholesome length about the private lives of the popes, their crimes and orgies, heterosexual and homosexual. But Ignatius has no trouble retaining his fiendish post of honor, the devil himself being afraid of him: "Therefore he determined to withdraw himself into his inward chamber, and to admit none but Ignatius: for he could not exclude him, who had deserved so well; neither did he think it safe to stay without, and give him more occasions to amplify his own worth."

A number of Donne's remarks are worthy of Swift. "For so the truth be lost, it is no matter how." "But if perchance once in an hundred years some one of the scum of the people be put to death for sodomy, and that, not so much for the offence, as for usurping the right of the ecclesiastic princes, we must not much lament . . . ." "But yet it must be an argument to us of no very nimble wit, if a man do so admire the Pope that he leave out the Devil, and so worship the image without relation to the prototype and first pattern." ". . . such as might be reduced to an art and method in licentiousness (for Jesuits never content themselves with the theory in anything, but straight proceed to practise)." The Jesuits spread rumors of miracles in the Indies "till one of our Order, in a simplicity and ingenuity fitter for a Christian than a Jesuit, acknowledged and lamented that there were no miracles done there." "Canonization is now grown a kind of declaration by which all men may take knowledge that such a one, to whom the Church of Rome is much beholden, is now made partaker of the principal dignities and places in Hell." Machiavelli entertains the Devil with a blasphemous parody of the Nicene Creed: "out of your abundant love, you begot this dearly beloved son of yours, Ignatius, which stands at your right hand."

The other point of interest in *Ignatius his Conclave* has to do with Donne's alertness to "the new philosophy," the new science, specifically the latest discoveries in

astronomy. Copernicus, Galileo, Tycho Brahe, and Kepler
are more than mentioned, and their discoveries or hypoth-
eses aired. Copernicus "was a soul to the earth and gave
it motion," "turned the whole frame of the world."
Galileo's latest book, out only a few months, is cited in
the margin, *Sidereus Nuncius*, or, to translate its full title,
"The Astronomical Messenger: Containing and setting
forth Observations lately made with the aid of a newly
invented Telescope respecting the Moon's Surface, the
Milky Way, Nebulous Stars, an innumerable multitude of
Fixed Stars, and also respecting Four Planets never before
seen, which have been named the Cosmian Stars." Wotton
had sent a copy on publication day to King James from
Venice. A work of Kepler's that had not even been published Donne may have seen a copy of and it may have
influenced the form of his satire. At least Kepler himself
thought that Donne had somehow made contact with a
manuscript of his *Somnium* (Dream), a piece of theoreti-
cally sound science fiction about a moon voyage. "I suspect
that the author of that impudent satire, *Ignatius his Conclave*, had got hold of a copy of this little work, for he
pricks me by name in the very beginning. Further on, he
brings up poor Copernicus to the judgment seat of Pluto—
if I don't mistake, the approach to that is through the
yawning chasms of Hecla" (in Iceland or "Islandia," the
original setting of *Somnium*). The beginning and ending
of *Ignatius his Conclave* carry the hint of a cosmic voyage,
it being proposed to translate the Jesuits to the moon.
Speculation over the plurality of worlds would soon run
wild, now that the telescope had brought the planets
nearer. No one was ever more up to date than—to give
the inevitable title of a recent article—"Donne the Space
Man." (As for *Biathanatos*, 1963 saw the ritual suicides of
Buddhist monks in South Vietnam.) An expression that
later centuries have made trite is his, and occurs in this
work: "modern man."

Donne (who ended up a Tychoist) had put to metaphorical use the heliocentric universe in a 1609 letter to
Goodyer. "I often compare not you and me, but the

sphere in which your resolutions are and my wheel, both I hope concentric to God: for methinks the new astronomy is thus appliable well, that we which are a little earth should rather move towards God, than that He which is fulfilling, and can come no whither, should move towards us." The revolution in astronomy turns up in various poems, dated and undated. What was blithe in *Ignatius his Conclave* became material for gloom in the first of the long poems on the death of Elizabeth Drury, *The First Anniversary*, 1611.

For, besides receiving now a steady income from his father-in-law, Donne won his way to the favor of a hospitable patron, Sir Robert Drury. This "gentleman of a very noble estate, and a more liberal mind, assigned him and his wife an useful apartment in his own large house in Drury Lane, and not only rent-free, but was also a cherisher of his studies, and such a friend as sympathized with him and his in all their joy and sorrows." But Donne was the first sympathizer, calculatingly and at a distance. When the Drurys' only child, Elizabeth, died in December, 1610, within two months of her fifteenth birthday, Donne, although "I never saw the gentlewoman," sent to the grief-stricken parents the first of a series of annual tributes. Thus commenced an important connection that led to Donne's being a tenant of the Drurys until 1621 and travel-ing with them abroad. Walton, especially in the later version of his Life, exaggerated the Donnes' dependence. Recently discovered documents indicate that they paid rent—though perhaps only a nominal rent—and occupied a separate establishment on Drury Lane, a "brick howse . . . with a little passage and a smale Court to the same belonginge." The Drurys helped with the furnishings.

Sir Robert Drury and Donne may have been acquainted previously. They had friends in common. Lady Drury's uncle was Sir Francis Bacon. Joseph Hall, who like Donne passed from satirist to cleric, served as rector at Hawstead, the country seat, in Suffolk, of this extremely wealthy family. He was there from 1601 to 1608. While there he complained of one who was none other than Donne's brother-in-law.

> I found there a dangerous opposite to the success of my ministry, a witty and bold atheist, one Mr. Lyly, who by reason of his travels and abilities of discourse and behavior had so deeply insinuated himself into my patron, Sir Robert Drury, that there was small hopes (during his entireness) for me to work any good upon that noble patron of mine, who by the suggestion of this wicked detractor was set off from me before he knew me.

Around 1594 Anne Donne, John's elder sister, had taken as her second husband this William Lyly, an ex-government agent. How the Catholic mother, who had striven so hard to indoctrinate her children in the old faith, must have grieved over her daughter's dereliction in passing from a recusant first husband to "a witty and bold atheist" that had actually served as an informer against papists abroad! He had certainly offended Hall, who took his death by plague in 1603 as an act of God.

> Finding the obduredness and hopeless condition of that man, I bent my prayers against him, beseeching God daily that He would be pleased to remove by some means or other that apparent hindrance to my faithful labors, who gave me an answer accordingly. For this malicious man going hastily up to London to exasperate my patron against me, was then and there swept away by the pestilence, and never returned to do any further mischief.

The widow may have stayed on at Hawstead and introduced her brother to Drury and spoken in terms that he did not forget of the hope and heir, the girl whose father's dream was said to be that she should marry Prince Henry, James's elder son—who also was destined to be cut off in his teens, two years after Elizabeth Drury, and be commemorated by Donne.

It is not certain what caused Elizabeth Drury's death.

Both in the only extant portrait and in the alabaster statue over her grave she lies on her left side, her head propped up on her elbow, looking tall and fragile, "One whose clear body was so pure and thin, / Because it need disguise no thought within." "Cullum records a tradition that Elizabeth died from a box on the ear; another, still current, alleges that she fell in love with a groom. To dispose of him, so the story goes, he was ordered to take out a dog to be destroyed, and instead he himself was, as if by accident, fatally shot. Elizabeth was so grief-stricken by his death that she was found some time later lying dead on his corn-bin!" Professor Bald adds, "Both tales, obviously apocryphal, are clearly *ex post facto*, creations of the rustic imagination to explain the posture of the figure on the monument." However, the Strindbergian Miss Julie tale has a certain fascination, and if Sir Robert was directly—by boxing her ears—or indirectly the cause of his daughter's death, he had added reason to indulge in an orgy of grief and to welcome Donne's hyperboles as nothing more than a proper crown to the tragedy.

Donne's shortest offering was "A Funeral Elegy," 106 lines. In print this was appended to "The First Anniversary," 474 lines. Although he was traveling abroad the next year, 1612, he was able to produce "The Second Anniversary," 528 lines. This program of annual commemoration threatened to be—already was—even more limitless than that monstrous epic, *The Progress of the Soul*. Had he met with less criticism, Donne might have gone on heaping monuments upon the slight dust of Elizabeth Drury till his own sands ran out. In the third poem he announces his "chaste ambition is / Yearly to bring forth such a child as this." But Jonson, the Countess of Bedford, and others brought him to his senses. On foundations like this was laid the future charge against the metaphysical poets—lack of judgment.

"The First Anniversary" was published with "A Funeral Elegy" in 1611, with a commendatory poem by Hall preceding. With the exception of an occasional piece or two, this was the first time any of Donne's poems had seen print—this at the instance of the proud father and, probably, Hall, who had the same publisher. The philosophical purpose of "The First Anniversary" or "An Anatomy of the World" is set forth in the subtitle, "wherein, by occasion of the untimely death of Mistress Elizabeth Drury the frailty and the decay of this whole world is represented." There is a further guide in the marginal notes. We see how this metaphysical poet widens out from the individual to the universal, "anatomy" meaning "analysis." The recurring line is, "She, she is dead; she's dead; when thou knowst this"—something is realized about the decline of the world. He said in "A Funeral Elegy," "she / Being spent, the world must needs decrepit be." A relationship between the death of a woman and the death of the world had been limned in a youthful poem, "A Fever."

> But when thou from this world wilt go,
>   The whole world vapors with thy breath.
> Or if, when thou, the world's soul, goest,
>   It stay, 'tis but thy carcass then.

The most famous passage in "The First Anniversary" is:

> So did the world from the first hour decay;
> That evening was beginning of the day,
> And now the springs and summers which we see,
> Like sons of women after fifty be.
> And new philosophy calls all in doubt,
> The element of fire is quite put out;
> The sun is lost, and th'earth, and no man's wit
> Can well direct him where to look for it.
> And freely men confess that this world's spent,
> When in the planets and the firmament
> They seek so many new; then see that this
> Is crumbled out again to his atomies.
> Tis all in pieces, all coherence gone;
> All just supply, and all relation:
> Prince, subject, father, son, are things forgot,
> For every man alone thinks he hath got

> To be a phoenix, and that there can be
> None of that kind, of which he is, but he.

Besides the upset wrought by the new astronomy, it was a
Christian concept that the world was going from bad to
worse in preparation for the final conflagration at the
Second Coming of Christ: "She, she is dead; she's dead;
when thou knowst this, / Thou knowst how dry a cinder
this world is." It was also a classical concept—the
worsening from the Golden Age to the Iron Age. "She,"
besides being Sir Robert Drury's daughter, has been taken
by one critic or another as standing for Jesus Christ (or
the Logos), the Virgin Mary, Astraea (Justice), the last of
the goddesses to flee the earth at the end of the Golden
Age, when she became the constellation Virgo, Elizabeth
the Virgin Queen, Wisdom personified as a female (God's
consort in the Old Testament and the Apocrypha) and
"the Idea of a Woman." The last phrase is Donne's in
answer to Jonson's criticism that the poems were "pro-
phane and full of blasphemies; that he told Mr. Donne if
it had been written of the Virgin Mary it had been something; to which he answered that he described the Idea
of a Woman, and not as she was."

So Donne paid a remarkable "first year's rent"—an
advance down payment, with cash and more verses to
follow. In 1612 "The Second Anniversary" came out, re-
employing the title of an unfinished poem, "Of the Progress of the Soul," "wherein, by occasion of the religious
death of Mistress Elizabeth Drury, the incommodities of
the soul in this life, and her exaltation in the next, are
contemplated." Another piece of Hall's acted as "The
Harbinger to the Progress," and the two earlier poems
were included in the volume, which again lacked Donne's
name, as did reprints in 1621 and 1625. The result has
been labeled by two modern critics "one of the great religious poems of the seventeenth century," although the
Anniversaries are not ordinarily classified among the
"Divine Poems." They are certainly the product of a
profound and searching melancholy.

The most often quoted lines in "The Second Anniversary" are: "her pure and eloquent blood / Spoke in her cheeks, and so distinctly wrought, / That one might almost say, her body thought." One who hailed this as in harmony with his philosophy was Thoreau. Emerson quoted the lines in his essay on "Love." Fielding used them to introduce Sophia Western.

Donne's interest in science is not confined to astronomy.

> Knowst thou but how the stone doth enter in
> The bladder's cave, and never break the skin?
> Knowst thou how blood, which to the heart doth flow,
> Doth from one ventricle to th'other go?
> And for the putrid stuff, which thou dost spit,
> Knowst thou how thy lungs have attracted it?

But the most medical pasage occurs as a simile at the beginning:

> Or as sometimes in a beheaded man,
> Though at those two red seas, which freely ran,
> One from the trunk, another from the head,
> His soul be sailed to her eternal bed,
> His eyes will twinkle, and his tongue will roll,
> As though he beckoned and called back his soul;
> He grasps his hands, and he pulls up his feet,
> And seems to reach, and to step forth to meet
> His soul . . . .

Donne must have attended the beheading of a noble, such as the Earl of Essex, on whom the headsman blundered so that he was nearly mobbed. Commoners were hanged.

The Anniversaries have received much academic attention in recent years, with agreement as to their importance but not as to their meaning. As noted, there has been a disposition to widen and strengthen the narrow shoulders of Elizabeth Drury—bearing an impossible weight—by transmogrifying her into a symbol. The

poems have been analyzed as traditional Ignatian meditations, with recurrent parts corresponding to the three parts
of the rational soul—memory, understanding, and will.
Where "The Second Anniversary" takes a "look upward,"
the First has touches of satire. One theory is that Donne
writes about two different worlds—one that died with
"Shee"—and this is the world with the dilemma we label
modern. But Donne and her mourners live in a different
world. Perhaps we should see the poems as Donne's first
sermons—*de contemptu mundi*. He says that all's wrong
with the world, but God's still in His heaven.

Although the work is reverenced in academic quarters
today, even to a separate edition in 1963—and has been
a happy hunting grounds for theorists—the author
received enough criticism, especially from jealous lady
friends, to regret publication. He wrote George Gerrard
from Paris in April, 1612:

> Of my Anniversaries, the fault which I acknowledge
> in myself is to have descended to print anything in verse,
> which, though it have excuse, even in our times, by
> example of men, which one would think should as little
> have done it as I; yet I confess I wonder how I declined
> to it, and do not pardon myself. But for the other part
> of the imputation of having said so much, my defence is,
> that my purpose was to say as well as I could; for since
> I never saw the gentlewoman, I cannot be understood to
> have bound myself to have spoken just truth; but I would
> not be thought to have gone about to praise anybody in
> rhyme, except I took such a person, as might be capable
> of all that I could say. If any of those ladies think that
> Mistress Drury was not so, let that lady make herself fit
> for all those praises in the book, and it shall be hers.

Sir Robert Drury had a perpetual desire to be an
ambassador—an ambition never fulfilled. Since he could
get no one to send him abroad, he sometimes sent himself.
John Chamberlain wrote Sir Dudley Carleton on December 4, 1611: "I cannot tell whether you have heard that

Sir Robert Drury and his lady have leave to travel for three years, and are already settled at Amiens, and with them John Donne." Actually the license providing for "twelve horses, coach and fifty pounds in money" had been granted five months before, but Sir Robert had many arrangements to make and Donne took some coaxing. Anne "was then with child"—as usual—"and otherways under so dangerous a habit of body as to her health that she professed an unwillingness to allow him any absence from her, saying, 'her divining soul boded her some ill in his absence,' and therefore desired him not to leave her. This made Mr. Donne lay aside all thoughts of the journey and really to resolve against it. But Sir Robert became restless in his persuasions for it; and Mr. Donne was so generous as to think he had sold his liberty when he received so many charitable kindnesses from him, and told his wife so; who did therefore with an unwilling-willingness give a faint consent to the journey." She received as a farewell present the "Song" "Sweetest love, I do not go / For weariness of thee," which attempts to soothe the fears that Walton mentions: "Let not thy divining heart / Forethink me any ill."

It could not have been an easy decision to undergo a separation, perhaps for years. Donne hesitated in a Latin letter to Goodyer. But he had debts, and he could not bear idleness. He was ready to grasp at any straw for secular employment. He could be useful to Sir Robert both as secretary and linguist. One disappointed courtier followed another. God and King James had not yet conquered. Mitcham was given up, and Anne and the children were sent off to the care of her sister, Lady Oglander, on the Isle of Wight. Goodyer was bid a somber farewell: "I speak to you at this time of departing, as I should do at my last upon my death-bed."[3]

At Amiens that winter, where two of the recreations were riding to the hounds and falconry, Donne busied

[3] Letter VI, Appendix.

himself with the civil law and with "The Second Anniversary." Morton's secretary tells of his study of the former:

> he passed over into France, where he gave himself to the study of the laws. And from Amiens (as I remember) he writ a letter to his always true friend Dean Morton, wherein he requested his advice whether taking of the degree of a doctor in that profession of the laws, it might not be conducible and advantageous unto him to practise at home in the, Arches, London. Unto whom the Dean then returned him answer, that in his judgment he thought the ministry in the Church of God would be safer and fitter for him: whereupon he desisted from further prosecution of those studies.

The concluding lines of "The Second Anniversary" refer to the country where the poem was composed: "Here in a place where misdevotion frames / A thousand prayers to saints, whose very names / The ancient Church knew not, Heaven knows not yet."

The party went on to Paris, where Donne had a clairvoyant experience (according to Walton, who, however, is so mixed up about place and dates and possible circumstances as to enhance doubt over an already doubtful episode—but good story).

> Two days after their arrival there, Mr. Donne was left alone in that room in which Sir Robert and he and some other friends had dined together. To this place Sir Robert returned within half an hour; and as he left, so he found Mr. Donne alone; but in such an ecstasy and so altered as to his looks as amazed Sir Robert to behold him. Insomuch that he earnestly desired Mr. Donne to declare what had befallen him in the short time of his absence. To which Mr. Donne was not able to make a present answer. But after a long and perplexed pause, did at last say, "I have seen a dreadful vision since I saw you. I have seen my dear wife pass twice by me through this room with her hair hanging about her shoulders and a dead child in her arms. This I have seen since I saw you." To which Sir

Robert replied, "Sure, Sir, you have slept since I saw you; and this is the result of some melancholy dream, which I desire you to forget, for you are now awake." To which Mr. Donne's reply was, "I cannot be surer that I live now than that I have not slept since I saw you, and am as sure that at her second appearing she stopped and looked me in the face and vanished." Rest and sleep had not altered Mr. Donne's opinion the next day. For he then affirmed this vision with a more deliberate and so confirmed a confidence that he inclined Sir Robert to a faint belief that the vision was true.

It is truly said that desire and doubt have no rest. And it proved so with Sir Robert, for he immediately sent a servant to Drury House with a charge to hasten back and bring him word whether Mrs. Donne were alive, and if alive, in what condition she was as to her health. The twelfth day the messenger returned with this account: that he found and left Mrs. Donne very sad and sick in her bed, and that after a long and dangerous labor she had been delivered of a dead child. And upon examination the abortion proved to be the same day and about the very hour that Mr. Donne affirmed he saw her pass by him in his chamber.

The dead child was buried January 22, 1612, when in fact the travelers were still in Amiens. Moreover, as late as April, letters from Donne to Goodyer show the husband still ignorant of the outcome of his wife's pregnancy. This explodes the last part of Walton's story, which, written sixty-three years after the event (it was added only to the last edition of the Life), may still preserve a modicum of truth, however "improved" in the retelling. (The story can be matched by others in the century, including a vision Jonson had—"his eldest son . . . with the mark of a bloody cross on his forehead," dead of the plague.)

The extra-sensory notification to Donne (a projection of his own anxieties?) would have taken place, if at all, around the latter part of March. On April 5 and 6 he witnessed elaborate celebrations in connection with the double betrothal of Louis XIII to Anne of Austria and his sister Elizabeth to the heir to the Spanish throne Religion aside, the Englishman was no unmitigated admirer of the French monarch, who had not yet reached his eleventh birthday. He had seen him once before on his previous visit to Paris. "That which was much observed in the King's more childish age, when I was last here, by those whom his father appointed to judge by an assiduous observation, his natural inclination is more and more confirmed, that his inclinations are cruel and tyrannous; and when he is any way affected, his stammering is so extreme as he can utter nothing." The visitor looked now at the "outward bravery" with perhaps a literally jaundiced eye, for besides his depression, he had had a sharp bout of illness, with vomiting followed by a fever. "The main bravery was the number of horses, which were above 800 caparisoned. Before the days the town was full of the five challengers' cartels, full of rodomontades; but in the execution there were no personal rencounters, nor other trial of any ability than running at the quintain and the ring."

In Gosse's words, "Nowhere is he so little of a divine as in these years immediately preceding his sudden resolution to enter the Church." This applies to his letters, at least. He stands on the sidelines of dispute. "I do (I thank God)," he wrote from Paris April 9, "naturally and heartily abhor all schism in religion so much, as, I protest, I am sorry to find this appearance of schism amongst our adversaries the Sorbonists." He was having his last fling at being a courtier, composing letters for a courtier and for that courtier's wife. A draft of a French letter in his hand survives, to be sent by Lady Drury to the Duchesse de Bouillon. The party had proceeded by slow stages to Frankfurt (which had the attraction of a reunion with Wotton) and were now in Heidelberg. Spa came next, for about a fortnight. In August they were at the Archduke's court at Brussels. The trip was nearly over, having lasted only ten months instead of the threatened three years. Donne could write, eagerly, that he expected to "sneak into London, about the end of August." He set out from

London for the Isle of Wight. By Michaelmas, September 29, the Donnes were back in the city as Sir Robert's tenants, in a house close to Drury House.

The memorializing of Elizabeth Drury was followed by "Elegy upon the Untimely Death of the Incomparable Prince Henry," which Jonson reported that Donne said "he wrote . . . to match Sir Edward Herbert in obscureness." This was published in the third edition of Joshua Sylvester's *Lachrymae Lachrymarum*, 1613, along with elegies by Herbert, Hall, Goodyer, and others. The history of England in the seventeenth century might have been very different if this elder brother of Charles had lived, instead of succumbing to typhoid fever at eighteen. As the poet (who had sent him his *Pseudo-Martyr* in 1610) conjectures, "What had his growth and generation done?" But the poem is unworthy of the young Prince of Wales' strong character. Grierson criticized its "tasteless extravagance." The point is that Donne was still working at being a courtier. He also produced "An Epithalamion, or Marriage Song" on the wedding of Henry's sister, Elizabeth (the youth in his last delirium had cried out for her rather than for his parents), to the Elector Palatine, a delayed ceremony which took place on St. Valentine's Day, 1613. Donne's opening stanza is the freshest tribute to birds (it was by tradition their mating day) since Chaucer:

> Hail Bishop Valentine, whose day this is,
> > All the air is thy diocese,
> > And all the chirping choristers
> And other birds are thy parishioners.
> > Thou marryest every year
> The lyric lark and the grave whispering dove,
> The sparrow that neglects his life for love,
> The household bird, with the red stomacher;
> > Thou mak'st the blackbird speed as soon
> As doth the goldfinch, or the halcyon.
> The husband cock looks out, and straight is sped,
> And meets his wife, which brings her featherbed.

This day more cheerfully than ever shine,
This day, which might inflame thyself, Old Valentine.

He commenced making up to Robert Ker, Viscount
Rochester, that favorite who rode high until a still prettier
one came along, the future Duke of Buckingham. Everybody was scrambling for office at this chaotic period that
followed the death of the able Lord Treasurer Salisbury.
Donne transcribed for Drury a document that showed
Rochester's eagerness for the post of Master of the Horse.
Drury himself tried for the ambassadorship to France,
which the ill-fated Overbury (soon to be murdered) had
gone to the Tower for refusing. Donne entertained high
hopes of official appointment.

He abruptly decided there would be "fortune" in
being a divine, after all. Base word, but that is not the
only base thing in the letter in which Lord Hay was
asked to pass on a letter to Rochester:

My Lord,-

I have told your Lordship often that I have no virtue
but modesty; and I begin to fear that I lose that in
saying so often that I have it; at least, if I were full
freighted with it before, I find that at this time I make
a desperate shipwreck of it. Either the boldness of putting
myself by this way of letter into my Lord of Rochester's
presence, or the boldness of begging from your Lordship
the favor of presenting it, would spend more of that virtue
than I have. But since I can strongly hope, out of the
general testimonies of his Lordship's true nobleness, that
he will allow me this interpretation, that I reserved myself
till now, when a resolution of a new course of life and
new profession makes me a little more worthy of his
knowledge; and that as soon as I had delivered myself over
to God, I deliver myself to him, I cannot doubt of your
Lordship's pardon for my boldness in using your mediation.

I did it not, my Lord, without some disputation. But
I thought it very unworthy to have sent a first letter to
his Lordship by a servant of my own, and to have made

it the business of any friend of mine who hath the honor of accesses to him. I thought myself tied by that to have communicated my purposes with him, that person, and so to have foreacquainted another with that which I desire his Lordship should first know. For I make account that it is in one instant that I tell his and your Lordship that I have brought all my distractions together, and find them in a resolution of making divinity my profession, that I may try whether my poor studies, which have profited me nothing, may profit others in that course; in which also a fortune may either be better made, or, at least, better missed, than in any other. One good fruit of it will be, that my prayers for your Lordship's happiness shall be, in that station, more effectual with God; and that, therein, I shall best show myself to be your Lordship's most humble and thankful servant.

It is hardly a Gospel certainty that a professional priest's "prayers for your Lordship's happiness shall be, in that station, more effectual with God." Donne is seen at his worst at this fawning time. His overture to Rochester couples service to God with the "virtues" of a catamite.

My Lord,-

I may justly fear that your Lordship hath never heard of the name which lies at the bottom of this letter; nor could I come to the boldness of presenting it now, without another boldness, of putting his Lordship, who now delivers it, to that office. Yet I have (or flatter myself to have) just excuses of this, and just ground of that ambition. For, having obeyed at last, after much debatement within me, the inspirations (as I hope) of the Spirit of God, and resolved to make my profession Divinity; I make account, that I do but tell your Lordship, what God hath told me, which is, that it is in this course, if in any, that my service presence, both in respect that I was an independent, and disobliged man, towards any other person in this State; and delivered over now (in my resolution) to be a household servant of God. I humbly beseech your Lordship that since these my purposes are likely to meet quickly a false and unprofitable dignity, which is the envy of others, you will vouchsafe to undertake, or prevent, or disable that, by affording them the true dignity of your just interpretations, and favorable assistance. And to receive into your knowledge so much of the history, and into your protection so much of the endeavors, of your Lordship's most humble and devoted servant.

All that can be said in extenuation is that this was the world Donne was born into—there are equivalent situations today—and that the writer, with his ailing wife and seven surviving children, still felt insecure, despite the material favors of his father-in-law and—putatively— Sir Robert Drury. The late Lord Treasurer had been frankly given by his father, the great Lord Burghley, the formula for getting ahead: "Be sure to keep some great man thy friend" and "Compliment him often." How did Bacon write when he sent one of the most glorious books of the age, *The Advancement of Learning*, to the author of this advice? He wrote humbly. "I humbly present one of the books to your Lordship.... Humbly desiring your acceptation thereof, with signification of humble duty, I remain...." In a realistic play of the period the needy hero is seen groveling to his patron: "I ... cast myself down at your worship's toes." It was not at all to the point that the feet were filthy, or of clay.

But Rochester did not encourage Donne's entry into the church, which was postponed till a sincerer time, two years later. However, the King's favorite did in some way respond to his overtures by planning useful work for him and by "buying" him. That is the word unabashedly employed in the next surviving letter.

My Most Honorable Good Lord,-
        After I was grown to be your

Lordship's by all the titles that I could think upon, it hath pleased your Lordship to make another title to me, by buying me. You may have many better bargains in your purchases, but never a better title than to me, nor anything which you may call yours more absolutely and entirely than me . . . .

One fruit of the purchase was an "Epithalamion" enclosed in an "Eclogue," celebrating the marriage of Ker, now become the Earl of Somerset, to Frances Howard, December 26, 1613. The "Epithalamion," which ends,

> This is joy's bonfire, then, where love's strong arts
> Make of so noble individual parts
> One fire of four inflaming eyes, and of two loving
> hearts.

has more nobility than the alliance it celebrates. Frances Howard, after being married for seven years to the third Earl of Essex, secured a divorce on outrageous grounds, in order to become the wife of her lover. She claimed Essex had never been able to consummate the marriage. Half the Commission found the evidence extremely doubtful, and the Archbishop of Canterbury, who presided, was of the opinion that the sort of divorce asked for did not exist in canon law at all. But James, who was remarkably free of jealousy when it came to the marital happiness of his minions, packed the court and forced the divorce or decree of nullity through. Meanwhile Lady Essex had seen to the murder of Overbury, who, eager to retain his own influence on Ker, stood in her way. When the scandal broke, it was the worst of the reign and showed the distance between the Court and the rest of the country. Donne, who in the Eclogue calls himself Idios, i.e. the private man who holds no place at court, voiced approval of the divorce, although he did not assist in the proceedings, as Gosse—confusing him with Sir Daniel Donne—thought. And he gave some of the blithest verses of his latter years to the criminal marriage, although prevented by illness from being personally present. "I deprehend in myself more than an alacrity, a vehemency to do service to that company, and so I may find reason to make rhyme."

He knew what was called for. Ignoring all rumors, outfacing them, indeed, he carefully adheres to the Epithalamion tradition that the bride and groom's confrontation on their wedding night was their first: "Their souls, though long acquainted they had been, / These clothes, their bodies, never yet had seen."

He missed the sight of that evil woman going to the altar with her hair shamelessly down on her shoulders as a virgin. Two days before Christmas he could hardly see. "It is one of my blind meditations to think what a miserable defeat it would be to all these preparations of bravery if my infirmity should overtake others; for, I am at least half-blind, my windows are all as full of glasses of waters as any mountebank's stall." For months he had been haunted, as Pepys was to be, by the fear of going blind: "my eyes do easily fall back to their distemper." "For if I do mine eyes a little more injury, I shall lose the honor of seeing you at Michaelmas; for by my troth I am almost blind." In March, 1614,[4] this and other ailments were followed by an influenza-like scourge. A week or so later a letter to Goodyer[5] portrays the family's condition as even worse. Yet the same epistle carries on with worldly ambition. There is chitchat of the Dean of St. Paul's "best living, worth above 300 pounds," of "a book of the nullity," of some expected bounty from Lady Huntingdon, of the forthcoming Parliament, in which Donne has received three separate offers of a seat and accepted the first.

The prospect of sitting as a member for Taunton evidently went to his head, for a week later he dares to ask Somerset for the ambassadorship to Venice:

[4] Letter VII, Appendix.
[5] VIII.

since I received a commandment, so much to assist myself, as to present to your Lordship whatsoever do appear to me likely to advantage me, and ease your Lordship, I am now bold, in obedience of that commandment, to tell your Lordship that that is told me, That Sir D[udley] C[arleton] is likely to be removed, from Venice to the States. If your Lordship have no particular determination upon that place, nor upon me, I humbly beseech your Lordship to pardon me the boldness of asking you, whether I may not be sent thither.

But this post was ultimately destined for Sir Henry Wotton, who was better fitted for it. Sir Robert also wanted it and, according to Chamberlain, would have paid 2000 pounds for it. Donne subsequently hinted at his willingness to accept the embassy at The Hague instead. But he got neither mission, and had only the experience of sitting in a short Parliament that passed no bills and therefore was labeled, rather unjustly, the Addled Parliament. Before the King dissolved it in disgust June 10 after two months and two days, it caused him trouble that was a hint of times to come, inasmuch as it refused to vote him any money until there was satisfaction of grievances. Donne's friend Hoskyns delivered such a blistering attack on James's Scottish favorites that with the end of his parliamentary immunity he was sent to the Tower. Donne, for the second time, failed to make any mark as an M.P., although he served on several committees.

As in the poem by his protégé George Herbert, "The Collar," he was struggling against the inevitable. He still imagined he had choices. The petitioning went on.

To the Earl of Somerset.

It is now somewhat more than a year since I took the boldness to make my purpose of professing divinity known to your Lordship, as to a person whom God had made so great an instrument of His providence in this kingdom, as that nothing in it should be done without your knowledge. Your Lordship exercised

upon me then many of your virtues, for besides that by
your bounty I have lived ever since, it hath been through
your Lordship's advice and inspiration of new hopes into
me that I have lived cheerfully.

The word "cheerfully" is quickly belied, since the letter
ends in a strain that is at once pathetic, properly
"humble," and morbidly flattering.

I humbly therefore beg of your Lordship that after you
shall have been pleased to admit into your memory that
I am now a year older, broken with some sickness, and in
the same degrees of honesty as I was, your Lordship will
afford me one commandment, and bid me either hope for
this business in your Lordship's hand, or else pursue my
first purpose or abandon all; for as I cannot live without
your favor, so I cannot die without your leave; because
even by dying I should steal from you one who is by his
own devotions and your purchase your Lordship's most
humble and thankful servant.

The seventh child, Mary Donne, died in May, 1614,
in her fourth year. The father writes about her in a
letter[6] to Somerset's namesake and protégé Sir Robert
Ker, which, in its abject apology for mentioning "no subject," the death of a child, is no more agreeable than the
others of this period. He devoted his verse this year to
"Obsequies to the Lord Harington, Brother to the Lady
Lucy, Countess of Bedford," who died at Twickenham, the
home of his sister. He proclaimed at the end of the 258
lines that these would be the last from his Muse:

Do not, fair soul, this sacrifice refuse,
That in thy grave I do inter my Muse,
Who, by my grief, great as thy worth, being cast
Behindhand, yet hath spoke, and spoke her last.

Fortunately, as Gosse remarks, "poets' vows are like those

[6] IX.

of lovers." The poetic vein had not yet dried up. But there was nothing left for Mary Donne, nor for Francis Donne, the fourth son, who passed away in November.

Between these two deaths lay a wretched summer. "We are condemned to this desert of London for all this summer, for it is company, not houses, which distinguishes between cities and deserts." There was so little health that the house let by Drury began to be designated, as Mitcham had been, "my poor hospital." There is wafted down to us from this period an odd detail: a carpenter's bill for the repair of a door.

> Item for the carpinder for takine of the dore in Mr.
>   Dunnes yarde and makine of it broder and hangine .. 0. 1. 0
> Item Layd out for mendine the Laches and sneches
>   of the same dore to the smeth 0.0. 2

So life somehow went on with its usual quiet—or hammer-ing—desperation.

In an epistle dated "From my Hospital, July 17, 1613" Donne had declared he was "busying myself a little in the search of the Eastern tongues." Walton said that in the years immediately before his ordination "he applied him-self to an incessant study of textual divinity, and to the attainment of a greater perfection in the learned lan-guages, Greek and Hebrew." The posthumously pub-lished *Essays in Divinity* "were the voluntary sacrifices of several hours, when he had many debates betwixt God and himself, whether he were worthy and competently learned to enter into Holy Orders." These somewhat unfinished meditations on the first verses of Genesis and Exodus con-stituted useful pre-professional practice both in theology and in prose. The author shows his wide acquaintance with the Scriptures, including the Apocrypha, and the Renaissance commentators. He continues to be the moder-ate for whom the Anglican church is a highly acceptable via media. "So synagogue and church is the same thing, and of the Church, Roman and Reformed, and all other distinctions of place, discipline, or person, but one Church, journeying to one Jerusalem, and directed by one guide, Christ Jesus." "Yet though we branch out East and West, that Church concurs with us in the root, and sucks her vegetation from one and the same ground, Christ Jesus, who (as it is in the Canticle) lies between the breasts of his Church and gives suck on both sides."

His lively fancy is still with him, obviously. At his best he can rise to what will be—a generation later—the music of Sir Thomas Browne.

> Truly, the Creation and the Last Judgment are the diluculum and crepusculum, the morning and the evening twilights of the long day of this world. Which times, though they be not utterly dark, yet they are but of uncertain, doubtful, and conjectural light. Yet not equally: for the break of day, because it hath a succession of more and more light, is clearer than the shutting in, which is overtaken with more and more darkness; so is the birth of the world more discernible than the death, because upon this God hath cast more clouds . . . . It is elder than darkness, which is elder than light; and was before Confusion, which is elder than Order, by how much the universal Chaos preceded forms and distinctions. A beginning so near Eternity that there was no Then, nor a minute of Time between them.

Their "curious and entangled wits"—to borrow a phrase from the *Essays*—kindle to the same subjects. The following could pass as an excerpt from the last chapter of *Urn-Burial*.

> Amongst men, all depositaries of our memories, all means which we have trusted with the preserving of our names, putrefy and perish . . . . The very places of the obelisks and pyramids are forgotten, and the purpose why they were erected. Books themselves are subject to the mercy of the magistrate: and as though the ignorant had not been enemy enough for them, the learned unnaturally and treacherously contribute to their destruction, by rasure and misinterpretation . . . . But names honored with a place

in this book, cannot perish, because the Book cannot. Next
to the glory of having his name entered into the Book of
Life, this is the second, to have been matriculated in this
Register, for an example or instrument of good. Lazarus
his name is enrolled, but the wicked rich man's omitted.

One sees the embryonic material of sermons to come.
There is an occasional self-flagellation, as in the words,
"Dig a little deeper, O my poor lazy soul." The first of
the Prayers placed at the end sounds repentantly autobiographical: "Thou hast set up many candlesticks, and
kindled many lamps in me; but I have either blown them
out, or carried them to guide me in by and forbidden
ways. Thou hast given me a desire of knowledge, and
some means to it, and some possession of it; and I have
armed myself with Thy weapons against Thee." This train
of thought was to emerge as great poetry five years later
in "A Hymn to Christ, at the Author's Last Going into
Germany":

> Seal then this bill of my divorce to all
> On whom those fainter beams of love did fall;
> Marry those loves, which in youth scattered be
> On Fame, Wit, Hopes (false mistresses) to Thee.
> Churches are best for prayer that have least light:
> To see God only, I go out of sight;
> And to 'scape stormy days, I choose
> An everlasting night.

We can trace the affinity with St. Augustine, who admitted
in his *Confessions*, "Bear with me, my God, while I say
somewhat of my wit, Thy gift, and on what dotages I
wasted it."

Donne made one last desperate try before he gave up.
He directed such importunity at Somerset as could no
longer be ignored by that worthy,

> who being then at Theobald's with the King, where one
> of the clerks of the council died that night, the Earl

posted a messenger for Mr. Donne to come to him immediately, and at Mr. Donne's coming said, "Mr. Donne, to
testify the reality of my affection and my purpose to prefer
you, stay in this garden till I go up to the King and bring
you word that you are clerk of the council. Doubt not my
doing this, for I know the King loves you, and know the
King will not deny me." But the King gave a positive
denial to all requests and, having a discerning spirit,
replied, "I know Mr. Donne is a learned man, has the
abilities of a learned divine, and will prove a powerful
preacher. And my desire is to prefer him that way, and in
that way I will deny you nothing for him."

The basic decision was arrived at in the latter part
of November, 1614. His father-in-law heard from him "At
my poor house 3 December," "I returned not till yester-
night from my expensive journey to Newmarket, where I
have received from the King as good allowance and
encouragement to pursue my purpose as I could desire."
A few more weeks were required for the necessary arrangements. It takes a mite of time to say farewell to the world
that one has loved so persistently. He even considered
flaunting the "false mistresses" by putting out an edition
of his poems, but was evidently told that this was a move
his spiritual superiors would deem exceedingly ill-timed.
He had debts to pay, also: it would not do for creditors
to be tugging at the surplice. He writes Goodyer, December 13, "fixing times to my creditors; for by the end of
next term, I will make an end with the world, by God's
grace."

So, after long but increasingly discouraged flirtation
with worldly things, after, in Gosse's words, "poverty and
anxiety dragged this beautiful nature down into the dust,"
Donne, at forty-three, flung himself into the bosom of the
Church. The witty sinner yielded to what the *Essays* call
"His exciting grace," and was ordained by the bishop of
his diocese, the Bishop of London, Dr. John King,
January 23, 1615.

On the day itself he sent off a letter to Sir Edward
Herbert.

Sir,-

Because since I had the honor to see you, or hear from you, I have received such a change as, if my unworthiness did not avile it, were an addition, I am bold to present to you the knowledge thereof: because thereby your power and jurisdiction, which is entirely over me, is somewhat enlarged. For, as if I should put any other stamp upon a piece of gold, the gold were not the less yours, so (if there be not too much taken by me in that comparison) by having, by the orders of our Church, received a new character, I am not departed from your title and possession of me. But, as I was ever, by my devotion, and your acceptance, your humble servant, so I am become, by this addition, capable of the dignity of being

Your very humble

chaplain

J. Donne

23 Jan. 1615, which was the very day wherein I took orders.

It must be admitted that this is not an exalted letter. Except for the announcement it contains it is indistinguishable from the writer's numerous other exercises in courtiership and courtesy. Whom is he serving, God or Mammon? How big *was* the "change"?

One can say of the Holy Sonnets that Donne had been composing since 1609 that literarily, at least, there was less change than would be expected. The clever sinner did not cease to be clever. He merely applied his individual style to a new object of affection, God. "God is love." In one of his early sermons Donne observed of Solomon that his "disposition was amorous, and excessive in the love of women: when he turned to God, he departed not utterly from his old phrase and language, but having put a new, and a spiritual tincture, and form and habit in all his thoughts and words, he conveys all his loving approaches and applications to God, and all God's gracious answers to his amorous soul, into songs and epithalamions and meditations upon contracts and marriages between God and his Church, and between God and his soul." The preacher knows whereof he speaks. In Holy Sonnet XIV (by the usual numbering) he assumes the posture of a woman begging to be ravished:

> Batter my heart, three-personed God; for You
> As yet but knock, breathe, shine, and seek to mend;
> That I may rise, and stand, o'erthrow me, and bend
> Your force, to break, blow, burn, and make me new.
> I, like an usurped town to another due,
> Labor to admit You, but oh! to no end;
> Reason, Your viceroy in me, me should defend,
> But is captived and proves weak or untrue.
> Yet dearly I love You, and would be loved fain,
> But am betrothed unto Your enemy.
> Divorce me, untie, or break that knot again,
> Take me to You, imprison me, for I
> Except You enthrall me, never shall be free;
> Nor ever chaste, except You ravish me.

There had been nothing like this since St. Teresa of Avila related how an angel appeared and pierced her with a dart of gold, thereby causing her sweet pain but inflaming her with an even greater passion for God, for the Spouse of whom she wrote, "The voice of the Well-Beloved causes in the soul such transports that she is consumed by desire, and yet does not know what to ask, because she sees clearly that her Lord is with her. What pain could she have? And for what greater happiness could she wish? To this I do not know what to answer; but that of which I am certain, is that the pain penetrates down to the very bottom of the bowels and that it seems that they are being torn away when the heavenly Spouse withdraws the arrow with which He has transpierced them." There would be nothing comparable again until the orgasms of Crashaw— on St. Teresa.

But let us not be too psychoanalytic, for this is very old. Dante would have understood it, because Dante illustrated it. The movements of the universe were an expression of divine love, or love of the divine. Also it was the first step in the Ignatian mode of meditation with which Donne was familiar, to fix vividly the New Testament scene. "Soul" is feminine in the languages that Donne knew. There was such a parallel poem as San Juan de la Cruz's "Coplas del alma que pena por ver a Dios" ("Verses of the Soul that Pines to See God"). Donne would use such locutions in his sermons as "Christ was married to my soul." He warned misunderstanders: "and therefore doth God, in more than this one place expect our love in a kiss; for if we be truly in love with Him, it will be a holy and an acceptable metaphor unto us: else it will have a carnal and a fastidious taste." The preacher could have quoted St. Barnard on the Canticles: "The kiss of his mouth signifies nothing else than to receive the inpouring of the Holy Spirit."

The first six of the twelve Holy Sonnets printed in 1633 have a darker theme, death and judgment, the Last Things. God moved the poet by fear, as well as by love (the theme of the second six). In such sonnets as "Oh my black soul" and "At the round Earth's imagined corners, blow" and "Death, be not proud" he frenetically endeavors to hope but is never far from despair. He knows full deeply that the soul is not guaranteed immortality in itself. As he observed in the *Essays*, "God hath made nothing which needs Him not, or which would not instantly return again to nothing without His special conservation." Salvation had to be worked out with fear and trembling.

4 / "A Preacher in Earnest"

In his lifetime Donne underwent three conversions. The first was from Catholic to Anglican. The second conversion was to true love, in the person of Anne More. The third conversion was to the priesthood.

When a man makes a change that improves his worldly state or prospects it is easy to accuse him of having only worldly motives. The most impulsive of Donne's conversions was the second; the *Cambridge History of English Literature* has enshrined, as we saw, a doubt even on this —the marriage to the well-connected Anne More—as possibly a calculating move. A 1949 writer denigrates it as "the hardiest of his gambles." The other two conversions, at first hearing, invite a cynical lift of the eyebrows. They were certainly opportune; were they opportunistic?

In regard to the first, it is obvious that Donne decided he would not be a martyr like his relatives. He joined the majority party. If he had been a citizen of Spain or Italy he would undoubtedly have remained a Roman Catholic. He took to himself the precept *cuius regio eius religio*—religion follows country. The doctrinal difference did not stick in his throat. "I never fettered nor imprisoned the word Religion, not straitening it friarly, . . . nor immuring it in a Rome, or a Wittenberg, or a Geneva:

they are all virtual beams of one Sun." After giving the problem due consideration as a secular person, he saw his way clear to follow the religion of the majority of his countrymen. As still a young man he declined, as Helen C. White puts it, "an odium that so social a temperament as his could hardly be expected to covet, and a restriction of experience that might well appal one who had taken all experience for his province." The one experience he could do without was hanging, drawing, and quartering. His mind found conviction; few of us are entitled to sneer at his mixed motives.

Ultimately he became the sort of convert who could tell a congregation, "Truly I have been sorry to see some persons converted from the Roman Church to ours, because I have known that only temporal respects have moved them, and they have lived after rather in a nullity or indifferency to either religion than in a true and established zeal."

What was originally a mixture of accommodation and conviction, if it spared him punishment, did not carry him where he expected to go. "The youthful Donne, the law student and courtier in London," Louis Bredvold reminds us, "would have been greatly astonished had he heard predicted his future failure at court and his subsequent greatness as a saintly divine." He did not get any of the futures that he had projected. He grew old and sick trying.

The third conversion is initially the most open to suspicion. We have overwhelming evidence that Donne took orders only when he saw that all other doors were closed to him. He used all the arts of flattery and got nowhere. The pearly gates he wanted to pass were the gates of Whitehall. King James said no. Jerusalem the Golden was not Donne's first choice. He would have preferred Venice or The Hague, even Ireland or Virginia, or a dozen other places, all mentioned in his letters. It took him painful years to fall, like an overripe peach, into the lap of Mother Church.

And when he did fall he was not suddenly and

miraculously changed. The letter he wrote on the official day itself is the old Donne—we may say, the old Adam. His servility to the great by no means ceases. He sounds no better than the clergymen such nineteenth-century novelists as Jane Austen and Anthony Trollope have made familiar. He is still looking for benefits, even if they are now to be called benefices. Here is further proof.

> Sir,-
>
> I have the honor of a letter from your Lordship, and a testimony that though better than any other you know my infirmity, yet you are not scandalized with my change of habit. I have, Sir, besides many other internal advantages this also by it, that besides the obligations of friendship and services towards you which bind me always to commend your fortunes to God in my prayers (having never had any other way of expressing myself), I am come now to do it by my office.
>
> And I may be credible to do my friend that service with much earnestness because as yet I have no other charge. For I do not so much as inquire of mine own hopes what the King will do with me: he forbade me at first, and I obey him still, and forbear so much as to remember him that he forbade me.

Thus the flatteries and the complaints continue. He himself acknowledged, "Thou art the same materials as before; / Only the stamp is changèd—but no more." And he said this years later, when it was no longer true of himself.

The same poem, "To Mr. Tilman After He had Taken Orders," asks,

> Why doth the foolish world scorn that profession
> Whose joys pass speech? Why do they think unfit
> That gentry should join families with it? . . .
> Let then the world thy calling disrespect,
> But go thou on, and pity their neglect.

It thus, wittingly or unwittingly, postulates another reason for Donne's reluctance: the lowly clergyman, scorned by the rich and worldly and lordly, with whom Donne had mixed. That would add to his self-consciousness. He had declined Dean Morton's offer in 1607 on the grounds that "maintenance" must not be the first consideration in choosing to be a priest. Now that he was a priest, he wondered where his maintenance would come from. He had not been ordained *to* anything: "I have no . . . charge." He is seen worrying a great deal, in a way that is human but sordid. Even when in a more settled state than he was, the clergy did not, the rank and file, find themselves in possession of incomes worth mentioning. A modern authority remarks, as if he were speaking of the teaching profession in our own time, "The wonder is . . . that any man, indeed, could be found to accept such posts, when their neighbors were becoming wealthy as merchants, lawyers, or doctors." After his momentous decision has been taken, Donne continues to scramble for favor and for money like a minister jumping over his master's stick at the court of Lilliput.

The question was, who was his master? Somerset, the Lord Chamberlain, had been, but the fact had not been generally known, and it was advisable now to endeavor to make headway, if possible, with a very different power, the Church's chief administrator. Donne confided to his father-in-law, "Before I go about to seek my Lord of Canterbury, I would gladly, if I could, discern his inclination to me, and whether he have any conjecture upon my relation to my Lord Chamberlain, which he is very like to have come to his knowledge since my going, by reason of his Lordship's more open avowing me than heretofore." George Abbot, the Archbishop of Canterbury (who was to outlive Donne), was a man of integrity who opposed the late divorce and marriage and who would not truckle to any of the King's minions or be ready to respect any of the minions' creatures.

There was also another reason to be modest about one's association with Somerset. He was on the way out as a favorite. In November the boyish slender-legged George Villiers (who was to be known to fame as the first Duke of Buckingham but would always be for the prematurely aging King "Baby Steenie") "received the appropriate appointment of cup-bearer to his Majesty." In December "Mr. Villiers" begins to figure knowingly in Donne's letters to Goodyer. "They are preparing for a masque of gentlemen, in which Mr. Villiers is." As to "whether Mr. Villiers have received from the King any additions of honor or profit: without doubt he hath yet none." "I have something else to say of Mr. Villiers, but because I hope to see you here shortly, and because new additions to the truths or rumors which concern him are likely to be made by occasion of this masque, I forbear . . . ." Jonson wrote the masque, in which the young man displayed his skill in dancing. In all attractive qualities he had the edge over the blond Scot, including English nationality.

Another patron was also proving less satisfactory— none other than the good Lady, the Countess of Bedford. She had been critical of his idolization of Elizabeth Drury. Now she helped to scotch his scheme of publishing his poems. And, as if these reminded her of his past sins, she looked askance at his ordination. More to the point, she failed to help enough with the debts that he had hoped to clear up. The return on his verse investment, the 258 lines on her brother, turned out to be 30 pounds.

> For her other way of expressing her favor to me, I must say, it is not with that cheerfulness as heretofore she hath delivered herself towards me. I am almost sorry that an elegy should have been able to move her to so much compassion heretofore, as to offer to pay my debts; and my greater wants now, and for so good a purpose, as to come disengaged into that profession, being plainly laid open to her, should work no farther but that she sent me £ 30, which in good faith she excused with that, which is in both parts true, that her present debts were burdensome, and that I could not doubt of her inclination, upon all future emergent occasions, to assist me. I confess to you her former fashion towards me had given a better confidence; and this diminution in her makes me see that I must use more friends than I thought I should have needed.

This is not a notably grateful missive to be sending behind the Countess's back to another of her protégés, Goodyer. Quite apart from Lady Bedford's numerous past favors, which are not being vividly recollected, 30 pounds was no mean nor stingy sum. It was fully the equivalent of two thousand dollars today. Thirty pounds is twice as much as Milton received for *Paradise Lost*, a poem that, if it flatters God, bows to no man or woman and rather outdistances "Obsequies to the Lord Harington."

If the Lady Bountiful was for once not bountiful enough, she had her reasons, as Donne grudgingly admits. She had lived lavishly. Her hospitality, like her collection of works of art, such as Holbeins, had been nothing less than princely. Her husband had been fined £20,000, later reduced to £10,000, for his minor part in the Essex rebellion (James had forgiven the last £3000 of this). With her father's and brother's death, her sister and she inherited an estate charged with debts of almost £40,000. The executors had been empowered "to sell all, or any part of the land, presently and speedily, and pay and discharge all." The Countess was a party to an expensive lawsuit that Sir John Harington had brought against her mother. She complained in October, 1614, that she was "feeling heavily the burden of" her "broken estate." Moreover, there was a Puritan at her ear.

> Of my Lady Bedford, I must say so much as must importune you to burn the letter; for I would say nothing of her upon record that should not testify my thankfulness for all her graces. But upon this motion, which I made to her by letter, and by Sir Thomas Roe's assistance, if any scruple should arise in her, she was somewhat more startling than I looked for from her; she had more suspicion of my calling, a better memory of my past life, than I had thought her nobility could have admitted; of all which, though I humbly thank God I can make good use, as one that needs as many remembrances in that kind as not only friends but enemies can present, yet I am afraid they proceed in her rather from some ill impression taken from Dr. Burges, than that they grow in herself.

John Burges had a double sway on the aging and increasingly pious Countess, who ceased to take part in masques. He was both her spiritual advisor and her physician. Donne had reason to be jealous of him, as Hall was once jealous of Donne's brother-in-law. This emotion was hard to avoid between rival favorites. Somerset went into a frenzy over Villiers. It was probably no accident when one of his servants spilt a bowl of soup over Villiers' new suit. It was certainly no accident that when the latter responded with a blow, the Lord Chamberlain demanded—of course in vain—the penalty for brawling in the King's presence: the striking off of the comely young man's right hand! In a transferred but still recognizable rivalry, Dr. Donne and Dr. Burges both preached at Paul's Cross in 1617. But by this time Lady Bedford, for all practical purposes, was no longer Donne's patron. Her letters from 1615 on refer only to Burges, never to Donne.

Repeating the (unheeded) caution about burning, Donne's letter to Goodyer resumes:

> I would you could burn this letter before you read it; at least do when you have read it. For I am afraid out of a contemplation of mine own unworthiness, and fortune, that the example of this Lady should work upon the Lady where you are; for though goodness be originally in her, and she do good for the deed's sake, yet, perchance, she may think it a little wisdom to make such measure of me as they who know no better do.

In other words, the debt-ridden man is turning anxious eyes in another direction, that of "the other Countess," the Countess of Huntingdon, his old friend whom he had known as the Lord Keeper's step-daughter. And she, it seems, responded generously. He rewarded her with verses, no longer feeling bound by the rash pledge at the end of the elegy on Lady Bedford's brother. When Goodyer insisted on praising the Twickenham Countess despite Donne's complaint of—or attempt at—her "diminution," his correspondent declined to join in, because of "my integrity to the other Countess, of whose worthiness, though I swallowed your opinion at first upon your words, yet I have had since an explicit faith, and now a knowledge; and for her delight (since she descends to them) I had reserved not only all the verses which I should make, but all the thoughts of women's worthiness."

Thus the evidence that, fortunately or unfortunately, has come down to us fails to make a winsome picture. Without necessarily being cynical one may also inquire whether Donne's dilatory abandonment of worldly things does not fit into what may be called the pattern of exhaustion. As George Herbert's God says in "The Pulley": "If goodness lead him not, yet weariness / May toss him to My breast." Many a saint has been a sensualist in his youth, reached a certain age, and then reformed. A recent book by a Congregationalist minister calls this the "rake's progress." Donne himself, in sermons of 1617 and 1619, speaks sarcastically of giving up "incontinence 'early,' that is, as soon as we are old or sick"—"when thy heats of youth are not overcome, but burnt out." Every rake, if he lives long enough, reforms. When surfeit—or a weakening of biological impulses—comes, someone like Augustine discovers he is "ready for religion." Donne was a tired paterfamilias who had attained the age of sobriety. He had reached the time of life when "lightness depresseth us." Forty-three was for a Jacobean a much more advanced age than we with our vitamins and other scientific aids like to think it is now. Does a face have to be furrowed at forty? Shakespeare thought so: "When forty winters shall besiege thy brow, / And dig deep trenches in thy beauty's field." In fact the average expectation of life was barely forty. Salisbury at forty-four was described by Jonson as having entered "the twilight of sere age." Cares and illness had, at least temporarily, drained Donne's energies. Years before, his wife had effectively weaned him away from other women as sexual objects. King James, with his blocking of all other avenues to advancement, stringently narrowed his occupational choices to one.

Morton's secretary seems uncertain as to whether it

was the Holy Spirit or King James that moved this
hesitator.

> For doubtless the Holy Spirit had the greatest stroke
> and power to incline and draw him to that sacred pro-
> fession. For myself have long since seen his picture in a
> dear friend's chamber of his in Lincoln's Inn, all enveloped
> with a darkish shadow, his face and feature hardly dis-
> cernible, with this ejaculation and wish written thereon:
> "Domine, illumina tenebras meas"; which long after was
> really accomplished, when (by King James his weighty and
> powerful persuasions) he took holy orders . . . .

What a mix-up, what a pious misreading of the inscrip-
tion around the Lover's Melancholy portrait, of "e" for
"a," "Domine" for "Domina"! But the writer could never
have been persuaded that he was confusedly juxtaposing
the Holy Spirit and King James. We are prone to think
of such a situation in either-or terms, but for seventeenth-
century man, the great amphibium, both-and was a
customary mode of thought. This is borne out in Donne's
Latin epitaph: "by the instinct and impulse of the Holy
Spirit, by the admonition and exhortation of King James,
[he] embraced holy orders." It is borne out in the in-
scription, also in Latin, Donne wrote in the Bible he gave
to the library at Lincoln's Inn: "After many years, the
Holy Spirit moving, the King persuading, [he was]
raised to holy orders." The fullest statement comes in
Expostulation VIII of the *Devotions Upon Emergent
Occasions*, where it is gratefully recalled "when he, first
of any man, conceived a hope that I might be of some
use in Thy church and descended to an intimation, to a
persuasion, almost to a solicitation, that I would embrace
that calling. And Thou who hadst put that desire into his
heart, didst also put into mine an obedience to it; and I,
who was sick before of a vertiginous giddiness and irresolution, and almost spent all my time in consulting how I
should spend it, was by this man of God, and God of men,
put into the pool and recovered: when I asked, perchance,
a stone, he gave me bread; when I asked, perchance, a

scorpion, he gave me a fish; when I asked a temporal
office, he denied not, refused not that; but let me see that
he had rather I took this." One would like to know what
"temporal office" it was that King James "denied not."

Walton provided the cue for a proper analysis when
he said:

> So now being inspired with an apprehension of God's par-
> ticular mercy to him in the King's and other solicitations
> of him, he came to ask King David's thankful question,
> "Lord, who am I that thou art so mindful of me?"—so
> mindful of me as to lead me for more than forty years
> through this wilderness of the many temptations and vari-
> ous turnings of a dangerous life, so merciful to me as to
> move the learnedest of kings to descend to move me to
> serve at the altar, so merciful to me as at last to move my
> heart to embrace this holy motion. Thy motions I will and
> do embrace. And I now say with the blessed Virgin, "Be
> it with thy servant as seemeth best in thy sight." And so,
> blessed Jesus, I do take the cup of salvation and will call
> upon thy name and will preach thy Gospel.

Such an analysis was furnished by Helen Gardner in 1952:

> In the end Donne accepted the advice of others, re-
> ceiving from them, and particularly from the king, what he
> regarded as a calling. It is true that by 1615 any hopes of
> secular preferment must have worn very thin. But Donne
> himself would not, I think, resent the implication that he
> took orders in the end because it was the only course
> open to him. He believed that each man's life is "guided
> and governed" by God's "good providence," and that the
> motion of the spirit may come through the voices of
> superiors or friends, or through the circumstances of daily
> life, as much—and perhaps with less danger of mistake—
> as through the voice of a man's own heart. Donne is to
> be honoured because, having received his vocation thus
> indirectly, he tried to fulfil it worthily and set himself an
> exacting standard of duty.

Another way of looking at it is to say that, however he began, Donne ended with sincerity, sincerity so earnest, so painful, and so articulate that for centuries (until the time of Newman) he stood alone in qualifying both as a saint (or a semi-saint) and as a master of eloquence in the English language.

Soon the death of his wife would confirm his calling.

In compliment to a new Chancellor, the Earl of Suffolk, the King was at Cambridge University from March 7 to 11, 1615. The new cleric, who became at a date unknown the King's Chaplain-in-Ordinary, attended him, and stayed behind after he departed. He was awaiting a royal mandate that there be conferred on him the Doctor of Divinity degree. He had won, for *Pseudo-Martyr,* an Honorary Master of Arts from Oxford, April 17, 1610. This, however, proved no recommendation to the sister university, which felt that it had been pressured into giving too many unearned degrees to the wrong persons and desired to call a halt to a corrupt practice. Sir Dudley Carleton gossiped to Chamberlain March 16: "the University is threatened with a mandate which, if it come, it is like they will obey, but they are resolved to give him such a blow withal, that he were better without his degree." Next Chamberlain informed Carleton, under date of April 7: "John Donne and one Cheke went out Doctors at Cambridge with much ado after our coming away by the King's express mandate, though the Vice-Chancellor and some other of the heads called them openly 'filios noctis' [sons of night] and 'tenebriones' [swindlers] that sought thus to come in at the window, when there was a fair gate open." (An early sermon of Donne's dares to refer to such a situation: "If the favor of a prince can make a man a doctor, *per saltum* [in one bound]—")

In the interval he would have learned of the death of Sir Robert Drury, who was carried off by a fever on April 2, having attained the mellow age of forty, but still no court office. The Donnes stayed on as the widow's tenants. On the fifth anniversary of his Oxford M.A.—

and while the ink was scarcely dry on his Cambridge D.D.
—the father self-consciously asked Ker[1] to stand godfather
to his tenth child and fifth daughter, Margaret: "I see that
I stand like a tree, which once a year bears, though no
fruit, yet this mast of children . . . I had rather be presently
under the obligations and the thankfulness towards you
than meditate such a trouble to you against another year."
Another year, another child. But how many more months
would there be for the true bearer of "this mast of children"?

Meanwhile he was serving his apprenticeship as a
preacher. He began humbly, as Walton relates. "And
though his long familiarity with scholars and persons of
greatest quality was such as might have given some men
boldness enough to have preached to any eminent auditory, yet his modesty in this employment was such that he
could not be persuaded to it but went, usually accompanied with some one friend, to preach privately in some
village not far from London, his first sermon being
preached at Paddington." This first sermon, unhappily,
has not been preserved. Paddington, before it became a
railroad station, was a village four or five miles west of
London, known for its watercourse running "to James-
head on the hill." The tiny parish church, dedicated to
St. Catherine, was in a state of disrepair. Its licentiate,
one Griffin Edwards, received a stipend of 28 pounds per
year—a sum two pounds less than Lady Bedford's not
very gratefully received present and all too typical of
clerical pay. In a couple of generations the church where a
small rural congregation witnessed Donne's debut would
be so ruined—"bare ruined choirs where late the sweet
birds sang"—a larger one would have to be built in its
place.

The earliest of the sermons that have come down to
us was "preached at Greenwich, April 30, 1615." It is
usually taken for granted that "Greenwich" means the
palace, Queen Anne's favorite residence, and that the

---

[1] Letter X.

Queen herself was present. Neither of these assumptions is probable, as the editors of the University of California Press edition of the sermons point out. In all likelihood Donne was still practicing before humble audiences, this time at the parish church in Greenwich. His text, Isaiah iii, 3—"Ye have sold yourselves for nought, and ye shall be redeemed without money"—was not one that could have been tactfully addressed to the Queen. She would not have listened complaisantly to a sermon against extravagance, when she was at that time spending considerable sums to improve the royal estate at Greenwich. No, Donne is speaking to businessmen or tradesmen. He was no prophet blasting the high and mighty, no reckless Savonarola or Amos. He trod softly, and he remembered his own sins, of which one was prodigality. "If a man waste so as that he becomes unable to relieve others, by this waste, this is a sinful prodigality; but much more, if he waste so as that he is not able to subsist, and maintain himself; and this is our case, who have even annihilated ourselves by our profuseness." Another sin is alluded to in the words, "a licentious man takes pleasure in the victory of having corrupted a woman, by his solicitation, but yet insensibly overthrows his constitution, by his sin." Did the speaker feel that the poor health of his middle age was a consequence of the wildness of his youth?

The sermon, rigid in structure, in sticking to its limited point, displays a knowledge of Hebrew and the law, tries to work on the listener by logic rather than emotional appeal. And, like the next surviving sermon, it deals more effectively with sin and damnation than with the Christian promise or hope.

This second of the dated sermons was preached a year later, "at Whitehall, April 21, 1616." A discourse on Ecclesiastes viii, 11, it likewise favors the formal cause over the efficient cause. "If a vehement fever take hold of him, he remembers where he sweat, and when he took cold; where he walked too fast, where his casement stood open, and where he was too bold upon fruit, or meat of hard digestion; but he never remembers the sinful and

naked wantonness, the profuse and wasteful dilapidations
of his own body, that have made him thus obnoxious and
open to all dangerous distempers." Some of Donne's soon
to be familiar devices are beginning to be used, such as
the sudden shift from the impersonal to the personal, the
swooping down upon the sinner who languidly fancied the
discussion was about someone else. We shall have, "Never
send to know for whom the bell tolls; it tolls for thee."
We have here, "Never ask what that hardness of heart is:
for, if thou know it not, thou hast it." Also, the man who
used to rhyme still jingles and alliterates: "all those curses
and maledictions with which He flings, and slings, and
stings the soul of the sinner." And the longing for suffering
has not ceased: it is just that it has been found to be good
for the soul: the sermon commences paradoxically: "We
cannot take into our meditation a better rule than that
of the stoic [Seneca], *Nihil infaelicius faelicitate
peccantium*: there is no such unhappiness to a sinner as
to be happy; no such cross as to have no crosses."

The King may or may not have been present on this
Sunday. At any rate he had by now heard the man who he
had insisted "will prove a powerful preacher." Walton
tells how "his Majesty sent and appointed him a day to
preach to him at Whitehall, and, though much were
expected from him both by his Majesty and others, yet he
was so happy (which few are) as to satisfy and exceed their
expectations, preaching the word so as showed his own
heart was possessed with those very thoughts and joys that
he labored to distil into others." This year, 1616, brought
more substantial recognitions, even as it completed the
downfall of Lord and Lady Somerset, who in May were
found guilty of Overbury's murder and were placed in the
Tower. Here lay a moral about how unsubstantial were
the vanities of this world. In the spring there fell to Donne
the living of Keyston, a small parish in Huntingdonshire.
In July he took on the emoluments of the rectorship of
Sevenoaks in Kent, which was in the gift of the Crown.
He would not have dreamt of leaving his beloved London
for actual residence at either of these places. Pluralism

was a practice that had not yet been held up to much
criticism. True, a legal decision forced him to relinquish
Keyston in 1622, but he hung to Sevenoaks for the
remainder of his life. His conscience was satisfied if he
preached occasionally in his parishes, leaving the rest to a
curate. He always had, it appears, more zest for his preaching than his pastoral duties. In the early years he often
preached twice a day.

That was one of the requirements of the far more
important post he was elected to on October 24, 1616:
Reader in Divinity to the Benchers of Lincoln's Inn. To
that sophisticated audience of lawyers and students he
began delivering about fifty sermons a year. They needed
to be learned and in every way convincing, for he was a
prodigal returned to his former classmates in shepherd's
clothing. They would put up with neither hypocritical
pretenses nor slovenly discourse. There was little chance
for him to pull the woolsack over their eyes.

With his varied sources of income he, large though
his family was, at last had enough. But his duties were
rigorous, as indeed his life had to be. Walton glows at
the transformation among "the companions and friends of
his youth," the opportunity "to renew his intermitted
friendship with those whom he so much loved and where
he had been a Saul, though not to persecute Christianity
or to deride it yet in his irregular youth to neglect the
visible practice of it, there to become a Paul and preach
salvation to his beloved brethren. And now his life was as
a shining light among his old friends."

On March 24, 1617, he had the honor of preaching
at Paul's Cross on the fourteenth anniversary of the King's
accession. An excerpt praising Elizabeth while compli-
menting James has been quoted. He was learning to vary
his approaches according to his audience, which this time
included "the Lords of the Council and other Honorable
Persons." (The King himself had departed for Scotland.)
There was a carry-over for him of the arts—and even of
some of the interests—of a courtier. A minister in the high
Anglican church does not, for instance, cease to care about

ceremony. The previous November 4 Donne had missed witnessing the creation of Charles as Prince of Wales. He wrote, with undoubted sincerity, "I was loth to be the only man who should have no part in this great festival." Now he made the most of his present opportunity, himself a spectacle. He held forth for two and a half hours, to judge by the printed text. Usually he was content to let the sands run through the hourglass once, but we know there were other times when in his zeal he turned it upside down, without inward or outward protest from a spellbound congregation. Besides, Paul's Cross sermons customarily ran to two hours. The pulpit just outside the cathedral, a public meeting place since the Middle Ages, was ideal for gathering a crowd, which sat or stood outdoors, while the nobility had stall or gallery seats as at a theater. A triptych has come down of such an audience being addressed by one of Donne's near predecessors as Dean of St. Paul's. All seem rapt, even two horses, except for a rearing dog that is being subdued by a tipstaff.

Death stalked his life more and more. His sister Anne Lyly died, leaving him the only surviving child of his mother, to whom he wrote a somber letter of consolation.[2] The tone of mortification would be equaled by Dr. Johnson's letters on similar occasions.

The sharpest wrench in Donne's becoming, as Walton puts it, "crucified to the world," was with Anne More's death. "A woman that is weak cannot put off her ninth month to a tenth for her delivery, and say she will stay till she be stronger" (Meditation XIX). That worn-out wife and mother gave birth to a still-born infant on August 8, 1617. The complications killed her August 15, at age thirty-three. Her monument spoke of a raging fever, no doubt puerperal fever. The father was left with seven children (out of twelve births), ranging from Constance, fourteen (old enough to take over housekeeping) to Elizabeth, one.

The Folger Shakespeare Library in Washington now

---

[2] XI.

harbors the widower's epitaph (it is of course in Latin) for his wife, in his own delicate handwriting. What is interesting about it is not the superlatives about what sort of woman, wife, and mother Anne was, but the dedication at the end that we know to transcend convention: "Very grievous to tell, the husband, once dear to this dear one, plights his ashes to hers, to be joined in this spot in a new matrimony, God willing."

The sermon he delivered afterwards is lost. "His first motion from his house was to preach where his beloved wife lay buried in St. Clement's Church, near Temple-Bar, London, and his text was a part of the Prophet Jeremy's lamentation, 'Lo, I am the man that have seen affliction.' And indeed, his very words and looks testified him to be truly such a man; and they with the addition of his sighs and tears expressed in his sermon did so work upon the affections of his hearers as melted and moulded them into a companionable sadness; and so they left the congregation; but then their houses presented them with objects of diversion; and his ·presented him with nothing but fresh objects of sorrow in beholding many helpless children, a narrow fortune, and a consideration of the many cares and casualties that attend their education."

Did he also go home to remorse? So Donne's two twentieth-century biographers have characteristically supposed. Hugh Fausset says, "And now his grief was barbed with bitter remorse.... now the consequences of his insatiable egoism stared him in the face, and even he could scarcely avoid drawing damaging conclusions. He had dragged his wife away from ease, to plunge her into poverty, and from life he had hurried her unsparingly to death." Evelyn Hardy asserts: "somewhere, deep in the recesses of his heart, he must have felt that he had killed her. He had used her selfishly for constant delight and propagation, with scarcely an interval for recovery. He had destroyed the very thing he loved in a fury of devitalizing fire." This is Oscar Wilde—"for all men kill the thing they love"—wed to Freud, but is it Donne? That complex, tortured man was emphatically no stranger to guilt—that is part of his modern fascination—but how much was his feeling of guilt ours? Just as our attitude towards birth control may be different from his ("To hinder it by physic or any other practice, nay to hinder it so far as by a deliberate wish or prayer against children, consists not well"—Sermon of May 30, 1621), so, beside his conscious, Christian guilt, doctrinaire speculation about the unconscious or half-conscious sounds a trifle exotic. He had a genius for self-awareness; this reduces it, perhaps gratuitously. In the earliest of his marriage sermons he flatly gives as the main reason for a man's having a wife the propagation of the human race. One cannot accuse him of having failed to practice what he preached. Maybe he was justifying himself, here, after his wife's death, but he ought to be given the benefit of the doubt, considering that the doctrine he set forth was—and is— so widely held. On the other hand, can Miss Hardy claim for her 1942 conclusion that it reaches out to the way the English thought 350 years ago? It would be difficult to produce evidence that even the women—the hapless victims—reasoned and felt that way, much less their victimizers the men. On this basis Milton killed two wives without giving them a single guilty thought, though he did memorialize one "late espousèd saint" in a sonnet.

Donne did similarly.

Since she whom I loved hath paid her last debt
To Nature, and to hers, and my good is dead,
And her soul early into heaven ravishèd,
Wholly in heavenly things my mind is set.
Here the admiring her my mind did whet
To seek Thee, God; so streams do shew the head.
But though I have found Thee, and Thou my thirst hast
        fed,
A holy thirsty dropsy melts me yet.
But why should I beg more love, when as Thou
Dost woo my soul, for hers offering all Thine:
And dost not only fear lest I allow
My love to saints and angels, things divine,

But in Thy tender jealousy dost doubt
Lest the world, flesh, yea Devil put Thee out.

Here is the dramatic apposition of human love and divine. After stating that his mind is wholly set on heavenly things, Donne, in powerful tribute to her who lay buried in the church of St. Clement Danes, backslides: "A holy thirsty dropsy melts me yet." This is the human but holy longing for such "saints" as Anne was. D. Louthan sees a pun on her maiden name in line 9: "But why should I beg More love." In his characteristic self-centered way the poet tells how he feels without offering any characterization of the woman who unfortunately enjoyed neither of his periods of prosperity: "she is the mere passive vehicle of her husband's preoccupations," Tillyard notes. Perhaps that is what she was all their married life.

"Affliction is a treasure," says the famous Meditation XVII, "and scarce any man hath enough of it. No man hath enough of it that is not matured and ripened by it, and made fit for God by that affliction." Now, more than ever, this minister's "earthly affections were changed into divine love, and all the faculties of his own soul were engaged in the conversion of others, in preaching the glad tidings of remission to repenting sinners and peace to each troubled soul." He began to take on depth, as in his sermon, four months after his personal loss, on love. After another four months came his first warmly unmistakable message on redemption.

The audiences were moved. Paine the modern democratic man sarcastically labeled Burke's *Reflections on the Revolution in France* "a dramatic performance." In Donne's day this plain man's fear of rhetoric was still distant, and of course the freethinkers had not yet scoffed. Pulpit oratory, the most allowable entertainment on a Sunday, brought the masses and the connoisseurs flocking, as to a play. Donne knew whereof he spoke when he reproved those who went to church "out of . . . a perverse and sinister affection to the particular preacher." He was subjected to something very like applause—"periodical

murmurings and noises which you make"—with the result
that "many that were not within distance of hearing the
sermon will give a censure upon it according to the frequency or paucity of these acclamations." His chief com-
petitor, the learned Bishop Lancelot Andrewes, complained, apropos of the text "Be ye doers of the word and
not hearers only," that "sermon-hearing" had become "the
Consummatum est of all Christianity"; "hearing of the
word is grown into such request that it hath got the start
of all the rest of the parts of God's service." The Bishop
said of Ezekiel's contemporaries but meant of his own:
"they seemed to reckon of sermons no otherwise than of
songs: to give them the hearing, to commend the air of
them, and so let them go. The music of a song, and the
rhetoric of a sermon, all is one." Certainly this was true
of Donne, of the rhythms he now developed, the "preach-
able conceits," the analogical, rather than logical, reasoning, the bursts of esoteric learning, even jingles.

Rare is the student of literature who has ever read
an English sermon, except Donne's last, "Death's Duel."
But interest in this antique art is whetted by Walton's description: "A preacher in earnest, weeping sometimes for
his auditory, sometimes with them, always preaching to
himself like an angel from a cloud, but in none, carrying
some, as St. Paul was, to heaven in holy raptures and
enticing others by a sacred art and courtship to amend
their lives, here picturing a vice so as to make it ugly to
those that practised it and a virtue so as to make it be
beloved even by those that loved it not; and all this with
a most particular grace and an unexpressible addition of
comeliness." However, the 160 surviving sermons—as with
his letters, Donne survives in unparalleled bulk—are heavy
going for a modern, as might be expected. A few well-
chosen excerpts are what we are usually content to get.
Even a hundred years ago, Henry Hart Milman, a doctor
of divinity and himself one of Donne's most perspicacious
successors as Dean of St. Paul's, cast on the posthumously
published folios a cold and impatient eye.

It is difficult for a Dean of our rapid and restless days to imagine, when he surveys the massy folios of Donne's sermons—each sermon spreads out over many pages—a vast congregation in the Cathedral or at Paul's Cross, listening not only with patience but with absorbed interest, with unflagging attention, even with delight and rapture, to these interminable disquisitions, to us teeming with laboured obscurity, false and misplaced wit, fatiguing antitheses. However set off, as by all accounts they were, by a most graceful and impressive delivery, it is astonishing to us that he should hold a London congregation enthralled, unwearied, unsatiated. Yet there can be no doubt that this was the case. And this congregation con- sisted, both of the people down to the lowest, and of the most noble, wise, accomplished of that highly intellectual age. They sat, even stood, undisturbed, except by their own murmurs of admiration, sometimes by hardly suppressed tears.

Evidently even the Victorian professionals lagged in zest far behind the laity of King James's time, such as Nicholas Ferrar's mother, who happily calculated that she had attended twelve thousand sermons—most of them, we may be sure, abysmally inferior to those the mere thought of which bored Dean Milman.

Of the 160 sermons—just a small fraction, of course, of those Donne delivered in his lifetime—six were pub- lished while he was yet alive, the rest in three folios edited by his son, *LXXX Sermons*, 1640, *Fifty Sermons*, 1649, and *XXVI Sermons*, 1660. Donne used notes or spoke from memory. It was considered bad form to read. Walton said of Bishop Sanderson's sermons: "they were the less valued, because he read them," and the future Bishop Earle gave as virtually his only commendation of "A Young Raw Preacher," "that he never looks upon book." On the other hand, the Puritanical practice of depending upon the inspiration of the moment was equally frowned upon. Discoursing on Luke xxiii, 40, the words of the thief on the cross, Donne noted: "We have here one example of an extemporal sermon: this thief had premeditated nothing. But he is no more a precedent for extemporal preaching than he is for stealing. He was a thief before, and he was an extemporal preacher at last. But he teaches nobody else to be either." Later, from his notes or from his copy, Donne would "exscribe" his sermon in a form ready for publication. Sometimes he expanded. His Hague sermon of 1619 he went over in 1630: "revising my short notes of that sermon, I digested them into these two." Manuscript versions (none of them, alas, in the preacher's hand) occasionally enable us to trace an improvement: "in the fall, about September," got rhythm in print as "at the fall of the leaf, in the end of the year." But he had shifted his allegiance to oratory. "I know what dead carcasses things written are in respect of things spoken," he told the Countess of Montgomery early in his new career. The writing of verse he now spoke of as a "descending."

To his Lincoln's Inn congregations, individuals among whom had been his boon companions, he spoke without sentimentality of the sins of youth, leaving scarcely an aspect untouched, including self-pollution. Sometimes he tries the Swiftian tack of disgust: "thou wilt solicit an adulterous entrance into their beds, who, if they should but see thee go into thine own bed, would need no other mortification nor answer to thy solicitation." To readers of his love poems in the past and the present, and in the future, he proclaims: "their sin, that shall sin by occasion of any wanton writings of mine, will be my sin, though they come after." He warns minds used to difficult distinctions: "This is it that undoes us, that virtues and vices are contiguous, and borderers upon one another; and very often we can hardly tell to which action the name of vice, and to which the name of virtue appertains." He delivers a series of sermons on apparently contradictory texts, as if they were conflicting laws. He essays epigrams: "In Adam we were sold in gross; in ourselves we are sold by retail." He tries jokes, saying on a hot night, "I shall be short, and rather leave you to walk with God in the cool of the evening." He is facetious—or telling—about his listeners' profession: "If any man will sue thee at law for thy coat, let him have thy cloak too, for if thine adversary have it not, thine advocate will." He pictures heaven as the place "where all clients shall retain but one councillor, our advocate Christ Jesus." The eighteen known Lincoln's Inn sermons constitute persuasive arguments *ad hominem*, show Donne's growing skill in adapting to his audience. He had said before, "Religion is no sullen thing, it is not a melancholy." He said it again, "Religion is a serious thing, but not a sullen." He wanted to be urbane, before lawyers or before courtiers, even if greatness—or his own humour—lay in the direction of "melancholy."

He continued to suffer from stomach trouble, what ultimately turned into cancer. The King, realizing a vacation was in order for his brilliant but overstrained protégé, arranged that he should accompany Lord Hay, now Viscount Doncaster, on an embassy to Germany. The embassy was important, but Donne's duties were light: he was neither a secretary nor the principal chaplain. He would deliver a very occasional sermon in the course of a long tour during which Doncaster struggled with the complex situation that led to the Thirty Years' War. Catholics and Protestants were at odds over the succession to the throne of Bohemia. James, the peace-maker, hoped to mediate between the warring German princes, one of whom was his son-in-law.

Before his departure Donne acted as if he were not sanguine that he would return alive. He informed Goodyer at Polesworth, "It is true that Mr. Gerrard told you, I had that commandment from the King signified to me by my Lord and am still under it, and we are within fourteen days of our time for going. I leave a scattered flock of wretched children, and I carry an infirm and valetudinary body, and I go into the mouth of such adversaries as I cannot blame for hating me, the Jesuits, and yet I go." He sent to trusted friends copies of his unpublished writings— the poems and *Biathanatos*. His "Sermon of Valediction at my going into Germany, at Lincoln's Inn, April 18, 1619" bids a moving farewell.

Now to make up a circle, by returning to our first word, Remember: As we remember God, so for His sake let us remember one another. In my long absence and far distance from hence, remember me, as I shall do you in the ears of that God to whom the farthest East and the farthest West are but as the right and left ear in one of us; we hear with both at once, and he hears in both at once. Remember me, not my abilities . . . . remember my labors and endeavors, at least my desire, to make sure your salvation. And I shall remember your religious cheerfulness in hearing the word, and your Christianly respect towards all them that bring that word unto you, and towards myself in particular, far above my merit. And so as your eyes that stay here, and mine that must be far off, for all that distance shall meet every morning, in looking upon that same sun, and meet every night, in looking upon the same moon: so our hearts may meet morning and evening in that God, which sees and hears everywhere . . . . That if I never meet you again till we have all passed the gates of death, yet in the gates of heaven I may meet you all.

The imagery of sea and storm marks the close, as it does that of "A Hymn to Christ, at the Author's Last Going into Germany," written while waiting to pass from Dover to Calais. One must compare the sermon,

> Christ Jesus remember us all in His kingdom, to which, though we must sail through a sea, it is the sea of His blood, where no soul suffers shipwreck; though we must be blown with strange winds, with sighs and groans for our sins, yet it is the Spirit of God that blows all this wind, and shall blow away all contrary winds of diffidence or distrust in God's mercy;

with the poem:

> In what torn ship soever I embark,
> That ship shall be my emblem of Thy ark;
> What sea soever swallow me, that flood
> Shall be to me an emblem of Thy blood;

Though Thou with clouds of anger do disguise
Thy face, yet through that mask I know those eyes,
   Which, though they turn away sometimes,
      They never will despise.

The new love affair—or rendezvous with death—is marked
by jealousy:

Nor Thou nor Thy religion dost control
The amorousness of an harmonious soul,
But Thou wouldst have that love Thyself; as Thou
Art jealous, Lord, so I am jealous now,
Thou lov'st not, till from loving more Thou free
My soul: whoever gives, takes liberty:
   Oh if Thou car'st not whom I love,
      Alas, Thou lov'st not me.

At Heidelberg he renewed his acquaintance with the
Elector and Electress Palatine whose nuptials he had
celebrated in verse. Now he had, as Walton sings it, "a
true occasion of joy, to be an eyewitness of the health of
his most dear and most honored mistress, the Queen of
Bohemia, in a foreign nation and to be a witness of that
gladness which she expressed to see him, who, having
formerly known him a courtier, was much joyed to see
him in a canonical habit and more glad to be an ear-witness
of his excellent and powerful preaching." The sermon of
June 16, 1619, has come down to us, on the cheerful text,
"For now is our salvation nearer than when we believed"
(Romans xiii, 11). This seemed true for a while in a
worldly way for Frederick when he was invited by the
Protestant nobles to be their sovereign; but his reign would
topple in a year. All this lay months distant, however, as
did the end and failure of the embassy. With her husband
temporarily at Heilbronn Elizabeth insisted that the 150
visitors sent by her father repair to the castle for lavish
hospitality, and when Doncaster declined on the grounds
of the lord's absence she forced submission by forbidding
the markets of Heidelberg to cater to them. The enchanted

ambassador reported back that he could say "no more than that she is that same devout, good, sweet Princess your Majesty's daughter should be, and she ever was, obliging all hearts that come near her by her courtesy, and so dearly loving and beloved of the Prince her husband, that it is a joy to all that behold them."

The mission was to last longer than expected. They were to visit Ulm, Augsburg, Munich, Salzburg, Nuremberg, Maastricht, and in December, The Hague, where Donne delivered a lengthy sermon that earned him a medal that he was to bequeath to the son of the late Bishop of London in his will: "To Doctor King my executor I give that medal of gold of the Synod of Dort which the Estates [General] presented me withal at The Hague . . . ." Meanwhile the Lincoln's Inn Reader was missing the Michaelmas Term, and that had to be apologized for to the benchers by Viscount Doncaster:

When I received his Majesty's command for this negotiation in Germany, I received his command also to take Doctor Donne in my company. At that time I could not suspect that I should do an act so prejudicial to your service as to frustrate you of him so long a time. But since these businesses are not yet so composed as that his Majesty may receive full satisfaction in my present return, the same command that drew Doctor Donne forth lies upon him still. Since therefore I am a continual witness of his desire to return to the service of your society, I thought it fittest for me to give you this signification of the reason of his absence, with an undoubted assurance that he shall suffer no prejudice in your good opinions thereby, because he is not altogether absent from that society now, whilst he is with me, who, by your favor, have the honor of being a member of your society. Neither is he absent from the service of God's Church, and is in obedience to his Master's commandment. In my particular I shall receive it for a singular favor from you, that you would so long spare to me from yourselves a person so necessary to you and so agreeable to me. I hope to restore

him to you by the midst of Michaelmas term, and for
your favor to me and him shall ever apprehend any
occasion to show myself.

The trip lasted indeed eight months (at a total cost of
30,000 pounds!). Donne got back only in time for the
Hilary Term in January, 1620.

Nothing had been accomplished except his refreshment. The Church of Christ was being torn to pieces in
the religious wars. A sonnet mourned her plight.

> Show me, dear Christ, Thy Spouse, so bright and clear.
> What! Is it She which on the other shore
> Goes richly painted? or which, robbed and tore,
> Laments and mourns in Germany and here?
> Sleeps she a thousand, then peeps up one year?
> Is she self Truth and errs? now new, now outwore?
> Doth she, and did she, and shall she evermore
> On one, on seven, or on no hill appear?
> Dwells she with us, or like adventuring knights
> First travail we to seek and then make love?
> Betray, kind husband, Thy spouse to our sights,
> And let mine amorous soul court Thy mild Dove,
> Who is most true, and pleasing to Thee then,
> When she'is embraced and open to most men.

It takes Donne to present Christ in the guise of a wittol!
"With his sorrows moderated and his health
improved," the Reader cast his eyes upward—to the
Deanery of Salisbury, which he had heard the incumbent
was about to resign. A game of musical chairs was immi-
nent. A letter went off[3] to the reigning favorite,
Buckingham, that exaggerated his needs. "May it please
your Lordship,—." His material situation was certainly no
longer desperate, but his craving for advancement had not
been assuaged. His view, mentioned in his sermons, was
that the characteristic vice of a young man is lust, of an

[3] XIII.

older man—ambition. At first there was disappointment. The hoped-for vacancy at Salisbury did not develop, but the Bishop of Exeter died on the twenty-sixth of August, and Valentine Cary, who had been a thoroughly undistinguished Dean of St. Paul's, was slated to succeed to the see of Exeter. Buckingham received another begging letter: "I most humbly beseech your Lordship . . . ." This was dated two weeks before Cary was elected bishop. Donne certainly knew how to keep his ear to the ground. Nor was he kept long in suspense. "The King sent to Dr. Donne, and appointed him to attend him at dinner the next day. When His Majesty was sat down, before he had eat any meat, he said, after his pleasant manner, 'Dr. Donne, I have invited you to dinner, and, though you sit not down with me, yet I will carve to you of a dish which I know you love well; for, knowing you love London, I do therefore make you Dean of St. Paul's; and when I have dined, then do you take your beloved dish home to your study, say grace there to yourself, and much good may it do you."

After certain official delays the President and Chapter of that church duly elected Donne Dean of St. Paul's November 19, 1621. He preached his first sermon as Dean on Christmas Day—appropriately, right after the winter solstice, "in that dark time of the year," on light: "He was not that light, but was sent to bear witness of that light" (John i, 8).

As Richard Corbet, a minor poet, had been made Dean of Christ Church, Oxford, the busy letter-writer Chamberlain could not forego a jest, "and then we are like to have our new Dean Dr. Donne at Paul's, so as a pleasant companion said that if Ben Jonson might be made Dean of Westminster, that place, Paul's, and Christ Church should be furnished with three very pleasant poetical deans." However, Chamberlain himself became an admirer of Donne's sermons. The minimum requirement was that the Dean preach on Christmas Day, Easter Sunday, and Whitsunday. Of course in the years that remained to him Donne preached much more often than that—Walton gave the average as "once a week"—and his growth in popularity may be measured by the number of outside invitations he received (and accepted). His regular audiences were the people now, men, women, and children, not just lawyers and courtiers. He opened up his discourse accordingly. In the summers he visited his country parishes and friends. As he himself said, before the Virginia Company, "Preachers that bind themselves always to cities and courts and great auditories may learn new notes; they may become occasional preachers and make the emergent affairs of the time their text, and the humors of the hearers their Bible; but they may lose their natural notes, both the simplicity and the boldness that belongs to the preaching of the gospel, both their power upon low understandings to raise them, and upon high affections to humble them."

The benchers bade him a reluctant farewell, and he bade likewise to his Keyston living, under suit. However, he received from the Earl of Kent the rectory of Blunham, a village six miles east of Bedford. On the other hand, he refused to accept any more payments from his father-in-law, whose means extravagance and a multitude of dependents had straitened. "The next quarter following, when ... Sir George More (whom time had made a lover and admirer of him) came to pay to him a conditioned sum of twenty pounds, he refused to receive it, and said, as good Jacob did, when he heard his beloved son Joseph was alive, 'It is enough. You have been kind to me and mine: I know your present condition is such as not to abound: and I hope mine is or will be such as not to need it: I will therefore receive no more from you upon that contract'; and in testimony of it freely gave him up his bond." (This benign account does not allow for an element of prideful satisfaction in this declaration of independence.) Donne had money left over for investment: on July 3, 1622, he became a full-fledged member of that Virginia Company before whom he preached. His old friend Christopher Brooke was their legal adviser.

He gave his first attention to some needed repairs in the Deanery. He had shown a like solicitude as Lincoln's

Inn Reader, leading a campaign, during his incumbency, for a new chapel, which is still in use. The Bishop of London consecrated it on Ascension Day, May 22, 1623.

We can still go and stare at the ornate pulpit from which Donne preached that day, but Old St. Paul's, the scene of his major activity as a minister in the last nine years of his life, went down in the fire of 1666, and the architectural masterpiece that Sir Christopher Wren erected in its stead does not tell us much about the original edifice. For pictures of that we turn rather to the mid-seventeenth-century engravings of Wenceslaus Hollar. "The goodliest heap of stones in the world," the old church was big, a true cathedral, 720 feet long by 130 feet broad. Its steeple had been as high as the Washington Monument. St. Paul's was then a temple from which the money-changers had not been driven out. Merchants in their hats dared to use the font as a counter. The nave had become a popular gathering place for Londoners, who transacted business in the aisles—merchants, lawyers, masterless servants looking for new employment. "I bought him in Paul's," exclaims Falstaff of Bardolph. Gallants showed off their new clothes there. Horses and mules were sometimes led through. This part, Paul's Walk, was characterized by John Earle in 1628 as "a heap of stones and men, with a vast confusion of languages; and were the steeple not sanctified, nothing liker Babel. The noise in it is like that of bees, a strange humming or buzz mixed of walking tongues and feet: it is a kind of still roar or loud whisper." This secular hubbub, which reached its climax at noon, might be going on while services were conducted in the fenced-off choir. Donne sometimes had to rebuke his own audiences for irreverent behavior, such as failure to kneel or remove the hat. He spoke bluntly to those who, having done business in the nave, came casually up into the choir. "You meet below, and there make your bargains, for biting, for devouring usury, and then you come up hither to prayers, and so make God your broker. You rob, and spoil, and eat his people as bread, by extortion and bribery and deceitful weights and measures, and deluding oaths in buying and selling, and then come hither, and so make God your receiver and his house a den of thieves."

In old age Donne became so exasperated that he resorted to more than reprimand. On March 12, 1630, looking out over the congregation, he found a person who was not kneeling at the Friday service. What next happened is preserved in a court record. "Item, this day Christopher Ruddy, one of the yeomen to Mr. Sheriff Smyth, for sitting in the time of Divine Service in Paul's and refusing to kneel, notwithstanding he was thrice admonished by the vergers from the Dean then present, but in contempt did thereupon depart thence, was by this court committed to the gaol of Newgate, there to remain until other order be taken for his enlargement." When disrespectful Ruddy was released is not on record. Was the example made of him salutary? Did others finally learn that it did not pay to affront God—and the Dean?

He justified any action he might feel obliged to take.

And therefore I must humbly entreat them who make this choir the place of their devotion, to testify their devotion by more outward reverence there. We know our parts in this place, and we do them; why any stranger should think himself more privileged in this part of God's house than we, I know not. I presume no man will misinterpret this that I say here now; nor, if this may not prevail, misinterpret the service of our officers, if their continuing in that unreverent manner give our officers occasion to warn them of that personally in the place, whensoever they see them stray into that uncomely negligence. They should not blame me now—they must not blame them then— when they call upon them for this reverence in this choir. Neither truly can there be any greater injustice than when they who will not do their duties blame others for doing theirs.

In a medieval structure which, like the Deanery, needed repairs—the Bishop of London pleaded for funds in 1620—the Dean presided over a Chapter consisting of five Archdeacons, a Chancellor, a Treasurer, a Precentor, and thirty prebendaries. The prebendaries helped with the preaching, and of course the Bishop of London, whose cathedra or seat St. Paul's was, gave sermons there at will and performed ordinations. The Dean's only chance to outshine a bishop was by the power of the delivered word.

During his first full year as Dean, 1622, Donne received invitations to preach outside the cathedral on several occasions, and two of his sermons were published. Early in 1624 there was published *Devotions upon Emergent Occasions,* the curious product of the main event of his life in 1623, an illness that put into the shade all his previous illnesses, an illness that cast the long shadow of death that would follow him the rest of his days, "the spotted fever . . . whereof . . . many die in two or three days' space." It seized him a little before December 1. "In the same instant that I feel the first attempt of the disease, I feel the victory; in the twinkling of an eye I can scarce see; instantly the taste is insipid and fatuous; instantly the appetite is dull and desireless; instantly the knees are sinking and strengthless; and in an instant, sleep, which is the picture, the copy of death, is taken away, that the original, death itself, may succeed, and that so I might have death to the life . . . . I sweat again and again, from the brow to the sole of the foot." He had reason to think it was the end; it nearly was. A bacteriologist has diagnosed it as relapsing fever, without, fortunately, the relapse—though the physicians had to inform him of this strong possibility. By December 6 he was just past his crisis. Chamberlain wrote of this plague-like thing, after mentioning its ravages: "yet many 'scape as the Dean of Paul's is like to do though he were in great danger."

He took notes and told the story of the twenty-three "stations of the sickness," of which the last was "the fearful danger of relapsing." "Upon emergent occasions," a common phrase in his prose, means upon occasions of emergency. The twenty-three Devotions each have three divisions: "I. Meditations upon our Human Condition" (what phrase more fashionable today!); "2. Expostulations, and Debatements with God; 3. Prayers, upon the several Occasions, to Him." His dedication to the Prince of Wales cleverly speaks of having "had three births; one, natural, when I came into the world; one, supernatural, when I entered into the ministry; and now, a preternatural birth, in returning to life from this sickness."

One scarcely knows with what to compare so odd a book. Its force of minute observation is comparable to Barbellion's description of his creeping paralysis in *The Journal of a Disappointed Man*. Barbellion was a professional biologist; Donne's knowledge of medicine was professional. But Donne, unlike the twentieth-century diarist, is fortified by theology, and his book is a triumph of analogical application. When the doctors "apply pigeons, to draw the vapors from the head," he is inspired to remember the Holy Dove, to find "a type to us that, by the visitation of Thy Spirit, the vapors of sin shall descend, and we tread them under our feet." The microcosm of course reflects the macrocosm. "Is this the honor which man hath by being a little world, that he hath these earthquakes in himself, sudden shakings; these lightnings, sudden flashes; these thunders, sudden noises; these eclipses, sudden offuscations and darkening of his senses; these blazing stars, sudden fiery exhalations; these rivers of blood, sudden red waters?" He sees everything, and he draws a lesson from everything. In the latter aspect he is the Dean of St. Paul's; in the former he is eternally human. "I observe the physician with the same diligence as he the disease; I see he fears, and I fear with him; I overtake him, I overrun him, in his fear, and I go the faster, because he makes his pace slow; I fear the more, because he disguises his fear, and I see it with the more sharpness, because he would not have me see it." He has insights ahead of his time: "as wind in the body will counterfeit any disease, and seem the stone, and seem the gout, so fear will counterfeit any disease of the mind." If this is Freud and Breuer, this is Dickens: "How many are sicker (perchance) than all we, and have not this hospital to cover them, not this straw to lie in, to die in, but have their gravestone under them, and breathe out their souls in the ears and in the eyes of passengers, harder than their bed, the flint of the street?" He was too much a contented member of the class system to feel this way often; his desolation lent him fellow feeling leading to the great Meditation XVII: "No man is an island, entire of itself; every man is a piece of the continent, a part of the main." We must not imagine that Ernest Hemingway was the first to discover the eloquence of this particular essay. Bacon, while Donne's duodecimo was still fresh from the press, made the following addition to his essay "Of Goodness, and Goodness of Nature": "his heart is no island cut off from other lands, but a continent that joins to them." *Devotions upon Emergent Occasions* was popular enough to go through five editions within fourteen years.

The Meditations parts of the *Devotions* are in the clipped, Senecan style, and the Expostulations likewise set a breathless, feverish pace, while the Prayers have the Ciceronian periods of the semons, only more so.

Donne's rising from bed—a resurrection of the body— was, it does not go without saying, a type of the resurrection of his soul! The same illness inspired one of the finest religious poems in the language. "A Hymn to God the Father" puns on the author's name with complete effectiveness.

> Wilt Thou forgive that sin where I begun,
>   Which is my sin, though it were done before?
> Wilt Thou forgive that sin through which I run,
>   And do run still, though still I do deplore?
>   When Thou hast done, Thou hast not done,
>   For I have more.

> Wilt Thou forgive that sin by which I won
>   Others to sin? and made my sin their door?
> Wilt Thou forgive that sin which I did shun
>   A year or two, but wallowed in a score?
>   When Thou hast done, Thou hast not done,
>   For I have more.

> I have a sin of fear, that when I have spun
>   My last thread, I shall perish on the shore;
> Swear by Thyself that at my death Thy Son

> Shall shine as He shines now, and heretofore;
> And, having done that, Thou hast done,
> I have no more.

"That sin by which I won / Others to sin" presumably refers to his erotic poetry. "Thy Son / Shall shine" is of course another pun, paralleled in a sermon: "I shall see the Son of God, the sun of glory, and shine myself, as that sun shines." Walton reports that the author of the hymn "caused it to be set to a most grave and solemn tune and to be often sung to the organ by the choristers of St. Paul's Church in his own hearing, especially at the evening service, and at his return from his customary devotions in that place did occasionally say to a friend, 'The words of this hymn have restored to me the same thoughts of joy that possessed my soul in my sickness when I composed it. And, Oh the power of church-music! that harmony added to this hymn has raised the affections of my heart and quickened my graces of zeal and gratitude; and I observe, that I always return from paying this public duty of prayer and praise to God with an inexpressible tranquillity of mind and a willingness to leave the world.' "

On December 3, 1623, while the Dean of St. Paul's was hovering between life and death, his eldest daughter Constance got married. The wedding had been carefully planned; it would have seemed overly sentimental to postpone it on account of the father's sudden illness. He had been sick often enough before, and it would have taken more time than was available to realize the exceptional gravity of his latest fever and to react accordingly. He himself was wary of dying with the ceremony unaccomplished; who could be sure then that it would ever be? According to a later complaint of his son-in-law, he expressed the "desire" that "our marriage should be performed with as much speed as might be, for . . . the world took large knowledge of it." Middle-class marriages in those days were not remarkable for sentiment anyway, so much did they partake of the nature of business deals arranged between the respective parents or guardians. In this case the bridegroom was thirty-seven years older than the bride. She would not seem to have been looking for romance: perhaps rather a father figure, or even a grandfather figure (since the husband was six years older than her father—a difference that definitely turned out to be troublesome).

Donne, like Mr. Bennet, had more than one daughter whom he needed to marry off, and he had tried before to make an ostensibly much more suitable arrangement for Constance, who had had years of practice at housekeeping and mothering. He advised a friend on October 18, 1622:

> Tell both your daughters a piece of a story of my Con, which may accustom them to endure disappointments in this world: An honorable person (whose name I give you in a schedule to burn, lest this letter should be mislaid) had an intention to give her one of his sons, and had told it me, and would have been content to accept what I, by my friends, could have begged for her; but he intended that son to my profession, and had provided him already £ 300 a year of his own gift in church livings, and hath estated £ 300 more of inheritance for their children; and now the youth (who yet knows nothing of his father's intention nor mine) flies from his resolutions for that calling, and importunes his father to let him travel. The girl knows not her loss, for I never told her of it; but, truly, it is a great disappointment to me.

This was the way things were done. The lucky girl does not know who her husband is to be until her father tells her. This has the advantage of sparing her "disappointment" if the deal falls through.

The deal that went through was with the actor-manager Edward Alleyn, a tall man who had once dazzled audiences in the passion-tattering role of Tamburlaine. Now fifty-seven, he had retired from acting, although he was still in charge of the royal bear-baiting—a connection that earned him a sneer from Jonson. Considering his past profession (he still had a share in a London theater), he was fairly well respected, being a man of property who had endowed hospitals and founded Dulwich College. He met Constance Donne at Camberwell in 1622, where he moved in the same circles as Sir Thomas and Lady Grymes, the latter being the sister-in-law of Donne. All these and some others dined together on September 4. Donne, all his life, despite—or even because of—his delicate stomach, was not above being drawn to a good meal (no doubt the company counted, too). In his secular days he was addressed with Jonson, Christopher Brooke, and a score of other friends as among "the Right Worshipful Fraternity of Sireniacal [Cyrenaic] Gentlemen that meet the first Friday of every month, at the sign of the Mermaid in Bread Street in London." Francis Beaumont the playwright wrote of that gay and gifted company:

> What things have we seen
> Done at the Mermaid? heard words that have been
> So nimble, and so full of subtle flame,
> As if that everyone from whom they came
> Had meant to put his whole wit in a jest
> And had resolved to live a fool the rest
> Of his dull life.

Had not even St. Paul, the first Puritan, advised, "Drink no longer water, but use a little wine for thy stomach's sake and thine often infirmities" (I Tim. v, 23)? We shall hear more about wine shortly, but meanwhile Alleyn had had a chance, recorded in his diary, to see Constance. However, his first wife was then still alive: they had been happily married for thirty years, he and Joan Woodward, the stepdaughter of Philip Henslowe, the theatrical manager. When she died June 28, 1623, Alleyn saw no reason to wait even six months before entering the blissful state again, this time with a nonresistant girl of twenty. The father had certainly hoped to do better for his daughter. Chamberlain commented, "But the strangest match, in my opinion, is that Alleyn, the old player, hath lately married a young daughter of the Dean of Paul's, which I doubt will diminish his

charity and devotion towards his two hospitals." An Elizabethan pamphleteer had protested such heartless ways of
parents with children: they "match them with inequality,
joining burning summer with key-cold winter, their daughters of twenty years old or under, to rich cormorants of
threescore or upwards." As the preacher told a Paul's Cross
congregation, resignedly, "God hath placed his creatures in
divers ranks, and in divers conditions; neither must any
man think that he hath not done the duty of a father, if he
have not placed all his sons, or not matched all his daughters, in a condition equal to himself, or not equal to one
another." That young potential cleric who had skipped out
would have been better.

So the father must have reflected, and not for the first
time, on receiving a bill of querulous particulars from his
elderly son-in-law early in 1625, reviewing the events of the
last year and a half. This, the most critical letter to Donne
that has come down, begins (and also ends), significantly,
with the root of all evil.

> Sir,-
>
> The unkind, unexpected, and undeserved denial of
> that common courtesy afforded to a friend, I mean the
> loan of unuseful monies which yourself some days before,
> I making you acquainted with all my proceeding, did then
> so lovingly grant unto (besides the voluntary offer of
> 500 marks more than I entreated—and your after repeating
> it to Sir Thomas Grymes)—makes me wonder what so
> strangely alter[ed] your mind at the very pinch of my
> occasion. And truly, Sir, I can not dwell in quiet till I be
> in some sort resolved herein . . . .

There is dispute over jointure and investments. The father-
in-law is accused of fits of temper and several failures to
keep his word. Con looked forward, in vain, to "her mother's childbed linen," "promised . . . for a New Year's gift."
She also hoped for "a little nag" that Donne was not using,
"but to prevent her of that comfort the nag was suddenly
sent away to Oxenford." She was asked to exchange one of

her diamond rings for a "ring with five stones" worn by her father. "I brought you the one but the other you keep still." Moreover, Donne is inhospitable to one whom he has testily called "a plain man." Since he feels that way, perhaps he had better pay for Lucy's food on her visits to her sister.

We lack Donne's side of the haggling story. The hardest charge for him to escape—from those who no longer have or believe in a system of social degree—would seem to be that of snobbery. The ex-actor was a crude begging fellow not to be put up with, overnight or any other time. Donne respected wealth and was horrified to be applied to for a loan from a supposedly affluent man. Even as our bias may be in favor of the poor, he leaned—when he had to choose—towards the rich. He preached what he practiced. "But consider them in the highest and in the lowest, abundant riches, beggarly poverty, and it will scarce admit doubt but that the incorrigible vagabond is farther from all ways of goodness than the corruptest rich man is." There was logic in the persuasion that those who prospered in this world very likely deserved to do so. This professional follower of Christ can write unabashedly to a lord: "Our blessed Saviour establish in you, and multiply to you the seals of His eternal election, and testify His gracious purposes towards you in the next world for ever, by a right small succession of His outward blessings here." "Right small" means large. Where were the signs of grace in "those herds of vagabonds and incorrigible rogues that fill porches and barns in the country"? But again the historical apology can be educed. It was only in 1963 that a committee of the Church of England recommended dropping from the hymn "All Things Bright and Beautiful"—as feudalistic—the verses: "The rich man in his castle, / the poor man at his gate, / God made them high or lowly, / and ordered their estate."

Clearly by becoming Dean of St. Paul's Donne was not transported above worldly troubles and cares. A friend, probably the spendthrift Goodyer (who had endeavored more than once to secure for himself a rich widow), applied to him for money. He penned a pious denial, protesting that his first year in the deanship had been expensive, "hath thrown me £ 400 lower than when I entered this house." As a precaution he took to signing his letters, "At my poor house at St. Paul's"—as if he were back at Mitcham. He displayed more than one "sin of fear." If he feared loss of heaven, he also feared the displeasure of the mighty of this world. His pious biographer complacently tells a story of flexible knees, after His Majesty had heard from "some malicious whisperer" that the Dean "had put on the general humor of the pulpits, and was become busy in insinuating a fear of the King's inclining to popery." James accepted Donne's denial of this implausible charge.

> When the King had said this, Dr. Donne kneeled down and thanked His Majesty, and protested his answer was faithful, and free from all collusion, and therefore "desired that he might not rise till, as in like cases he always had from God, so he might from His Majesty, some assurance that he stood clear and fair in his opinion."

It was taken for granted that there was nothing wrong with paralleling God's anointed with God (in Charles's reign he would teach, "a religious king is the image of God"), or with professing that one "always" received affirmation of the latter's favor. Walton's quotation is contradicted by some of the divine poems, which greatly doubt.

Offices multiplied. Besides being Dean and one of the King's chaplains, in which latter capacity he often was called on to preach at Whitehall, Donne held, as has been mentioned, the not unprofitable livings of Sevenoaks and Blunham and had not given up Keyston without a struggle. In March of 1624, after his convalescence, he received another benefice, the reversion of which had long since been promised him by the Earl of Dorset. He became vicar of St. Dunstan's in the West, near Fleet Street, where he was to have as an idolizing parishioner Izaak Walton. By royal grant a dispensation was drawn up empowering him to hold these several livings simultaneously. He attended to his duties as conscientiously as a pluralist can, paying a curate to be his substitute and preaching in the country churches in the summer. None of these rural sermons did he think worthy of preserving, but a half dozen of the St. Dunstan's sermons are in the collections, including the first of April 11 on the duties of the pastor and his flock.

If on the one hand such a pastor was worthy of his hire, the hire should have amounted to enough now to satisfy the pastor, even if he could point to five or six dependent children. John was at Oxford; George entered the army. Lucy took over Constance's duties as housekeeper. The aged Catholic mother moved into the Deanery. The Vicar of St. Dunstan's answered criticism by declaring, "I make not a shilling profit of St. Dunstan's as a Churchman, but as my Lord of Dorset gave me the lease of the Impropriation for a certain rent, and a higher rent than my predecessor had it at" and "This I am fain to say often, because they that know it not have defamed me of a defectiveness towards that Church; and even that mistaking of theirs I ever have, and ever shall endeavor to rectify, by as often preaching there as my condition of body will admit." But emoluments there definitely were. The Vestry Minutes of June 25, 1624, state: "This day the parishioners of this parish of St. Dunstan's being assembled have lovingly condescended to give £ 200 per annum unto the Vicar ... for the tithes of the parish to be paid unto him quarterly by even portions." Donne dined and wined so lavishly with the vestrymen that the money spent on banquets was subject to criticism. Moreover, like a poet laureate, he was sent sack for Christmas. An energetic refurbisher, he directed a building program that resulted in reparations, a new pulpit and new pews. He rented seats in the chancel for his profit, and made some money on memorial sermons.

If, as he said, the besetting sin of youth was lust, of soberer years ambition, he added, too—now that he was in his fifties (the equivalent of the sixties or seventies today)— that the old had to be on guard against covetousness. In the available sermons, many of which are mediocre, all of which are conventional in their theology and tend to be tiresome in their *divisio,* their eternal text-chopping, we get flashes of inspired passion—perhaps self-inspired, as if he saw the sinner within, the man he knew best, the man that never could be sure of salvation. At such times he hypnotized his audiences with his obsessions. "What Tophet is not Paradise, what brimstone is not amber, what gnashing is not a comfort, what gnawing of the worm is not a tickling, what torment is not a marriage bed to this damnation, to be secluded eternally, eternally, eternally from the sight of God?" So warned the cavernous voice, the increasingly rugose face, the mortal that looked frailer with each sickness-ridden year.

5 | *The Longed–For Release*

March, 1625, brought two deaths that Donne commemorated in different ways. "An Hymn to the Saints and to Marquis Hamilton" consists of twenty-one couplets written at Ker's request, one of Donne's last performances as a poet. This Scotch gallant, James Hamilton—Chamberlain had "not heard a man generally better spoken of than the Marquis, even by all the English"—had been an opponent of Buckingham's war policy; there were rumors that it was not, after all, "a malignant fever" but poison that brought about his sudden demise. Chamberlain was not of Ker's mind that it became the Dean to revert to verse. "I send you here certain verses of our Dean of Paul's upon the death of the Marquis Hamilton, which, though they be reasonable witty and well done, yet I could wish a man of his years and place to give over versifying."

The elegy had scarcely been written when another James died. A tertian ague and complications ended the reign of James I on March 27. In his dotage he had ceased to matter: Baby Steenie and Charles were running him. "The wisest fool in Christendom," he had been, at best, an ineffectual ruler. But Donne felt a personal loss. While the body lay in state, as it did for a month, he ruminated sadly.

"It was not so hard a hand when we touched it last, nor so cold a hand when we kissed it last." His sermon supported the official view that England had lost her "Solomon."

At least it had been possible—that was both James's weakness and his strength—to draw close to, to become somewhat familiar with, the late king. As for the new king, he was reserved and impersonal. No one was close to him except Buckingham, who "lay the first night of the reign in the King's bedchamber."

That was what a Gentleman of the Bedchamber was for. The seclusion of the two at St. James's Palace lasted for a week. Suddenly there went out an order. The Dean of St. Paul's was to preach before the new king Sunday, April 3. The Dean's nervous stomach quivered at the fearful opportunity.[1]

Charles listened palely, with an air "very attentive and devout." Did he approve what he heard? Who could read those aquiline, inscrutable features? Donne's nervousness was soon relieved. The King found the sermon so much to his liking that he commanded it be printed, as it promptly was: *The First Sermon Preached to King Charles.* Shortly afterwards it was offered to the public again, as the fourth of Donne's first collected volume, *Four Sermons upon Special Occasions.* Where James was a pedantic arguer, Charles (the first monarch to be brought up from childhood in the Church of England) had a quiet spiritual passion that responded to the painful sincerity of the greatest preacher in his realm. From this signal beginning, Donne was called on again and again. His only possible rival, Lancelot Andrewes, died in 1626, and there would be nobody remotely comparable again until Jeremy Taylor, then a boy of twelve.

Besides fasting on the day of the delivery of the sermon, he was accustomed to spend a week in preparation. "The latter part of his life may be said to be a continued study; for as he usually preached once a week, if not oftener, so after his sermon he never gave his eyes rest till he had

[1] Letters XIV and XV.

chosen out a new text, and that night cast his sermon into form and his text into divisions; and the next day betook himself to consult the fathers, and so commit his meditations to his memory, which was excellent. But upon Saturday he usually gave himself and his mind a rest from the weary burden of his week's meditations and usually spent that day in visitation of friends or some other diversions of his thoughts, and would say, 'that he gave both his body and mind that refreshment that he might be enabled to do the work of the day following, not faintly, but with courage and cheerfulness.' "

It was a wet, tainted spring. "God can call up damps and vapors from below, and pour down putrid defluxions from above, and bid them meet and condense into a plague, a plague that shall not be only uncurable, uncontrollable, unexorable, but indisputable, unexaminable, unquestionable." Bad outbreaks of the plague are associated, like a judgment of history, with the Stuarts—the last and worst under Charles II, but the coronation of James I was marred in 1603, and now there was a steady increase in deaths in April and May, and in June the mortality rate soared, when the new king was to receive his fifteen-year-old bride from France, Henrietta Maria. The people stayed to see the royal couple enter London by barge, but the people were dropping suddenly in the streets in the midst of the joyful bonfires and the commanded seven hours' ringing of bells. The bells tolled for them, for 5000 of them in July, 19,000 in August. Parliament had been convened in June, but the members began fleeing well before the enforced adjournment on July 11. Trinity Term was halted on June 18; six days later all trials by jury were called off. No one who could get away, including John Donne, lingered in the doomed city that dreadful summer. September brought 40,000 deaths. "Donne's little parish of St. Dunstan's in the West suffered with more than average severity. Many of the city churches were closed for want of a congregation." It was not known that the fleas on the black rats were spreading the plague, but it was sensed that the thing to do was to avoid crowds and company. Scattering his children in outlying districts, Donne withdrew to the suburb of Chelsea, maintaining such a strict quarantine that he was thought to be dead.

By contemporary reports all that was heard in the stricken city was "the howling of dogs, the raving of the sick, and the mourning of the bereaved." "Within a few weeks" in Chelsea, too "the infection multiplied so fast as that it was no good manners to go to any other place." As if "in a secular monastery," Donne meditated with moral horror on how some people had behaved. "The citizens fled away, as out of a house on fire, and stuffed their pockets with their best ware, and threw themselves into the highways, and were not received so much as into barns, and perished so, some of them with more money about them than would have bought the village where they died. A justice of peace, into whose examination it fell, told me of one that died so with £ 1400 about him." Those whose desperate attitude was eat, drink, and be merry "were cut off by the hand of God, some even in their robberies, in half-empty houses; and in their drunkenness in voluptuous and riotous houses; and in their lusts and wantonness in licentious houses; and so took in infection and death, like Judas' sop, death dipt and soaked in sin. Men whose lust carried them into the jaws of infection in lewd houses, and seeking one sore perished with another; men whose rapine and covetousness broke into houses, and, seeking the wardrobes of others, found their own winding-sheet in the infection of that house where they stole their own death; men who sought no other way to divert sadness but strong drink in riotous houses, and there drank up David's cup of malediction, the cup of condemned men, of death, in the infection of that place."

The preacher explained in a letter "how I have spent this summer in my close imprisonment. I have revised as many of my sermons as I had kept any note of, and I have written out a great many, and hope to do more. I am already come to the number of eighty, of which my son, who, I hope, will take the same profession or some other in the world of middle understanding, may hereafter make some use." He was indeed like a monk cloistered from the world, busy at his scriptorium. As he told Goodyer, "the report of my death hath thus much of truth in it, that though I be not dead yet I am buried." But he was buried in excellent company, his hosts being Sir John and Lady Danvers. He wrote in expectation and appeal to his brother-in-law Sir Nicholas Carew on June 21: "I go to a family to which I owe much, and therefore must entreat you to be my surety for one debt to them, which is, sometime this summer to bestow a buck upon me." Lady Danvers was the former Magdalen Herbert. Her brilliant and thoughtful son George, now thirty-two, was with them. It was years before, probably, that he and Donne had exchanged Latin poems on Donne's seal of Christ upon the Anchor (an emblem of hope). Now, the difference in their ages no longer mattering, their relationship could be described as Walton describes it: "a long and dear friendship made up by such a sympathy of inclinations that they coveted and joyed to be in each other's company; and this happy friendship was still maintained by many sacred endearments." Having distinguished himself in the post of University Orator at Cambridge, Herbert was undergoing "many conflicts with himself, whether he should return to the painted pleasures of a court life, or betake himself to a study of divinity and enter into sacred orders (to which his dear mother had often persuaded him)." His consumptive body was as frail as his soul was anguished. "He would often say, 'He had too thoughtful a wit: a wit like a pen-knife in too narrow a sheath, too sharp for his body.' " As he hovered on the threshold of the church of which he became at last, at Bemerton, a pastoral saint, his life as well as his poetry underwent a pervasive influence during those months of seclusion.

The two geniuses were shut up with the remarkable mother, while the grave-diggers knocked on doors, asking, "Have ye any dead?" As her friend related in her funeral sermon, that charitable lady did not cease even then "to minister relief to the sick."

It was the worst outbreak of the plague in Donne's

lifetime, but the winter brought the customary abatement. People ventured back to their homes in time for Christmas. On January 15, 1626, the Dean gave at St. Dunstan's "The First Sermon after our Dispersion by the Sickness." Two Sundays later, at St. Paul's, his theme was again joy, a joy that took the sting out of death. He concluded: "But as in the face of Death, when he lays hold upon me, and in the face of the Devil, when he attempts me, I shall see the face of God (for everything shall be a glass, to reflect God upon me), so in the agonies of death, in the anguish of that dissolution, in the sorrows of that valediction, in the irreversibleness of that transmigration, I shall have a joy, which shall no more evaporate than my soul shall evaporate, a joy that shall pass up and put on a more glorious garment above, and be joy superinvested in glory. Amen."

He was in demand for funeral sermons. One of the best was "preached at the funeral of Sir William Cokayne, Knight, Alderman of London, December 12, 1626." It is a rational, as distinguished from an emotional, masterpiece. Donne wanted to do well by one of his richest parishioners. He perhaps did not know that the worthy he eulogized had been guilty of shady dealing in a textile bubble called the New Merchant Adventurers, a well-bribed attempt at a monopoly that, being more grandiose than usual, brought about the depression of 1620 when it collapsed. What the Dean noticed with appreciation was the alderman's outer piety, his good church manners: "I have observed him to enter with much reverence, and compose himself in this place with much declaration of devotion." Also he died well, saying, " 'Little know ye what pain I feel this night, yet I know I shall have joy in the morning,' and in that morning he died," repeating the name of Jesus. Anyway he showed "industry," and "Not to hope well of him that is gone is uncharitableness." The speaker reserves his keenness of analysis for other directions, being generous with epigrams, such as the opening one, "God made the first marriage, and man made the first divorce;" or one a little further on, "Young men mend not their sight by using old men's spectacles." He employs an architectural comparison well, as he will do in "Death's Duel": "There is no form of building stronger than an arch, and yet an arch hath declinations, which even a flat-roof hath not. The flat-roof lies equal in all parts; the arch declines downwards in all parts, and yet the arch is a firm supporter. Our devotions do not the less bear us upright, in the sight of God, because they have some declinations towards natural affections." He draws on the new science to brighten a commonplace: "I need not call in new philosophy, that denies a settledness, an acquiescence in the very body of the earth, but makes the earth to move in that place where we thought the sun had moved. I need not that help, that the earth itself is in motion, to prove this, that nothing upon earth is permanent." (But he still uses the Ptolemaic system when it suits him.) He tries out different degrees of Latinity in his phrases, from "thy holy amorousness" to "a vicissitudinary transmutation." He is capable of Anglo-Saxon vividness: "A merchant condensed, kneaded, and packed up in a great estate becomes a lord"; "Though a man knew not that every sin casts another shovel of brimstone upon him in Hell—." Or he anticipates, as he had done in the *Essays in Divinity,* the mournful splendors of Sir Thomas Browne: "They said in their hearts to all the world, 'Can these bodies die?' And they are dead. Jezebel's dust is not amber, nor Goliah's dust *terra sigillata,* medicinal; nor does the Serpent, whose meat they are both, find any better relish in Dives' dust than in Lazarus'."

The year 1626 was the least marked with ill health and other tribulations of Donne's declining years. Pain he found trivial, calling it "but a caterpillar got into one corner of my garden, a mildew fallen upon one acre of my corn." He made a note: "This year God hath blessed me and mine with *multiplicatae sunt super nos misericordiae tuae*" (Thy mercies over us have been multiplied).

Those who get on in years—and it all happened sooner in those days—inevitably find their relatives and friends dropping away, immobilized by illness or by death. Donne suffered a succession of losses in 1627 and 1628. On January 9, 1627, his eldest surviving unmarried daughter, Lucy,

eighteen, was buried at Camberwell. Her place as housekeeper at the Deanery was taken by Bridget, seventeen. But
of course her place could never be taken, any more than
Anne's could, and there are wistful passages in the sermons
that sound as if the new loss were being touched on. George,
so much the favorite son that when Con wanted that "little
nag" from her father, she employed him "to move you for
it," was taken prisoner after Buckingham's disastrous attempt to aid the Huguenots at the Isle of Rhe. His father
never saw him again. The original Lucy, Countess of Bedford, childless, outlived her invalid husband but a month,
dying on May 31, followed within a few days by Lady Danvers. That favorite correspondent Goodyer went on March
18, 1628, preceded by Christopher Brooke, February 7. Before that year was out, Ben Jonson suffered a paralytic
stroke that left him bed-ridden for his remaining years. He
outlived Donne (if living it could be called), reaching what
the Earl of Clarendon labeled the "very old" age of sixty-
four.

In the funeral sermon Donne portrayed Magdalen
Herbert Danvers with unusual vividness, even passing on a
direct quotation that showed her eagerness for church. "She
ever hastened her family and her company hither, with that
cheerful provocation, 'For God's sake, let's go. For God's
sake, let's be there at the Confession.'" Her friends ad-
mired "her inclination and conversation naturally cheerful
and merry, and loving facetiousness and sharpness of wit."
But alas, it was true even of her, "some sicknesses, in the
declination of her years, had opened her to an overflowing
of melancholy." How much truer was it of him, with his
"sickly inclination" towards the grave!

In this very sermon, he struggled in public with the
death wish. "If we could wish our own death as innocently,
as harmlessly, as they did the Day of Judgment, if no ill
circumstances in us did vitiate our desire of death, if there
were no dead flies in this ointment (as Solomon speaks), if
we had not at least a collateral respect (if not a direct and
principal) to our own ease from the incumbrances and
grievances and annoyances of this world, certainly we

might safely desire, piously wish, religiously pray for, our own death. But it is hard, very hard, to divest those circumstances that infect it. For if I pretend to desire death merely for the fruition of the glory, of the sight of God, I must remember that my Saviour desired that glory, and yet stayed his time for it. If I pretend to desire death that I might see no more sin, hear no more blasphemies from others, it may be I may do more good to others than I shall take harm by others if I live. If I would die that I might be at the end of temptations in myself, yet, I might lose some of that glory which I shall have in Heaven, by resisting another year's temptation, if I died now. To end this consideration, as this *looking for* the day of the Lord (which is the word of our text) implies a joy and a gladness of it when it shall come (whether we consider that as the day itself, the Day of Judgment, or the even of the day, the day of our death), so doth this *looking for it* imply a patient attending of God's leisure." Of course there was the alternative, spoken of four months before, of wishing, like Job, that one had never been born. "If there were any other way to be saved and to get to Heaven than by being born into this life, I would not wish to have come into this world."

The *Sermon of Commemoration of the Lady Danvers* was immediately published, accompanied by nineteen elegiac poems in Latin or Greek by George Herbert. If George Herbert had not yet chosen to display his powers in English verse, John Donne had abandoned his old harmonies (or discords)—but not his ingenuity. The public was permitted to witness, as a prime example, his conjuring away of the discrepancy between the lady's age and her husband's: "For, as the well tuning of an instrument makes higher and lower strings of one sound, so the inequality of their years was thus reduced to an evenness, that she had a cheerfulness agreeable to his youth, and he a sober staidness conformable to her more years. So that I would not consider her, at so much more than forty, nor him, at so much less than thirty, at that time, but as their persons were made one and their fortunes made one by marriage, so I would put their years into one number, and, finding a sixty be-

tween them, think them thirty apiece, for, as twins of one
hour, they lived. God, who joined them, then, having also
separated them now, may make their years even this other
way too: by giving him as many years after her going out of
this world as He had given her before his coming into it;
and then, as many more, as God may receive glory and the
world benefit by that addition, that so, as at their first meeting she was, at their last meeting he may be, the elder
person.''

In the midst of other clouds, Donne was suddenly visited with Charles's suspicion, as he had once been with
James's. On April 1, 1627, he had preached at Whitehall
what he considered to be—and the surviving text bears him
out—a perfectly harmless sermon. Among the auditors was
that energetic High Church busybody, the rising Bishop of
Bath and Wells, William Laud, who whispered into the
King's ear that they had been hearing Low Church doctrine
consonant with an offensive sermon that had been preached
a little earlier by Abbot, the Primate who was thoroughly
out of favor for more than one reason, including the daring
to ally himself on occasion with the Puritans. The day after,
the Dean in trepidation despatched the following letter to
Ker at court.

Sir,-

A few hours after I had the honor of your letter, I
had another from my Lord of Bath and Wells, commanding
from the King a copy of my sermon. I am in preparations
of that, with diligence, yet this morning I waited upon
his Lordship and laid up in him this truth, that of the
Bishop of Canterbury's sermon, to this hour, I never heard
syllable, nor what way, nor upon what points he went. And
for mine, it was put into that very order, in which I
delivered it, more than two months since.

Freely to you I say, I would I were a little more
guilty: only mine innocency makes me afraid. I hoped for
the King's approbation heretofore in many of my sermons;
and I have had it. But yesterday I came very near looking
for thanks; for, in my life, I was never in any one piece
so studious of his service. Therefore, exceptions being

taken and displeasure kindled at this, I am afraid it was rather brought thither than met there. If you know any more fit for me (because I hold that unfit for me, to appear in my master's sight as long as this cloud hangs, and therefore this day forbear my ordinary waitings), I beseech you to intimate it to your very humble and very thankful servant,

J. Donne

April 2, 1627

In his age he was even less ready than in his youth for foolish, heroic resistance to the powers that be. What was the telling phrase in *Pseudo-Martyr:* "a just love of your own safety"? He searched the text he had written out for indiscretions. Where had he been—against his custom and his character—"overbold"?—he who ever since the Cokayne sermon had pointedly defended his Church against the attacks of the Puritans? Had there been the shadow of an allusion to Charles's Catholic queen? He begged for any opportunity to apologize and retract and explain, if his shaken health permitted. His courtier friend was sent off a second letter twice as long.[2]

> Sir,-
>
> I was this morning at your door, somewhat early; and I am put into such a distaste of my last sermon as that I dare not practise any part of it, and therefore, though I said then that we are bound to speak aloud, though we awaken men and make them froward, yet after two or three modest knocks at the door I went away . . . .

What priceless self-characterization, worthy of Boswell's *London Journal!*

Hay and Buckingham came to the rescue. Laud noted in his diary: "April 4, Wednesday, when His Majesty King Charles forgave to Doctor Donne certain slips in a sermon preached on Sunday."

[2] XVI.

The next month Donne informed his St. Dunstan's congregation: "Every minister of God is to have ... the courage of a lion .... In every minister I look for such an invincible courage as should be of proof against persecution,—which is a great, and against preferment,—which is a greater, temptation; that neither hopes nor fears shake his constancy—neither his Christian constancy, to stagger him, nor his ministerial constancy, to silence him." That, to be sure, was the ideal. In the discerning words of Arthur Symons, "to a brain so abstract, conduct must always have seemed of less importance than it does to most other people."

If he did not practice one virtue he practiced another. With fewer dependents, "he was enabled to become charitable to the poor, and kind to his friends." On two occasions he lent Sir John Danvers sums equivalent to thousands of dollars that had not yet been paid at the time that Donne, in his last illness, made out his will. "He gave an hundred pounds at one time to an old friend"—doubtless the thriftless Goodyer. "He was inquisitive after the wants of prisoners, and redeemed many from thence that lay for their fees or small debts. He was a continual giver to poor scholars, both of this and foreign nations." Never forgetting his own stay in prison, he sent around presents to the city jails on festive occasions, notably Christmas and Easter.

He kept busy and he kept social, health permitting. He served on church commissions on which his legal knowledge was of special use. He wrote letters of recommendation, a power himself now. There circled around him younger friends and protégés—Herbert, Henry King, Thomas Carew (poets all), Walton, the exotic Brian Duppa, who, after Donne-like explorations and hesitations in secular realms, was led by his patron to the Deanship of Christ Church in 1629 as the necessary preliminary to rising to three bishoprics. All that Donne had to do to become a bishop himself was to live long enough.

After Goodyer's death in the spring of 1628, his place as Donne's chief correspondent was assumed by a lady whom the knight had probably introduced to the Dean at

Polesworth. Mrs. Thomas Cokayne's husband was related to
the wealthy Sir William, the late alderman, but had behaved in a most unbourgeois fashion, having abandoned
his wife in the country to hide in London and incubate,
under the alias Brown, an English-Greek lexicon. Never
was a wife left for so unexpected a reason; they had had
seven children, of whom the eldest, Aston Cokain, now on
the threshold of manhood, became a comic dramatist.
Whether or not her name Anne worked a spell, Donne
addressed to Mrs. Cokayne letters[3] unusually warm and
free of artificiality. They chatted with the intimacy of
invalids. She is seeking a cure at Bath; he has suffered
"a violent falling of the uvula," in addition to fever and
quinsy. A teacher without a voice, he ventured to preach
only once, at St. Dunstan's, before November. Moreover, as he feared, his sickness *was* "presented by rumor
worse than God" had "been pleased to make it." Again, as
in the plague year, word went out that the Dean was dead:
so eremitically had he lived.

The four sermons that survive for the winter of 1628-29
are lacking in eloquence—that is, in energy, as if the
preacher were conserving what strength he had. He avoids
melodrama, keeps to an area that always leaves him calm—
the class system. His letter to Anne Cokayne,[4] when she
lost her son Thomas, seventeen, is also calm. It is one of
two letters that survive for 1629.

As he entered upon the last twelve months of his active
ministry, he returned, for three sermons, to Genesis. "My
end is my beginning": that had been the interesting motto
of that troublesome Catholic, Mary Queen of Scots. The
preacher continues to avoid excitement, with scarcely an
allusion to death and no passion over sin. He served on an
ecclesiastical commission in June of 1629, then visited one
of his country parishes. Both these activities are alluded to
in a dunning letter he addressed his father-in-law from
"Paul's house" June 22, 1629.[5] Surely, whatever the

[3] See Appendix.
[4] XX.
[5] XXI.

worry about repayment, it was better to be a lender than a borrower, in a spectacular reversal of position between an aging and an aged man.

The aging man's health did not break down completely until August, 1630. His last sermons at St. Paul's were preached in the spring of 1630.

In August, 1630, Charles was making arrangements contingent upon Donne's being "advanced to a bishopric." But that was the very time when the Dean of St. Paul's unmistakably ceased to be fit for anything but the contemplation of the grave. He had gone to visit his daughter Constance, who, well widowed, had married her second husband Samuel Harvey on June 24. They lived in style at Aldborough Hatch—shortened as Abury Hatch—at Epping Forest in Essex. There her father "fell into a fever, which, with the help of his constant infirmity—vapors from the spleen—hastened him into so visible a consumption that his beholders might say, as St. Paul of himself, 'he died daily.' " The modern diagnosis is cancer of the stomach. (Here, too, he was ahead of his time.)

There, tended by his valet Robert Christmas, "he was forced to spend much of that winter, by reason of his disability to remove from that place." George Gerrard, who had become Master of the Charterhouse, and Mrs. Cokayne received his last letters.

On December 13, with death three and a half months off, he drew up a new will, in which he made no claim to be sound of body. He left equal portions to his unmarried children, the rich sum of 500 pounds apiece being mentioned. As his father had been in his will, he was charitable to the local poor, though on a less lavish scale. He distributed paintings among his friends, Carlisle receiving "the picture of the blessed Virgin Mary which hangs in the little dining-room" and Gerrard "the picture of Mary Magdalen in my chamber." To Dr. Winniff, who was to succeed him as Dean, he bequeathed—for his sober contemplation—"the picture called the Skeleton which hangs in the Hall." Walton relates that he caused his emblem of Christ-upon-the-anchor "to be engraven very small in heliotropean stones and set in gold, and of these he sent to many of his dearest friends to be used as seals or rings and kept as memorials of him and of his affection to them." His father had made provisions for death's-head rings. It was an age that treasured such remembrances, the *memento mori* that was easily transformed, for a Christian, into *memento vivere,* Death as the gateway of Life.

The rumor that he was dead already did not trouble him so much as the opposite charge that he was malingering. One

> writ unto me that some (and he said of my friends) conceived that I was not so ill as I pretended, but withdrew myself to save charges, and to live at ease, discharged of preaching. It is an unfriendly and, God knows, an ill-grounded interpretation: for in these times of necessity, and multitudes of poor, there is no possibility of saving to him that hath any tenderness in him; and for affecting my ease, I have been always more sorry when I could not preach than any could be that they could not hear me. It hath been my desire (and God may be pleased to grant it me) that I might die in the pulpit; if not that, yet that I might take my death in the pulpit, that is, die the sooner by occasion of my former labors.

He was to come close to dying in the pulpit. He had plans already for making the alternative wish a reality, that a last exertion there hasten his end. He would answer his detractors in a way they would never forget.

At Mrs. Cokayne's importuning he supplied clinical details. On top of his chronic complaint he suffered from what was perhaps a malarial fever.

He managed to journey back to London the beginning of February. There he was pressed to try a milk diet—still a standard procedure. But this he deemed a fate worse than death:

> Dr. Foxe, a man of great worth, ... told him, "That by cordials and drinking milk every twenty days together there

was a probability of his restoration to health"; but he passionately denied to drink it. Nevertheless, Dr. Foxe, who loved him most entirely, wearied him with solicitations till he yielded to take it for ten days; at the end of which time he told Dr. Foxe, "He had drunk it more to satisfy him than to recover his health and that he would not drink it ten days longer upon the best moral assurance of having twenty years added to his life, for he loved it not, and was so far from fearing death, which to others is the king of terrors, that he longed for the day of his dissolution."

Izaak Walton tells the rest like the spectator he probably was.

He was appointed to preach upon his old constant day, the first Friday in Lent; he had notice of it, and had in his sickness so prepared for that employment that, as he had long thirsted for it, so he resolved his weakness should not hinder his journey; he came therefore to London some few days before his appointed day of preaching.

At his coming thither, many of his friends—who with sorrow saw his sickness had left him but so much flesh as did only cover his bones—doubted his strength to perform that task, and did therefore dissuade him from undertaking it, assuring him, however, it was like to shorten his life; but he passionately denied their requests, saying he would not doubt that that God, who in so many weaknesses had assisted him with an unexpected strength, would now withdraw it in his last employment; professing an holy ambition to perform that sacred work.

And when, to the amazement of some beholders, he appeared in the pulpit, many of them thought he presented himself not to preach mortification by a living voice, but mortality by a decayed body and a dying face. And doubtless many did secretly ask that question in Ezekiel: "Do these bones live? or, can that soul organise that tongue to speak so long as the sand in that glass will move towards its center, and measure out an hour of this dying man's unspent life? Doubtless it cannot." And yet, after some faint pauses in his zealous prayer, his strong desires enabled his weak body to discharge his memory of his preconceived meditations, which were of dying; the text being, "To God the Lord belong the issues from death." Many that then saw his tears, and heard his faint and hollow voice, professing they thought the text prophetically chosen, and that Dr. Donne had preached his own funeral sermon.

Being full of joy that God had enabled him to perform this desired duty, he hastened to his house; out of which he never moved, till, like St. Stephen, "he was carried by devout men to his grave."

The next day after his sermon, his strength being much wasted, and his spirits so spent as indisposed him to business or to talk, a friend that had often been a witness of his free and facetious discourse asked him, "Why are you sad?" To whom he replied, with a countenance so full of cheerful gravity as gave testimony of an inward tranquillity of mind and of a soul willing to take a farewell of this world; and said—

"I am not sad; but most of the night past I have entertained myself with many thoughts of several friends that have left me here, and are gone to that place from which they shall not return; and that within a few days I also shall go hence, and be no more seen. And my preparation for this change is become my nightly meditation upon my bed, which my infirmities have now made restless to me. But at this present time I was in a serious contemplation of the providence and goodness of God to me; to me, who am less than the least of His mercies; and looking back upon my life past, I now plainly see it was His hand that prevented me from all temporal employment; and that it was His will I should never settle nor thrive till I entered into the ministry; in which I have now lived almost twenty years—I hope to His glory—and by which, I most humbly thank Him, I have been enabled to requite most of those friends which showed me kindness when my fortune was very low, as God knows it was: and—as it hath occasioned the expression of my gratitude—I thank God most of them have stood in need of my requital. I have lived to be useful and comfortable to my good father-in-law, Sir George More, whose patience God hath been pleased to exercise with many temporal crosses; I have maintained my own mother, whom it hath pleased God, after a plentiful fortune in her younger days, to bring to great decay in her very old age. I have quieted the consciences of many, that have groaned under the burden of a wounded spirit, whose prayers I hope are available for me. I cannot plead innocency of life, especially of my youth; but I am to be judged by a merciful God, who is not willing to see what I have done amiss. And though of myself I have nothing to present to Him but sins and misery, yet I know He looks not upon me now as I am of myself, but as I am in my Saviour, and hath given me, even at this present time, some testimonies by His Holy Spirit, that I am of the number of His Elect: I am therefore full of inexpressible joy, and shall die in peace."

In "Holy Sonnet I" he had said, "I run to death, and death meets me as fast, / And all my pleasures are like yesterday." The last sermon, published after his decease under the title "Death's Duel," was delivered before the King at Whitehall on the twenty-fifth of February, 1631. The editor of *The Christian Century* has commented, "There is no sermon like it in the whole literature of the Christian pulpit." However, in a marked way Donne had been preparing for it all his life. Literarily as well as psychically and biologically he had been dueling with death ever since his martyr-surrounded youth. The very titles of his early poems are indicative: "The Funeral," "The Relic," "The Will," "The Dissolution." As a modern critic points out, "death is constantly making its appearance in metaphorical form, in the poems of secular love. Absence is death; intercourse is death; the beloved's scorn is death." The "bracelet of bright hair about the bone" might have come from one of Poe's tales: there is something of the romantic or neurotic *frisson nouveau* in Donne. "The Damp" and "The Apparition" both imagine the poet as dead. Then he went on to such ghoulish prose works as

Biathanatos and *Devotions upon Emergent Occasions.* He preached his first extant sermon on death on Easter Sunday, 1619, with Psalm lxxxix, 48 as his text, "The King being then dangerously sick at Newmarket."

The author of *Donne's Imagery,* Milton Rugoff, finds (with statistics to prove it) a

> sense of man's mortality, decay ever present, and the skull beneath the skin which pervades Donne's work and links him with that considerable group of Elizabethan and Jacobean writers whose works are shot through with the melancholy or morbid consciousness of death. The reasons why this sense of death should have been so extraordinarily pervasive in the early seventeenth century are complex; it is probable that many forces contributed: the tradition of the *carpe diem* theme; the fanatic emphasis of the medieval clergy on the vanity of the flesh; the depression and cynicism of spirit that seem to follow eras which, like the Elizabethan, are characterized by inordinate expansions in every direction; and life itself rendered as cheap as ever by disease and war, the former raging unchecked, the latter accepted like daily bread. If some personal circumstance is needed to explain why Donne may have been even more sensitive to these forces than most men, we find it in his lifelong ill-health; it is the pathetic burden of his letters and the theme of his *Devotions*; in fact, Donne's images from this source are merely a sombre counterpoint in those lofty and impassioned fugues wherein he welcomes death, inveighs against the flesh, or dwells with almost pathological fervor on physical corruption and the ghastly work of the worm.

Like the Pontic king Mithridates, who legendarily became immune to poison by taking it in ever increasing doses, Donne had meditated so long on death that he could stare "the king of terrors" in the face without flinching.

> God accustomed St. Paul, no doubt, to such notifications from Him, and such apprehensions in himself of death, as, because it was not new, it could not be terrible. When

St. Paul was able to make that protestation, "I protest by your rejoicing, which I have in Christ Jesus our Lord, I die daily," and again, "I am in prisons oft, and often in deaths—I die often"—no executioner could have told him, You must die tomorrow, but he could have said, Alas, I died yesterday, and yesterday was twelve-month, and seven year, and every year, and month, and week, and hour, before that. There is nothing so near immortality as to die daily, for not to feel death is immortality; and only he shall never feel death that is exercised in the continual meditation thereof: continual mortification is immortality.

He penetrated to the very core, and found it soft:

When of the whole body there is neither eye nor ear nor any member left, where is the body? And what should an eye do there where there is nothing to be seen but loathsomeness? or a nose where there is nothing to be smelt but putrefaction? or an ear where in the grave they do not praise God? . . . Painters have presented us with some horror the skeleton, the frame of the bones of a man's body; but the state of the body in the dissolution of the grave no pencil can present to us. Between that excremental jelly that thy body is made of at first and that jelly which thy body dissolves to at last there is not so noisome, so putrid a thing in nature.

The last sentence, which takes a remarkable revenge on sex, will find no rival in grisliness until the romantic period: its like will not be seen again until the entombment scenes of Matthew Gregory Lewis's Gothic novel, *The Monk* (1795). It is a shock mixture of science and imagination: how modern we can appreciate by quoting from a short story by John Updike ("Lifeguard," published in 1962) a sentence that has the same mixture: "Young as I am, I can hear in myself the protein acids ticking; I wake at odd hours and in the shuddering darkness and silence feel my death rushing toward me like an express train."

But the other side of this is Donne's belief, not only in the immortality of the soul, but in the resurrection of that so despised body. No Christian ever envisioned the Judgment Day miracle more vividly, or was so sympathetic with the details of God's problem: the quick accomplishment, the accomplishment "in the twinkling of an eye," of atomic recomposition.

> At the round earth's imagined corners blow
> Your trumpets, angels, and arise, arise
> From death, you numberless infinities
> Of souls, and to your scattered bodies go.

But the resurrection of the body is discernible by no other light but that of faith, nor could be fixed by any less assurance than an article of the Creed. Where be all the splinters of that bone which a shot hath shivered and scattered in the air? Where be all the atoms of that flesh which a corrasive hath eat away, or a consumption hath breathed and exhaled away from our arms and other limbs? In what wrinkle, in what furrow, in what bowel of the earth, lie all the grains of the ashes of a body burnt a thousand years since? In what corner, in what ventricle of the sea lies all the jelly of a body drowned in the general flood? What coherence, what sympathy, what dependence maintains any relation, any correspondence, between that arm that was lost in Europe and that leg that was lost in Africa or Asia, scores of years between? One humour of our dead body produces worms, and those worms suck and exhaust all other humour, and then all dies, and all dries, and molders into dust, and that dust is blown into the river, and that puddled water tumbled into the sea, and that ebbs and flows in infinite revolutions, and still, still God knows in what cabinet every seed-pearl lies, in what part of the world every grain of every man's dust lies; and ... He whispers, He hisses, He beckons for the bodies of His saints, and in the twinkling of an eye that body that was scattered over all the elements is sate down at the right hand of God, in a glorious resurrection.

If Hamlet speculated whether the dust of Caesar or Alexander was stopping a bunghole, Donne looked around the church and observed: "Every puff of wind within these walls may blow the father into the son's eyes or the wife into her husband's or his into hers or both into their children's or their children's into both. Every grain of dust that flies here is a piece of a Christian." But God will perform His miracle—though this proto-scientific mind wonders how.

Thus "Death's Duel," from which none of these quotations have come, is a fitting, not a surprising, climax, its superlativeness residing in the force of its logic and its passion. No sermon was ever more carefully structured. Its threefold division, like the form of Dante's *Comedy,* pays tribute to the Trinity. Beginning with an architectural analogy, the preacher sets up for consideration three kinds of deliverance: a deliverance from death, a gift of God the Father; a deliverance in death, when the Holy Ghost is comforter; and a deliverance through death, through the death of the Blessed Saviour.

> First, then, we consider this *exitus mortis*, to be *liberatio a morte*, that with God the Lord are the issues of death, and therefore in all our deaths and deadly calamities of this life we may justly hope of a good issue from Him. And all our periods and transitions in this life are so many passages from death to death. Our very birth and entrance into this life is *exitus a morte*, an issue from death, for in our mother's womb we are dead so as that we do not know we live, not so much as we do in our sleep, neither is there any grave so close, or so putrid a prison, as the womb would be unto us if we stayed in it beyond our time, or died there before our time .... In the womb the dead child kills the mother that conceived it, and is a murderer, nay a parricide, even after it is dead .... The womb, which should be the house of life, becomes death itself if God leave us there.

Supposing one does manage to escape this womb-tomb, what then?

But then this *exitus a morte* is but *introitus in mortem,* this issue, this deliverance from that death, the death of the womb, is an entrance, a delivering over to another death, the manifold deaths of this world. We have a winding-sheet in our mother's womb, which grows with us from our conception, and we come into the world wound up in that winding-sheet, for we come to seek a grave. And as prisoners discharged of actions may lie for fees, so when the womb hath discharged us, yet we are bound to it by cords of flesh, by such a string as that we cannot go thence, nor stay there. We celebrate our own funerals with cries, even at our birth.

What is biological change but death? "That which we call life is but *hebdomada mortium,* a week of deaths, seven days, seven periods of our life spent in dying, a dying seven times over—and there is an end. Our birth dies in infancy, and our infancy dies in youth, and youth and the rest die in age, and age also dies and determines all."

The change goes on, spontaneously, after burial: "this dissolution after dissolution, this death of corruption and putrefaction, of vermiculation and incineration, of dissolution and dispersion in and from the grave."

Donne's second division, the manner of dying, gets the least attention. After all, he was showing them one manner in person. He hastens on to the third part, which involves a triple, ascending wonder: "That God, this Lord, the Lord of life, *could* die is a strange contemplation..., but that God *would* die is an exaltation of that. But even of that also it is a superexaltation that God *should* die, must die."

In conclusion he looks at Jesus' last day and applies it to his audience, ending with a pun: "There we leave you in that blessed dependency, to hang upon Him that hangs upon the Cross...."

So the genius who had first entered Whitehall Palace as a courtier during the reign of the great Queen left it as a living *memento mori,* having "preached his own funeral sermon" in a "faint and hollow voice." He looked sufficiently spiritualized. Years before, he had quoted St. Jerome to recommend slimness to his congregation. "The attenuation, the slenderness, the deliverance of the body from the encumbrance of much flesh, gives us some assimilation, some conformity to God and His angels; the less flesh we carry, the liker we are to them, who have none." He got "liker" with each passing day, as he reposed in the Deanery, listening to the great bell of St. Mary-le-Bow in Cheapside (which was the bell that tolled in the 17th Meditation and the bell that made all, like him, born within its range, Cockneys). Was the morality play played out? Not yet. In the five weeks left him Donne was not yet done with ceremony and lesson-giving.

His physician alerted him to the advisability of a monument, whereupon

> Dr. Donne sent for a carver to make for him in wood the figure of an urn, giving him directions for the compass and height of it, and to bring with it a board of the just height of his body. These being got, then without delay a choice painter was got to be in a readiness to draw his picture, which was taken as followeth: Several charcoal fires being first made in his large study, he brought with him into that place his winding-sheet in his hand and, having put off all his clothes, had this sheet put on him and so tied with knots at his head and feet and his hands so placed as dead bodies are usually fitted to be shrouded and put into their coffin or grave.
>
> Upon this urn he thus stood with his eyes shut and with so much of the sheet turned aside as might show his lean, pale, and death-like face, which was purposely turned toward the East, from whence he expected the second coming of his and our Saviour, Jesus. In this posture he was drawn at his just height; and when the picture was fully finished, he caused it to be set by his bed-side, where it continued and became his hourly object till his death and was then given to his dearest friend and executor, Doctor Henry King, then chief residentiary of St. Paul's, who caused him to be thus carved in one entire piece of white marble, as it now stands in that church.

Thus he turned himself into a Mannerist work of art. The marble was executed by Nicholas Stone, who had expensively carved memorials for the Countess of Bedford. Walton may be exaggerating, however, as to Donne's having posed standing. "The folds of the drapery show the statue was modelled from a recumbent figure." But what counts is that the statue, engravings from which were used for several of Donne's works, stood—and still stands, representing a figure rising from its urn for the Last Judgment. This was the only thing that survived intact from the conflagration that leveled old St. Paul's: so indeed "it now stands" in Christopher Wren's St. Paul's, having weathered the damage of World War II also.

Walton may also be wrong in dating "A Hymn to God, my God, in My Sickness" as having been written eight days before the end:

> Since I am coming to that holy room,
>> Where, with Thy Choir of Saints, for evermore
> I shall be made Thy music, as I come
>> I tune my instrument here at the door,
> And, what I must do then, think here before . . . .

One manuscript associates it with the Dean's "great sickness in December, 1623." In either case, the author thought he was dying.

> Upon Monday after the drawing this picture, he took his last leave of his beloved study, and, being sensible of his hourly decay, he retired himself to his bedchamber, and that week sent at several times for many of his most considerable friends, with whom he took a solemn and deliberate farewell, commending to their considerations some sentences useful for the regulation of their lives; and then dismissed them, as good Jacob did his sons, with a spiritual benediction. The Sunday following [March 20] he appointed his servants, that if there were any business yet undone, that concerned him or themselves, it should be prepared against Saturday next [March 26]; for after that

day he would not mix his thoughts with anything that concerned this world; nor ever did; but, as Job, so he "waited for the appointed day of his dissolution."

And now he was so happy as to have nothing to do but to die; to do which, he stood in need of no longer time; for he had studied it long, and to so happy a perfection, that in a former sickness he called God to witness (in his book of *Devotions* written then) "he was that minute ready to deliver his soul into His hands, if that minute God would determine his dissolution." In that sickness he begged of God the constancy to be preserved in that estate forever; and his patient expectation to have his immortal soul disrobed from her garment of mortality makes me confident that he now had a modest assurance that his prayers were then heard, and his petition granted. He lay fifteen days earnestly expecting his hourly change; and in the last hour of his last day [March 31, 1631], as his body melted away and vapored into spirit, his soul having, I verily believe, some revelation of the beatifical vision, he said, "I were miserable if I might not die"; and after those words closed many periods of his faint breath by saying often, "Thy Kingdom come, Thy will be done."

His speech, which had long been his ready and faithful servant, left him not till the last minute of his life, and then forsook him, not to serve another master (for who speaks like him?), but died before him; for that it was then become useless to him that now conversed with God on earth, as angels are said to do in heaven, *only by thoughts and looks.* Being speechless, and seeing heaven by that illumination by which he saw it, he did, as St. Stephen, "look stedfastly into it, till he saw the Son of Man standing at the right hand of God" His Father; and being satisfied with this blessed sight, as his soul ascended and his last breath departed from him, he closed his own eyes, and then disposed his hands and body into such a posture, as required not the least alteration by those that came to shroud him.

It was, as the first biographer noted, an "exemplary" death. (Significantly, Walton's title as first published was,

"The Life and Death of Dr. Donne.") In his youth he had put forth the view that virtuous men make quiet exits:

As virtuous men pass mildly away,
  And whisper to their souls to go,
Whilst some of their sad friends do say,
  The breath goes now, and some say, no:
So let us melt, and make no noise.

But it befitted an eminent churchman to preach until the last, to make of himself an inspiring spectacle, last words and all, like the saints of yore, the saints who, by God's grace, had traveled far from their early sins.

When the soul had gone, and the body had been carried out of the Deanery, two remarkable portraits were left to contemplate each other. One was of a handsome young blade, arms folded over his heart in the game of lover's melancholy, teasing his mistress to lighten his darkness. The other, also by "a choice painter," showed an emaciated, white-bearded man in his shroud, eyes shut, his face "turned toward the East, from whence he expected the Second Coming."

6 | Donne Redivivus: The Twentieth–Century Discovery of Donne

The last sentence of Walton's biography is: "But I shall see it reanimated." He was referring to Donne's "small quantity of Christian dust." But his words were prophetic also of Donne's reputation and living influence: Walton, who did not die until 1683, saw the poet, whom he had played down in favor of the preacher, posthumously found a school that included some of the most brilliant stars of what has been called "the century of genius": in the first generation George Herbert, his brother Edward Lord Herbert of Cherbury, Henry King; in the second generation, Richard Crashaw, Abraham Cowley, Andrew Marvell, Henry Vaughan, and Thomas Traherne. Before the century was out the influence reached Edward Taylor, a Puritan minister in W.estfield, Massachusetts; like Traherne this best of Colonial poets was not published until the twentieth century. All the others Walton himself could have read, even Marvell's posthumous collection of 1681.

Donne composed a Latin poem on how much more a manuscript was to be respected than a book. As we know, this poet was fairly content in his lifetime to circulate in handwritten copies only. This was the gentlemanly thing to do, to remain "unclapperclawed by the vulgar." In his case it became at last the seemly thing, as his friends hastened to point out to him when, on the verge of ordination, he contemplated a limited edition, "not for much public view, but at mine own cost, a few copies." To be a coterie poet, to be caviar to the general—had that not always been his direction anyway? Besides, hiding his light under a bushel served to render glimpses of it more tantalizing and copyists more eager. Drayton complained in the Preface to *Polyolbion,* 1612: "there is this great disadvantage against me, that it cometh out at this time, when verses are wholly deduced to chambers, and nothing esteemed in this lunatic age but what is kept in cabinets and must only pass by transcription." Donne was still alive when Constantine Huyghens, Dutch poet and diplomat, father of the scientist Christian, wrote zestfully to his friend and fellow-poet Hooft in 1630.

> I think I have often entertained you with reminiscences of Dr. Donne, now Dean of St. Paul's in London, and on account of this remunerative post (such is the custom of the English) held in high esteem, in still higher for the wealth of his unequalled wit, and yet more incomparable eloquence in the pulpit. Educated early at Court in the service of the great; experienced in the ways of the world; sharpened by study; in poetry he is more famous than anyone. Many rich fruits from the green branches of his wit have lain mellowing among the lovers of art, which now, when nearly rotten with age, they are distributing.

Huyghens enclosed some translations. "In poetry he is more famous than anyone": this is a remarkable thing to say of an unpublished poet. Thomas Freeman had begged in 1614, at the very time when Donne was about to give up secular poetry:

> *The Storm* described hath set thy name afloat,
> Thy *Calm* a gale of famous wind hath got;
> Thy Satires short, too soon we them o'erlook:
> I prithee, Persius, write a bigger book.

On reading some further translations by Huyghens, made in 1633, the Amsterdam Latinist Casper Barlaeus made the thoroughly modern comment: "I believe that I have never read any love poetry equal or even second to this in its acuteness and perception."

The *Poems* went through seven editions between 1633 and 1669. Accompanying were some sixteen "Elegies upon the Author" that often are interesting as constituting literary criticism in verse (a common medium for it, as witness Jonson's couplets on Shakespeare, in the period when there were no reviews). For instance, John Chudleigh, "a frequent hearer of his sermons," made a point so valid that Walton quoted it in his Life: "He kept his loves, but not his objects; wit / He did not banish, but transplanted it." The best of the elegies was by Thomas Carew, who ended:

> Here lies a king that ruled as he thought fit
> The universal monarchy of wit;
> Here lies two flamens, and both those the best,
> Apollo's first, at last the true God's priest.

Carew emphasized Donne's break with "the mimic fury" of poets who were mere copyists: "They each in other's dust had raked for ore." This was the 1633 reading; the 1640 version was stronger: "They each in other's dung had searched for ore."

A traditionalist like Drummond took a different stand. What the multilingual Scot singled out for admiration were the Epigrams, which were classical, or the Second Elegy, "The Anagram," which follows the Italian line of paradox by demonstrating that it is better to have an old and ugly wife than a young and pretty one. Drummond expressed his utter distrust of baffling and freakish innovation in a letter to a Latinist friend:

> In vain have some men of late, transformers of everything, consulted upon [Poetry's] reformation, and endeavored to abstract her to metaphysical ideas and scholastical

quiddities, denuding her of her own habits and those ornaments with which she hath amused the world some thousand years. Poesy is not a thing that is yet in the finding and search, or which may be otherwise found out, being already condescended upon by all nations, and as it were established *jure gentium* amongst Greeks, Romans, Italians, French, Spaniards. Neither do I think that a good piece of poesy, which Homer, Virgil, Ovid, Petrarch, Bartas, Ronsard, Boscan, Garcilasso (if they were alive and had that language) could not understand and reach the sense of the writer.

Suppose these men could find out some other new idea like poesy, it should be held as if Nature should bring forth some new animal—neither man, horse, lion, dog—but which had some members of all, if they had been proportionably and by right symmetry set together. What is not like the ancients and conform to those rules which hath been agreed unto by all times, may, indeed, be something like unto poesy, but it is no more poesy than a monster is a man. Monsters breed admiration at the first, but have ever some strange loathsomeness in them at last.

As J. B. Leishman remarks, "Milton would probably have subscribed to every word of this." Yet Drummond, like Bacon, was not above borrowing from Donne for his prose; he worked some phrases from *The Anniversaries* into his funereal essay, *A Cypress Grove*.

So the term *metaphysical* came gradually to be applied to Donne and his followers. Mrs. Cokayne's son, Sir Aston, wrote in 1658:

> Stifle therefore, my muse, at their first birth
> All thoughts that may reflect upon the earth;
> Be metaphysical, disdaining to
> Fix upon anything that is below.

It was a term of disapproval, in the age of classicism and clarity and end-stopped couplets. Dryden complained, as quoted before, "He affects the metaphysics." Donne

retained some reputation as a wit—the same critic acknowledged him "the greatest wit, though not the best
poet, of our nation"—but was evidently little read. After
the 1669 edition of his poems there was not another for
fifty years: the well-known publisher Jacob Tonson issued
one at about the time that Pope condescended to smooth
out, by rewriting, Satires II and IV. Then there was not
another edition for sixty years. Lewis Theobald,
Shakespeare's editor, summed up the eighteenth-century
attitude: "Thus became the poetry of Donne (though the
wittiest man of that age) nothing but a continued heap of
riddles."

In his *Lives of the English Poets*, 1779, Samuel
Johnson (taking his cue from Pope) set the seal on the
term "metaphysical" and gave a vigorous description—
which is also an indictment—of the peculiarities of the
school. The collected poets for whom Dr. Johnson was
writing biographical and critical prefaces started with the
mid-seventeenth century only, with Cowley and Milton;
Johnson's reversion to Donne was something of a digression. "About the beginning of the seventeenth century,"
he explains, "appeared a race of writers that may be
termed the metaphysical poets; of whom in a criticism on
the works of Cowley it is not improper to give some
account."

The metaphysical poets were men of learning, and to
show their learning was their whole endeavor; but,
unluckily resolving to show it in rhyme, instead of writing
poetry, they only wrote verses, and, very often, such verses
as stood the trial of the finger better than of the ear; for
the modulation was so imperfect that they were only found
to be verses by counting the syllables . . . .

Those, however, who deny them to be poets allow
them to be wits . . . . If . . . that be considered as wit which
is, at once, natural and new, that which, though not
obvious, is, upon its first production, acknowledged to be
just; if it be that which he that never found it wonders
how he missed; to wit of this kind the metaphysical poets

have seldom risen. Their thoughts are often new, but seldom natural; they are not obvious, but neither are they just; and the reader, far from wondering that he missed them, wonders more frequently by what perverseness of industry they were ever found.

But wit, abstracted from its effects upon the hearer, may be more rigorously and philosophically considered as a kind of "discordia concors" [a phrase from Horace]; a combination of dissimilar images, or discovery of occult resemblances in things apparently unlike. Of wit, thus defined, they have more than enough. The most heterogeneous ideas are yoked by violence together; nature and art are ransacked for illustrations, comparisons, and allusions, their learning instructs, and their subtilty surprises; but the reader commonly thinks his improvement dearly bought, and, though he sometimes admires, is seldom pleased.

Johnson's objection was partly moral—to the poets' detachment:

From this account of their compositions it will be readily inferred that they were not successful in representing or moving the affections. As they were wholly employed on something unexpected and surprising, they had no regard to that uniformity of sentiment which enables us to conceive and to excite the pains and the pleasure of other minds: they never inquired what, on any occasion, they should have said or done; but wrote rather as beholders than partakers of human nature; as beings looking upon good and evil, impassive and at leisure; as epicurean deities, making remarks on the actions of men and the vicissitudes of life, without interest and without emotion. Their courtship was void of fondness, and their lamentation of sorrow. Their wish was only to say what they hoped had never been said before.

This was not a promising line for a poet to take, since

Great thoughts are always general, and consist in positions not limited by exceptions, and in descriptions not des-

cending to minuteness.... Those writers who lay on the
watch for novelty could have little hope of greatness; for
great things cannot have escaped former observation....

Yet great labor, directed by great abilities, is never
wholly lost; if they frequently threw away their wit upon
false conceits, they likewise sometimes struck out unexpected truth; if their conceits were far-fetched, they were
often worth the carriage. To write on their plan it was,
at least, necessary to read and think. No man could be
born a metaphysical poet, nor assume the dignity of a
writer by descriptions copied from descriptions, by imitations borrowed from imitations, by traditional imagery, and
hereditary similes, by readiness of rhyme and volubility of
syllables.

Thus Johnson, like Carew, gives credit for originality.

There follow numerous quotations from Cowley and
Donne. Citing the second stanza of "A Valediction: Of
Weeping," the critic dryly advises, "If the lines are not
easily understood, they may be read again." This sets the
scene, as it were, for present-day *explication de texte*.
Other key items appear in this classic account, such as
"conceit": it is objected of Cowley, "Whatever he writes
is always polluted with some conceit." Where a modern
praises Donne for his colloquial language, in Ben Jonson's
phrase, "language such as men do use," Dr. Johnson
attacks on the same basis. *He* believed in poetic diction.
Wordsworth did not: Such is the seesaw of taste. Johnson
can justify his.

Language is the dress of thought: and as the noblest mien,
or most graceful action, would be degraded and obscured
by a garb appropriated to the gross employments of rustics
or mechanics; so the most heroic sentiments will lose their
efficacy, and the most splendid ideas drop their magnifi-
cence, if they are conveyed by words used commonly upon
low and trivial occasions, debased by vulgar mouths, and
contaminated by inelegant applications.

Prejudiced or not, Dr. Johnson, one of the indubitably great critics (who are rarer in English than great poets), has remained to this day a force, an eternal No, to be reckoned with. Twentieth-century criticism had no other place to take off from but him. Coleridge made some passing remarks on Donne, as on everything else, but there was no major criticism in the nineteenth century. That was, rather, a time of scholarship and informal appreciation. New attempts were made to make available Donne's texts. The standard biography was written by Edmund Gosse. In his last paragraph, Gosse notes the kinship with Browning. For one thing, they were partners in metaphysical "obscurity." There was even a biographical parallel. In the words of Joseph E. Duncan, "Browning may have felt an increasing personal sympathy with Donne as he too flouted an irate father-in-law to make a secret marriage inspired by a deep love, saw the marriage flower despite hardship and sickness, and then lost his wife just when real success seemed assured." Are not such poems as "The Canonization" and "The Flea" and "Break of Day" dramatic monologues? Two other kindred poets— possibly by a sort of spiritual metempsychosis, for neither of them can be proved to have known Donne—were Gerard Manley Hopkins and Emily Dickinson, but they were themselves twentieth-century discoveries.

The Donne revival did not get under full sail until Grierson's edition of the Poetical Works in 1912. The scholar, in this case a doughty Scot, Herbert J. C. Grierson of the University of Aberdeen, had to provide a comparatively definitive text before the critics could go to work. As Donne did not supervise the publication of his poems there were many problems presented by variant readings in the printed texts and in dozens of manuscript collections and also by attribution to him of Donne-like poems that may or may not have been his. Grierson in his old age (he lived until 1960) explained to a scholar that "it had occurred to him during the 1890's that Donne's poems needed textual study similar to that he had recently given Aristotle's *Nicomachean Ethics* while studying at

Oxford . . . . he realized that both the canon and text of Donne's poems needed careful re-examination." The result was the two-volume Oxford University Press edition, Volume One containing the text with variant readings, Volume Two consisting of 425 pages of commentary. Both jobs were done so well that an independent and meticulous editor coming after Grierson in 1929, John Hayward, felt constrained to say (or sigh), "The present text of the poems is substantially his text, for the simple reason that it is wellnigh impossible to improve on his recension," and no one ventured again on an annotated edition of any of the poems until the 1950's. However, scholarship progresses. Grierson himself put out in 1929 a one-volume text with changes; R. E. Bennett made an independent edition in 1942, and Helen Gardner's recension of the *Divine Poems*, 1952, had much that was new (and she is presently at work on the *Songs and Sonets*). Grierson included in the canon poems no longer thought to be Donne's; new manuscripts have turned up; more thorough collations are being made. It is enough of a feat that the two-volume Oxford edition, happily kept in print, was standard for a generation. And not the least of Grierson's original—if now outmoded—services was to provide a sympathetic, though far from blindly partial, introduction on "The Poetry of Donne" that stirred the modern reader's interest and helped to balance the famous strictures of Dr. Johnson.

A later book edited by Grierson was to have T. S. Eliot as reviewer. This one had Rupert Brooke, of "The Great Lover" and the "1914" sonnets fame, one of the last of the romantics, the idol of the young, the unbelievably handsome tennis player, as fine a poet (not forgetting Sidney) as a war ever cut off—World War I, when, sailing towards Gallipoli with the B. E. F., he was stricken with sunstroke and blood poisoning and buried on Skyros. Brooke, of course, wrote glitteringly about Donne.

In his own words he "loved to be subtle to plague himself." He would startle the soul from her lair with unthinkable paradoxes, and pursue her, with laughter and tears, along all the difficult coasts between sense and madness. At one moment he knows the most unworldly ecstasy of the communion of two souls:

> And whilst our souls negotiate there,
>> We like sepulchral statues lay,
> All day the same our postures were,
>> And we said nothing all the day.

At another he contemplates the consummation of human love within the black, bright walls of a flea. He compares his lady to a primrose, an angel, the number five, Mary Magdalen, a gingerbread figure, Newfoundland, the stationary leg of a compass, God. And one can never doubt his sincerity.

The last assertion is doubtful, considering the reasons there are to believe that, in accordance with some practice and much aesthetic theory of the time, Donne was often bent on merely displaying his wit, on producing "evaporations" ("I do not condemn in myself that I have given my wit such evaporations" — to Goodyer). The modern danger is to take him too seriously, as perhaps the tendency among his contemporaries was to take him too lightly. In any case, "sincerity" is a question no longer raised in literary criticism, Yeats's doctrine of "the mask" having succeeded. We consider old-fashioned the indignation of an English professor in 1936 because "in a number of studiously scandalous 'elegies' and 'songs'" Donne "unfolds his sage and serious doctrine of promiscuity; presents that view of human nature which Othello greeted simply with the words 'Goats and monkeys' as the only true view; describes his adventures on these unlit levels; boasts of his conquests, mocks at injured husbands, and, in short, is at pains to present himself as a coxcomb."

To return to Brooke, in the second of two 1913 articles he was to say some things that anticipated the renowned analysis of Eliot.

The whole composition of the man was made up of brain, soul, and heart in a different proportion from the ordinary prescription. This does not mean that he felt less keenly than others; but when passion shook him, and his being ached for utterance, to relieve the stress, expression came through the intellect. Under the storm of emotion, it is common to seek for relief by twisting some strong stuff. Donne, as Coleridge said, turns intellectual pokers into love-knots. An ordinary poet, whose feelings find far stronger expression than a common man's, but an expression according to the same prescription, praises his mistress with some idea, intensely felt . . . Donne, equally moved and equally sincere, would compare her to a perfect equilateral triangle, or to the solar system. His intellect must find satisfaction.

Donne was immediately espoused by a group of Georgian poet-critics that included, in addition to Brooke, John Drinkwater and Walter de la Mare. The latter compared Brooke himself and his period to the Jacobean poet and age.

After the Great War, Grierson published, with another influential Introduction, a 215-page anthology, *Metaphysical Lyrics and Poems of the Seventeenth Century*. The author of the London *Times Literary Supplement* leading article on this was T. S. Eliot. The same year, 1921, being the tercentenary of Marvell's birth, Eliot also took on the assignment of commemorating him. The two critiques, reprinted in *Selected Essays, 1917-1932*, have been incalculably seminal, and are far better known than Eliot's "John Donne" article of 1923, which the same volume omitted. Eliot propagated phrases, two of which "alone have enabled several later writers to set up in business and drive quite a prosperous trade as literary and historical critics." That generation and more ago Eliot was decisively on his way to his commanding eminence as poet and critic, a critic conditioned by his own poetic practice and his sense of what modernity must consist of. Donne's stock soared; that of Milton and the Victorians slumped.

Eliot commended in Donne and his compeers their "direct sensuous apprehension of thought," their "recreation of thought into feeling."

A thought to Donne was an experience; it modified his sensibility. When a poet's mind is perfectly equipped for its work, it is constantly amalgamating disparate experience; the ordinary man's experience is chaotic, irregular, fragmentary. The latter falls in love, or reads Spinoza, and these two experiences have nothing to do with each other, or with the noise of the typewriter or the smell of cooking; in the mind of the poet these experiences are always forming new wholes.

We may express the difference by the following theory: The poets of the seventeenth century, the successors of the dramatists of the sixteenth, possessed a mechanism of sensibility which could devour any kind of experience.... In the seventeenth century a dissociation of sensibility set in, from which we have never recovered; and this dissociation, as is natural, was aggravated by the influence of the two most powerful poets of the century, Milton and Dryden.... The language went on and in some respects improved; the best verse of Collins, Gray, Johnson, and even Goldsmith satisfies some of our fastidious demands better than that of Donne or Marvell or King. But while the language became more refined, the feeling became more crude. The feeling, the sensibility, expressed in the *Country Churchyard* (to say nothing of Tennyson and Browning) is cruder than that in the *Coy Mistress*.

Could a unified sensibility ever be regained? "In one or two passages of Shelley's *Triumph of Life*, in the second *Hyperion*, there are traces of a struggle toward unification of sensibility. But Keats and Shelley died, and Tennyson and Browning ruminated."

In this first essay Donne was praised for the very quality that had alienated readers for generations—his difficulty. "Poets in our civilization, as it exists at present, must be *difficult*." The French symbolists are quoted.

In the Marvell essay, the same position is developed by opposing wit, seen in this poet as "a tough reasonableness beneath the slight lyric grace," to Milton's magniloquence and William Morris's vagueness.

Eliot went on to other interests, in fact cooled towards Donne, and eventually—by way of Dante and a growingly serious involvement in Anglo-Catholicism—warmed towards Milton. But he had set a rage for the metaphysicals that it was beyond his power to extinguish, had he wished. "Dissociation of sensibility," "a mechanism of sensibility which could devour any kind of experience"— these became the cant references in quarterlies and cocktail parties and college classrooms. Minds eager to show their powers and build their reputations went to work on the alleged difficulties. A 1939 bibliography, *Studies in Metaphysical Poetry*, covering the years 1912-1938, listed 540 books and articles, most of them post-Eliot.

And this was before Hemingway, in 1940, called popular attention to the fact that Donne also wrote prose. When *For Whom the Bell Tolls* became a best-seller, Donne became a best-seller, too, in that he went promptly out of print in the Random House edition, the edition, John Hayward's, of the poetry and selected prose that contained the passage that the novel quoted as a call to involvement—involvement in Spain's troubles, and, by implication, now Europe's, since no man is an island. There was a rush to publish the Seventeenth Meditation, all two pages of it. Oxford Press reported a run on its editions of Donne's poetry, while "Fifteen hundred sheets ordered by Random House from England were bombed out of existence."

Of course titles are among the indexes of currency. Edna St. Vincent Millay, who berated the America-Firsters with such verses as, "Dear isolationist, you are / So very, very insular," called a book of sonnets *Fatal Interview*, from the first line of Elegy XVI, "By our first strange and fatal interview." Another American favorite, Dorothy Parker, entitled a book of short stories *After Such Pleasures*. After what pleasures? Not every reader was immediately alive to the context of line 23 of "Farewell to Love"—the pleasures of copulation. But the divine Donne was not neglected either. When John Gunther issued his moving account of his son's losing fight with a

brain tumor, he named it, after the opening of Holy
Sonnet X, *Death Be Not Proud.*

It was inevitable, too, that Donne be made the subject of a novel or a romance. Richard Ince's *Angel from
a Cloud* (London, 1939) is less well written and less well
known than Robert Graves' fictional attack on Milton,
Wife to Mr. Milton. A sugar-and-water dilution of Gosse's
biography, it commences:

> Mr. Nicholas Hilyard, Court Painter to Queen
> Elizabeth, was at work on the young man's portrait. His
> rugged old face, framed in thin grey hair, was tense with
> concern. From time to time he grunted.

The "concern" and the grunts seem to have been well
warranted. On page 149 "The Ecstasy" is paraphrased. It
happened when John and Anne, not yet married, got lost
in the woods eight miles from Harefield, the Egerton
estate.

> They ate in silence and then lay side by side upon the
> bank, their hands interlaced, his eyes looking with a
> lover's longing into hers. Neither spoke. The hours slipped
> by. A state of exalted, ecstatic happiness possessed them.
> Simply to lie there, hand in hand, while the brook went
> murmuring and bubbling by brought them to the very
> brink of bliss.

Twenty-five years later, Elizabeth Gray Vining tried her
hand at the same subject in *Take Heed of Loving Me,
A Novel about John Donne* (New York, 1964) that is
eloquent on the couple's struggle with births and penury.
Her Ecstasy occurs in London on page 94:

> The girl beside him said nothing; her small hands lay
> loosely clasped and still in her lap. He took one of them
> gently in his own but made no effort to draw her closer.
> Their eyes met. He lost himself. The thongs of convention
> fell away . . . .

What a contrast to the critical approaches to the same
key poem that our times have witnessed, such as Merritt
Y. Hughes' 1960 article in the *Publications of the Modern
Language Association* (a sequel to his 1932 *Modern Language Review* article), which has 78 footnotes! Keeping up
with the literature on Donne has become almost as difficult
as keeping up with the literature on Shakespeare or
Milton. Geoffrey Keynes' *Bibliography*, not complete, for
1900-1957 adds up to 632 items, exclusive of editions and
reviews.

Eliot's famous phrases are of course questionable.
Unified sensibility? All good poets, surely, have unified
sensibility and in most of the best it is also multiple. And
to boost Donne was it necessary to attack Milton, as if
there could be only one kind of acceptable poet? A battle
of the books raged between the Donneans and the
Miltonists, between the critics and the professors.
F. L. Leavis announced in 1936: "Milton's dislodgment in
the past decade, after his two centuries of predominance,
was effected with remarkably little fuss." On the contrary,
the fuss was enormous. But Eliot turned against his own
critical positions. By 1931 he was saying, "In Donne, there
is a manifest fissure between thought and sensibility."
Donne went down and Milton up, leaving Eliot's echoers
high and dry. In the wake of Eliot's British Academy
Lecture of 1947 that welcomed Milton back into the fold,
Leavis put out, self-consciously, another essay, insisting "no
intimation of Mr. Eliot's alters my own finding."

All the while both Milton and Donne, for different
reasons, remained caviar to the general. When Donne
went out of print in 1941 it was because a thousand
copies were sold: even doctoral dissertations have been
known to equal that figure. For the man in the street his
poems perish for want of being understood and for not
living up to—or down to—the expectation of what poetry
should be. Virginia Woolf, writing in 1931, the death
tercentenary, discriminates cautiously: "Far be it from us
to suggest even in this year of celebration and pardonable
adulation that the poems of Donne are popular reading or

that the typist, if we look over her shoulder in the Tube, is to be discovered reading Donne as she returns from her office." The legendary secretary who explained she did not want a book for Christmas because she already had a book did not, we may be sure, have Donne: she probably had Edgar Allan Poe. The Donne revival was and is kept going by sophisticates and academics, by those who are taking, have taken, or wish they had taken, a poetry course in college (to say nothing of the givers of such courses). A widely used textbook, Coffin and Witherspoon's *Seventeenth-Century Prose and Poetry* (1946), does some lyrical summarizing:

> It took a world war, the bitter discovery of the discord within a man, and a lost generation, to lift John Donne's name from among the forgotten and make this poet of paradox a power among English-speaking poets, three hundred years after his hot body had gone to the cool dust under Paul's pavements.
>
> Donne had an immense impact on the temper and trend of the poetry of his day. But he was lost sight of completely in the riotous and rollicking Restoration days, and remembered only by a few scholars in the nineteenth century. And then when the assurances of empire, outside and inside man, fell upon evil days, this cynic-singer, this doubter, this analytic lyricist, this lover of intellectual approach to passion, this Elizabethan and Jacobean breaker of Elizabethan and Petrarchan peace of mind, this man of the fever-like figurativeness, came alive and came into his own. As he had founded—against his wishes, once he was within the church—a school of the metaphysical in his own time, so now he was responsible for the Fugitives, in a new world he knew only as a wilderness, and a whole generation of young poets, in America and his own country, whose minds hurt them and made them say bitter and beautiful things about the very bones and sinews of their bodies and of their beliefs. T. S. Eliot, Elinor Wylie, Archibald Mac-Leish, Auden, Spender, MacNeice, Dylan Thomas, Robert Penn Warren, and a host of other modern poets have

learned from Donne to probe the emotions with a scalpel, cut appearances to the bone, and use intellectual acumen to riddle and confound.

Coffin and Witherspoon strangely omit Yeats from their list, Yeats who boasted, "And I may dine at journey's end / With Landor and with Donne." The Irish poet also sought "unity of being" through correspondences, and his poems as well as his letters show how carefully he read the edition by his friend Grierson. There was a similarity of reaction to Armageddon, to a world that was disintegrating. Odette de Mourgues has said of the earlier poet's era:

> We all know the rough outlines of that crisis which originated in the impact of Renaissance and Reformation on the medieval universe of Christendom: the clash between the pagan and the Christian worlds, and inside Christianity between Protestants and Catholics; political unrest and religious wars; the absence of a systematized philosophy which could have suggested some coherent answer to these new problems. We are used to thinking of the period as an era of pessimism, chaos, and violence succeeding the optimism of the Renaissance when Man, having asserted his birthright as the centre of the universe, felt the world was his, and himself and the world were one harmonious whole.

Donne was to sum up this crisis of modernity in the remarkable lines previously quoted from "An Anatomy of the World" on the "new philosophy calls all in doubt" and " 'Tis all in pieces, all coherence gone," and on the disrupting Phoenix-like egotistic insistence on uniqueness. Measurably, the world was decaying, was going from bad to worse, in fulfillment of the conditions prophesied for the Second Coming. What are Yeats's parallel lines in "The Second Coming"?

> Turning and turning in the widening gyre
> The falcon cannot hear the falconer;

> Things fall apart; the centre cannot hold;
> Mere anarchy is loosed upon the world,
> The blood-dimmed tide is loosed, and everywhere
> The ceremony of innocence is drowned;
> The best lack all conviction, while the worst
> Are full of passionate intensity.[1]

History made Donne seem timely. If he were Nostradamus, we should say he foresaw the ultimate disaster of nuclear warfare: "this [world] Is crumbled out again to his atomies." In any case, his disciple Dame Edith Sitwell, as Duncan points out, "has adapted the metaphysical style to the poetic scrutiny of modern warfare more distinctively and successfully than any other poet," as in "The Shadow of Cain," in which "Christ, man, and the atomic bomb are brought together in a conceit." Donne redivivus indeed!

On the other hand, he said with Othello, "When I love thee not, chaos is come again." First he said, "When I love thee not." Afterwards he went on to, "When I love Thee not." As a love poet he makes an incisive appeal to undergraduates, adolescent intellectuals who are struggling with similar ranges of mood, and with the teasing problems of mind-body equilibrium, the carnal and the spiritual in love. Appropriately, Donne is the first to use the word sex in its modern sense.

> This ecstasy doth unperplex
>   (We said) and tell us what we love,
> We see by this, it was not sex,
>   We see, we saw not what did move.

>   should she
> Be more than woman, she would get above
>   All thought of sex, and think to move
>   My heart to study her, and not to love.

---

[1] Reprinted with permission of the publisher from *Collected Poems*, by William Butler Yeats. Copyright 1924 by The Macmillan Company. Renewed 1952 by Bertha Georgie Yeats.

His jokes on the relations of the sexes are still lively. He tells his congregation that he need not say much about the submission of wives, "because husbands at home are likely enough to remember them of it." He hits at the celibacy of the priesthood: "When God had made Adam and Eve in Paradise, though there were four rivers in Paradise, God did not place Adam in a monastery on one side and Eve in a nunnery on the other, and so a river between them." Elegy XVIII, "Love's Progress," which begins with the mistress's head and works its way down to her waist, then darts to her feet and creeps up, could, surreptitiously printed, have a lively undercounter sale. It needs only to be discovered and banned. As for the closing lines of Elegy XIX, according to the (disputable) 1954 analysis of Clay Hunt, "they do nothing less than identify a woman's genitals with the Essence of God." It was an age capable of much frankness, but never, at least among its artists, just for frankness' sake, as witness that decorative offspring of Elegy XVIII, Carew's "The Rapture." "Death's Duel" slips with startling but instructive ease from Judas's kiss to the *homme moyen sensuel*: "About midnight He was taken and bound with a kiss. Art thou not too conformable to Him in that? Is not that too literally, too exactly, *thy* case—at midnight to have been taken and bound with a kiss?" For his sermon at St. Dunstan's on New Year's Day, 1624, on Genesis xvii, 24, Donne pursues his anatomical-moral point unabashedly, even as he considered it a legitimate effect to end "Farewell to Love" with brutal bluntness. But if the naked human anatomy lies at the bottom of his spectrum, at the top the soul soars. No one has ever written more cogently of complete love, besides which "Nothing else is."

Donne's modernity is woven of three related strands—his interest in science, his skepticism, and his insight as a psychologist. We can find him writing about the resurrection of the body as if it were a laboratory problem. We often catch him using beliefs for their illustrative value, seemingly not caring which was right, veering back and forth, for instance, between the heliocentric system and the

geocentric. "And one soul thinks one, and another way /
Another thinks, and 'tis an even lay." Nescient, undog-
matic, as if there were no infallible authority left, he tries
out—sometimes quite mischievously—different attitudes
just for size—or for effect. He ruffles what might have
been a smooth surface by a doubt or a hesitation. He is
as skeptical as a believing Christian can be: "At the round
earth's *imagined* corners." He wonders (in Holy
Sonnet IX) why God does not send animals to hell for
faults for which men have to go there: "If lecherous
goats, if serpents envious / Cannot be damned, alas, why
should I be?" He can put himself perfectly in an outsider's
place.

> He that should come to a heathen man, a mere natural
> man, uncatechized, uninstructed in the rudiments of the
> Christian religion, and should at first, without any prepara-
> tion, present him first with this necessity, "Thou shalt burn
> in fire and brimstone eternally except thou believe a
> Trinity of Persons, in an unity of one God; except thou
> believe the incarnation of the Second Person of the
> Trinity, the Son of God; except thou believe that a virgin
> had a son, and the same son that God had, and that God
> was man too, and being the immortal God, yet died"—he
> should be so far from working any spiritual cure upon this
> poor soul as that he should rather bring Christian mysteries
> into scorn than him to a belief. For that man, if you proceed
> so, "Believe all, or you burn in hell," would find an easy,
> an obvious way to escape all. That is, first not to believe
> hell itself, and then nothing could bind him to believe
> the rest.

Another sermon recalls the Indian king that interrupted
his would-be converter, "Is your God dead and buried?
Then let me return to the worship of the sun, for I am
sure the sun will not die."

Preaching on Matthew xxviii, 6, he is not at ease
about the statement at the beginning of the chapter that
the two Marys "came . . . to see the sepulchre." He fusses
over what their reasons might be. "What then intended

these women to do more than was done already?" They
really had no business going. Also, come to think of it,
angels ought to have better memories, because what they
say in Luke xxiv, 7, is not exactly what Jesus said in
Matthew xvii, 22-23. Donne knew outrageously much.
Studying himself, he knew anxieties can make a man sick,
and he found the death wish in history as well as in
himself. On guilt he was a specialist. We can even catch
him worrying about a Freudian slip: "some misinterpreta-
tion of a word in my prayer, that may bear an ill sense."

We must not claim everything for him, must not, as
Professor Hughes warns, "kidnap" him totally into our
time. Who does not feel much more at home with
Montaigne, who died when Donne was twenty and who
had a more agreeable personality? (Neither was heroic, a
fact that contributes to modern acceptance, according to
Eliot's 1923 essay on Donne: "The age objects to the
heroic and sublime....") (Yet to mention Eliot again is
to recall that he and Mann and Hemingway have Donne's
themes—self-division, love, time, death and sickness.) A
divided man, Donne was a crippled genius; he is great in
flashes. For example, a serious novel published in 1962
puts to good psychological use the haunting lines from
Elegy XVI: "Oh, oh, / Nurse, oh, my love is slain; I saw
him go / O'er the white Alps alone." His sharp mind has
sharp limitations. For instance, he could scarcely pass as
an authority on children, as the following from a sermon
(even allowing for didactic purpose) sufficiently demon-
strates:

> An artificer of this city brought his child to me, to
> admire (as truly there was much reason) the capacity, the
> memory especially, of the child. It was but a girl, and not
> above nine years of age—her parents said less, some years
> less. We could scarce propose any verse of any book or
> chapter of the Bible, but that that child would go forward
> without book. I began to catechize this child, and truly,
> she understood nothing of the Trinity, nothing of any of
> those fundamental points which must save us; and the
> wonder was doubled, how she knew so much, how so little.

On the other hand, how long we have to wait before we get again such a picture of the casual tickings of the mind (Virginia Woolf's characters were good at that) as he candidly holds up in his Sir William Cokayne sermon:

But when we consider with a religious seriousness the manifold weaknesses of the strongest devotions in time of prayer, it is a sad consideration. I throw myself down in my chamber, and I call in and invite God and His angels thither, and when they are there I neglect God and His angels for the noise of a fly, for the rattling of a coach, for the whining of a door. I talk on, in the same posture of praying, eyes lifted up, knees bowed down, as though I prayed to God. And if God or His angels should ask me when I thought last of God in that prayer, I cannot tell. Sometimes I find that I had forgot what I was about, but when I forgot it I cannot tell. A memory of yesterday's pleasures, a fear of tomorrow's dangers, a straw under my knee, a noise in mine ear, a light in mine eye, an anything, a nothing, a fancy, a chimera in my brain—troubles me in my prayer.

James Harvey Robinson quotes this in *The Mind in the Making*, along with excerpts from depth psychologists. In a few honest words Donne explodes the pretensions of centuries, including centuries of educators, that the mind is an orderly, logical mechanism, not subject to divagations except maybe in women, children, and imbeciles. And, *a fortiori*, prayer is a monolithic thing. The logician and the divine, in not the least of his confessions, opens his humanness to us, letting us know what he is like, letting us—who had so long pretended differently—know what we are like.

In all the literature one cannot find a more beautiful and penetrating benediction than the words of Yeats to Grierson—the great poet to the great scholar—in a congratulatory letter on the 1912 edition:

... the more precise and learned the thought the greater the beauty, the passion; the intricacy and subtleties of his imagination are the length and depths of the furrow made by his passion. His pedantry and his obscenity—the rock and loam of his Eden—but make me more certain that one who is but a man like us all has seen God.

Appendix

Supplementary Letters

I

To Sir Henry Wotton

[November? 1599]

Sir,

But that I have much earnest sorrow for the loss of many dear friends in Ireland, I could make shift to grieve for the loss of a poor letter of mine which sought you there after your return: in which, though there were nothing to be commended but that it was well suited for the place and barbarous enough to go thither, yet it should have brought the thanks and betrothed to you the love and services of one who had rather be honest than fortunate.

This letter hath a greater burden and charge, for it carries not only an assurance of myself to you but it begs a pardon that I have not in these weeks sought you out in England by letters and acknowledged how deep root the kindness of your letter hath taken in me. But as in former innocent times estates of lands passed safely in few words (for these many entangling clauses are either intended at least to prevent or breed deceit), so unchangeable friendship, being ever the same and therefore not subject to the corruption of these times, may now in these few and ill lines deliver me unto you and assure you none hath better title than you in

Your poor friend and lover

II

[To Sir Henry Wotton?]

[December? 1599]

Sir,

That love which went with you follows and overtakes and meets you. If words sealed up in letters be like words spoken in those frosty places where they are not heard till the next thaw, they have yet this advantage, that where they are heard they are heard only by one or such as in his judgment they are fit for. I am no courtier, for without having lived there desirously I cannot have sinned enough to have deserved that reprobate name. I may sometimes come thither and be no courtier as well as they may sometimes go to chapel and yet are no Christians. I am there now where, because I must do some evil, I envy your being in the country—not that it is a vice will make any great show here, for they live at a far greater rate and expense of wickedness; but because I will not be utterly out of fashion and unsociable, I glean such vices as the greater men (whose barns are full) scatter, yet I learn that the learnedest in vice suffer some misery, for when they have reaped flattery or any other fault long, there comes some other new vice in request wherein they are unpractised. Only the women are free from this charge, for they are sure they cannot be worse, nor more thrown down, than they have been. They have perchance heard that God will hasten his judgment for the righteous' sake, and they affect not that haste, and therefore seek to lengthen out the world by their wickedness.

The Court is not great, but full of jollity and revels and plays, and as merry as if it were not sick. Her Majesty is well disposed and very gracious in public to my Lord Mountjoy. My Lord of Essex and his train are no more missed here than the angels which were cast down from Heaven, nor (for anything I see) likelier to return. He withers still in his sickness and plods on to his end in the same pace where you left us. The worst accidents of his sickness are that he conspires with it, and that it is not here believed. That which was said of Cato, that his age understood him not, I fear may be averted [reversed] of your Lord: that he understood not his age. For it is a natural weakness of innocency: That such men want locks for themselves and keys for others.

III

[c. 1600?]

Sir,

Only in obedience I send you some of my Paradoxes. I love you and myself and them too well to send them willingly, for they carry with them a confession of their lightness and your trouble and my shame. But, indeed, they were made rather to deceive Time than her daughter Truth; although they have been written in an age when anything is strong enough to overthrow her. If they make you to find better reasons against them, they do their office, for they are but swaggerers—quiet enough if you resist them. If perchance they be prettily gilt, that is their best, for they are not hatched. They are rather alarms to truth to arm her, than enemies: and they have only this advantage to scape from being called ill things, that they are nothings. Therefore take heed of allowing any of them lest you make another.

Yet, sir, though I know their low price, except I receive by your next letter an assurance upon the religion of your friendship that no copy shall be taken for any respect of these or any other my compositions sent to you,

I shall sin against my conscience if I send you any more. I speak that in plainness which becomes (methinks) our honesties, and therefore call not this a distrustful but a free spirit: I mean to acquaint you with all mine, and to my Satires there belongs some fear, and to some Elegies and these, perhaps, shame. Against both which affections although I be tough enough, yet I have a riddling disposition to be ashamed of fear and afraid of shame. Therefore I am desirous to hide them without any over reconning of them or their maker.

But they are not worth thus much words in their dispraise. I will step to a better subject, your last letter, to which I need not tell I made no answer but I had need excuse it. All your letter I embrace and believe it when it speaks of yourself, and when of me too, if the good words which you speak of me be meant of my intentions to goodness. For else, alas! no man is more beggarly in actual virtue than I.

I am sorry you should (with any great earnestness) desire anything of P. Aretinus. Not that he could infect, but that it seems you are already infected with the common opinion of him. Believe me, he is much less than his fame and was too well paid by the Roman Church in that coin which he coveted most, where his books were by the Council of Trent forbidden, which, if they had been permitted to have been worn by all, long ere this had been worn out. His divinity was but a syrup to enwrap his profane books to get them passage, yet in these books which have divine titles there is least harm, as in his letters most good. His others have no other singularity in them but that they are forbidden.

The psalms which you ask, if I cannot shortly procure you one to possess I can and will at any time borrow for you. In the meantime, sir, have the honor of forgiving two faults together: my not writing last time and my abrupt ending now.

IV

[1600?]

Sir,

I am no great voyager in other men's works, no swallower nor devourer of volumes, nor pursuant of authors. Perchance it is because I find born in myself knowledge or apprehension enough, for (without forfeiture or impeachment of modesty) I think I am bond to God thankfully to acknowledge it, to consider Him and myself—as when I have at home a convenient garden I covet not to walk in others' broad meadows or woods, especially because it falls not within that short reach which my foresight embraceth, to see how I should employ that which I already know. To travail for inquiry of more were to labor to get a stomach and then find no meat at home.

To know how to live by the book is a pedantry, and to do it is a bondage. For both hearers and players are more delighted with voluntary than with set music. And he that will live by precept shall be long without the habit of honesty, as he that would every day gather one or two feathers might become brawn [all muscle, no fat] with hard lying before he make a featherbed of his gettings. That Earl of Arundel that last died (that tennis ball whom Fortune, after tossing and banding, brickwalled into the hazard) in his imprisonment used more than much reading, and to him that asked him why he did so he answered, he read so much lest he should remember something. I am as far from following his counsel as he was from Petruccio's:[1] but I find it true

---

[1]The only footnoter this letter has had proposes: "Perhaps Petruccio Ubaldini, an Italian pensioner of Elizabeth, man of letters and illuminator, in England 1562-86." This goes far astray. What we have is Donne's only reference to Shakespeare. He had seen *The Taming of the Shrew* (not printed till the 1623 Folio). It was notorious that Arundel was dominated by his wife. Even the short article in the *Dictionary of National Biography* mentions this: "His wife was a woman of strong character, and of a religious disposition, and her influence soon made itself felt upon her husband." Thus he was at "far" remove from Shakespeare's famous wife-tamer.

that after long reading I can only tell you how many leaves I have read.

I do therefore more willingly blow and keep awake that small coal which God hath pleased to kindle in me than far off to gather a faggot of green sticks which consume without flame or heat in a black smother: yet I read something. But indeed not so much to avoid as to enjoy idleness.

Even when I begun to write these I flung away Dante the Italian, a man pert enough to be beloved and too much to be believed. It angered me that Celestine, a pope [so] far from the manners of other popes that he left even their seat, should by the court of Dante's wit be attached and by him thrown into his purgatory. And it angered me as much that in the life of a pope he should spy no greater fault than that in the affectation of a cowardly security he slipped from the great burden laid upon him. Alas! what would Dante have him do?

Thus we find the story related: he that thought himself next in succession, by a trunk through a wall whispered in Celestine's ear counsel to remove the papacy. Why should not Dante be content to think that Celestine took this for as immediate a salutation and discourse of the Holy Ghost as Abraham did the commandment of killing his son? If he will needs punish retiredness thus, what hell can his wit devise for ambition? And if white integrity merit this, what shall *male* or *malum* [badly done or evil], which Seneca condemns most, deserve? But as the chancellor Hatton, being told after a decree made, that his predecessor's was of another opinion, he answered, he had his genius and I had mine. So say I of authors that they think and I think both reasonably, yet possibly both erroneously. That is manly, for I am so far from persuading, yea counselling, you to believe others that I care not that you believe not me when I say that others are not to be believed: only believe that I love you and I have enough.

I have studied philosophy, therefore marvel not if I make such accompt of arguments *quae trahuntur ab effectibus* [which are drawn from effects].

V

To Sir H. Goodyer

[September, 1608]

Sir,

Every Tuesday I make account that I turn a great hour-glass, and consider that a week's life is run out since I writ. But if I ask myself what I have done in the last watch, or would do in the next, I can say nothing; if I say that I have passed it without hurting any, so may the spider in my window. The primitive monks were excusable in their retirings and enclosures of themselves; for even of them every one cultivated his own garden and orchard, that is, his soul and body, by meditation and manufactures; and they ought [owed] the world no more since they consumed none of her sweetness, nor begot others to burden her. But for me, if I were able to husband all my time so thriftily, as not only not to wound my soul in any minute by actual sin, but not to rob and cozen her by giving any part to pleasure or business, but bestow it all upon her in meditation, yet even in that I should wound her more and contract another guiltiness. As the eagle were very unnatural if because she is able to do it, she should perch a whole day upon a tree, staring in contemplation of the majesty and glory of the sun, and let her young eaglets starve in the nest.

Two of the most precious things which God hath afforded us here, for the agony and exercise of our sense and spirit, which are a thirst and inhiation after the next life, and a frequency of prayer and meditation in this, are often envenomed and putrefied, and stray into a corrupt disease; for as God doth thus occasion, and positively concur to evil, that when a man is purposed to do a great sin, God infuses some good thoughts which make him choose a less sin, or leave out some circumstance which aggravated that; so the devil doth not only suffer but provoke us to some things naturally good, upon condition that we shall omit some other more necessary and more obligatory. And this is his greatest subtlety, because herein we have the deceitful comfort of having done well, and can very hardly spy our error because it is but an insensible omission and no accusing act. With the first of these I have often suspected myself to be overtaken, which is with a desire of the next life; which though I know it is not merely out of a weariness of this, because I had the same desires when I went with the tide, and enjoyed fairer hopes than now; yet I doubt worldly encumbrances have increased it. I would not that death should take me asleep. I would not have him merely seize me, and only declare me to be dead, but win me and overcome me.

When I must shipwreck, I would do it in a sea where mine impotency might have some excuse; not in a sullen weedy lake, where I could not have so much as exercise for my swimming. Therefore I would fain do something, but that I cannot tell what is no wonder. For to choose is to do; but to be no part of any body is to be nothing. At most, the greatest persons are but great wens and excrescences; men of wit and delightful conversation but as moles for ornament, except they be so incorporated into the body of the world that they contribute something to the sustentation of the whole.

This I made account that I begun early, when I understood the study of our laws; but was diverted by the worst voluptuousness, which is an hydroptic, immoderate desire of human learning and languages—beautiful ornaments to great fortunes; but mine needed an occupation, and a course which I thought I entered well into when I submitted myself to such a service, as I thought might employ those poor advantages which I had.

And there I stumbled too, yet I would try again; for to this hour I am nothing, or so little, that I am scarce subject and argument good enough for one of mine own letters; yet I fear, that doth not ever proceed from a good root, that I am so well content to be less, that is dead. You, sir, are far enough from these descents, your virtue keeps you secure, and your natural disposition to mirth will preserve you; but lose none of these holds, a slip is often as dangerous as a bruise, and though you cannot fall

to my lowness, yet in a much less distraction you may meet
my sadness; for he is no safer which falls from an high
tower into the leads, than he which falls from thence to
the ground; make therefore to yourself some mark, and go
towards it alegrement. Though I be in such a planetary
and erratic fortune that I can do nothing constantly, yet
you may find some constancy in my constant advising you
to it.

Your hearty true friend,

J. Donne.

I came this evening from Mr. Jones his house in
Essex, where Mr. Martin hath been and left a relation
of Captain Whitlock's death. Perchance it is no news to
you, but it was to me; without doubt want broke him;
for when Mr. Holland's company by reason of the plague
broke, the Captain sought to be at Mrs. Jones' house, who
in her husband's absence declining it, he went in the
night, his boy carrying his cloak-bag, on foot to the Lord
of Sussex, who going next day to hunt, the Captain not
then sick, told him he would see him no more. A chaplain
came up to him, to whom he delivered an account of his
understanding, and I hope, of his belief, and soon after
died; and my Lord hath buried him with his own an-
cestors. Perchance his life needed a longer sickness, but a
man may go faster and safer when he enjoys that daylight
of a clear and sound understanding, than in the night or
twilight of an ague or other disease. And the grace of
Almighty God doth everything suddenly and hastily, but
depart from us; it enlightens us, warms us, heats us,
ravishes us, at once. Such a medicine, I fear, his inconsideration needed; and I hope as confidently that he had
it. As our soul is infused when it is created, and created
when it is infused, so at her going out, God's mercy is
had by asking, and that is asked by having. Lest your
Polesworth carrier should cozen me, I send my man with
this letter early to London, whither this Tuesday all the
Court come to a christening at Arundel House, and stay

in town so that I will sup with the good Lady, and write again to-morrow to you if anything be occasioned there which concerns you, and I will tell her so; next day they are to return to Hampton, and upon Friday the King to Royston.

VI

[To Sir Henry Goodyer]

[November, 1611]

Sir,

I am near the execution of that purpose for France; though I may have other ends, yet if it do but keep me awake, it recompenses me well. I am now in the afternoon of my life, and then it is unwholesome to sleep. It is ill to look back, or give over in a course; but worse never to set out.

I speak to you at this time of departing, as I should do at my last upon my deathbed; and I desire to deliver into your hands a heart and affections as innocent towards you, as I shall to deliver my soul into God's hands then. I say not this out of diffidence, as though you doubted it, or that this should look like such an excuse as implied an accusation; but because my fortune hath burdened you so, as I could not rectify it before my going, my conscience and interpretation (severer I hope than yours towards myself) calls that a kind of demerit, but God who hath not only afforded us a way to be delivered from our great many debts, contracted by our executorship to Adam, but also another for our particular debts after, hath not left poor men unprovided for discharge of moral and civil debts; in which acknowledgment and thankfulness is the same as repentance and contrition is in spiritual debts; and though the value and dignity of all these be not perchance in the things, but in the acceptation, yet I cannot doubt of it, either in God, or you.

But, sir, because there is some degree of thankfulness in asking more (for that confesses all former obligations and a desire to be still in the same dependency) I must entreat you to continue that wherein you have most expressed your love to me, which is, to maintain me in the same room in my Lady Bedford's opinion, in the which you placed me. I profess to you that I am too much bound to her for expressing every way her care of my fortune, that I am weary before she is; and out of a loathness, that so good works should be bestowed upon so ill stuff, or that so much ill-fortune should be mingled with hers, as that she should miss anything that she desired, though it were but for me; I am willing to depart from further exercising her endeavors in that kind. I shall be bold to deliver my poor letters to her ladyship's hands, through yours, whilst I am abroad, though I shall ever account myself at home whilst I am in your memory.

Your affectionate servant and lover,

J. Donne.

VII

[To Sir Henry Goodyer?]

[March? 1614]

Sir,

I gave no answer to the letter I received from you upon Tuesday, both because I had in it no other commandment by it but to deliver your letter therein, which I did, and because that letter found me under very much sadness, which (according to the proportion of ills that fall upon me) is since also increased, so that I had not written now, if I had been sure to have been better able to write next week, which I have not much appearance of; yet there was committed to my disposition (that is, left at my house in my absence) a letter from Sir W. Lover, but it was some hours after all possibility of sending it by the carrier, so that Mr. W. Stanhope giving me the honor of a visit at that time, and being instantly to depart, for your parts, did me the favor to undertake the delivery of it to you.

With me, Sir, it is thus; there is not one person (besides myself) in my house well. I have already lost half a child, and with that mischance of hers, my wife fallen into an indisposition, which would afflict her much, but that the sickness of her children stupefies her; of one of which, in good faith, I have not much hope. This meets a fortune so ill-provided for physic and such relief, that if God should ease us with burials, I know not well how to perform even that. I flatter myself in this, that I am dying too; nor can I truly die faster, by any waste, than by loss of children.

But, Sir, I will mingle no more of my sadness to you, but will a little recompense it, by telling you that my Lord Harrington, of whom a few days since they were doubtful, is so well recovered that now they know all his disease to be the pox and measles mingled. This I heard yesterday; for I have not been there yet. I came as near importunity as I could for an answer from Essex House, but this was all, that he should see you shortly himself.

Your servant,

J. Donne.

I cannot tell you so much, as you tell me, of anything from my Lord of Som[erset] since the epithalamium, for I heard nothing.

VIII

To Sir H[enry] G[oodyer]

[March 14, 1614]

Sir,

I receive this 14th your letter of the 10th, yet I am not come to an understanding how these carriers keep days; for I would fain think that the letters which I sent upon Thursday last might have given you such an account of the state of my family, that you needed not have asked by this. But, Sir, it hath pleased God to add thus much to my affliction, that my wife hath now confessed herself to be extremely sick; she hath held out thus long to assist me, but is now overturned, and here we be in two beds, or graves; so that God hath marked out a great many of us, but taken none yet. I have passed ten days without taking anything; so that I think no man can live more thriftily. I have purged and vexed my body much since I wrote to you, and this day I have missed my fit; and this is the first time that I could discern any intermission.

This is enough; the rest I will spend upon the parts of your letter; your letter at Paul's is delivered. In the history of that remove, this only perchance may be news to you, that Mr. Alabaster hath got of the King the Dean's best living, worth above £300, which the Dean had good hope to have held a while.

Of that which you wrote concerning a book of the nullity, I have heard no syllable any other way. If you have received it by good hands, I believe it with you; otherwise the report is naturally very incredible. Though the answering of it be a work for some, both of better abilities really, and in common reputation also, yet I was like enough to have had some knowledge thereof.

You mention again something which it seems you are not willing I should understand of my Lady Huntingdon; some of your former letters (which I never saw), which speak of the matter as of a history and thing done; and these later letters speak of it prophetically, as of a future contingent. I am glad the often remembrance of it gives me often occasion of thankfulness to her, for retaining me in her memory, and of professing myself in my end, and ways, her most humble servant.

For your Parliament business, I should be very sorry, if you came not up, because I presume you had supposed many businesses to have been done at that time; but in the ways wherein you have gone, I protest I am diffident. For the first, for that Lord whom you solicited by letters through me, I tell you with the whispering of a secret, but the confidence of a friend, that you will be deceived whensoever you think that he should take any delight in doing you a courtesy. And I am afraid, the true heartiness of the other noble gentleman, Mr. Howard, will be of small use in this particular, if he have but solicited my Lord his father to reserve a blank for his friend, for my Lord hath suffered more denials, even in places where he sent names, than could have been feared. Besides Mr. Howard hath not written to his father therein, but to Mr. Woodward, who perceiving those letters to be written, before his purpose of being Knight for the shire, thinks these letters extinguished. You made me offer so long since of a place (it was when you wrote into the west), yet I could think it no merit to have offered you one since, otherwise it hath been since in my power, for since the Master of the Rolls provided me one, Sir Edward Herbert, who makes haste away, made me a present of his; and I have had a third offer.

The business of your last week's letter concerning the widow, is not a subject for a feverous man's consideration. Therefore I only send you back those letters which you sent; and ask you leave to make this which I am fain to call my good day, so much truly good, as to spend the rest of it with Dr. Layfield, who is, upon my summons, at this hour come to me. My physicians have made me afraid that this disease will work into my head, and so put me into lightnesses, therefore I am desirous that I be understood before any such danger overtake me.

Your true poor servant,

J. Donne.

IX

To the Honorable Knight Sir Robert Ker

[May, 1614]

Sir,

Perchance others may have told you that I am relapsed into my fever; but that which I must entreat you to condole with me, is that I am relapsed into good degrees of health; your cause of sorrow for that is, that you are likely to be the more troubled with such an impertinency, as I am; and mine is, that I am fallen from fair hopes of ending all; yet I have scaped no better cheap than that I have paid death one of my children for my ransom. Because I loved it well, I make account that I dignify the memory of it by mentioning of it to you, else I should not be so homely. Impute this brevity of writing to you upon no subject to my sickness, in which men use to talk idly; but my profession of desiring to be retained in your memory, impute to your own virtues, which have wrought so much upon your humble servant,

John Donne.

X

To the Honorable Knight Sir Robert Ker, Gentleman
of his Highness's Bedchamber

[April 17, 1615]

Sir,

I have often sinned towards you, with a presumption of being pardoned, but now I do it without hope, and without daring to entreat you to pardon the fault. In which there are thus many degrees of importunity. That I must beg of you to christen a child, which is but a daughter, and in which you must be content to be associated with ladies of our own alliance, but good women, and all this upon Thursday next in the afternoon.

Sir, I have so many and so indelible impressions of your favor to me as they might serve to spread over all my poor race. But since I see that I stand like a tree, which once a year bears, though no fruit, yet this mast of children, and so am sure that one year or other I should afflict you with this request, I had rather be presently under the obligations and the thankfulness towards you than meditate such a trouble to you against another year. I was desirous this paper might kiss your hands as soon as you came, that if any other diversions made this inconvenient to you, I might have another exercise of your favor, by knowing so much from you, who in every act of yours make me more and more

> Your humble and thankful servant,

> J. Donne.

XI

To Elizabeth Rainsford

[1616]

My Most Dear Mother,

When I consider so much of your life as can fall within my memory and observation, I find it to have been a sea, under a continual tempest, where one wave hath ever overtaken another. Our most wise and blessed Saviour chooseth what way it pleaseth Him to conduct those which He loves to His haven and eternal rest. The way which He hath chosen for you is strait, stormy, obscure, and full of sad apparitions of death, and wants, and sundry discomforts; and it hath pleased Him that one discomfort should still succeed and touch another, that He might leave you no leisure, by any pleasure or abundance, to stay or step out of that way, or almost to take breath in that way, by which He hath determined to bring you home, which is His glorious kingdom.

One of the most certain marks and assurances that all these are His works, and to that good end, is your inward feeling and apprehension of them, and patience in them. As long as the Spirit of God distils and dews His cheerfulness upon your heart, as long as He instructs your understanding to interpret His mercies and His judgments aright, so long your comfort must needs be as much greater than others as your afflictions are greater than theirs. The happiness which God afforded to your first young time, which was the love and care of my most dear and provident father, whose soul, I hope, hath long since enjoyed the sight of our blessed Saviour, and had compassion of all our miseries in this world, God removed from you quickly, and hath since taken from you all the comfort that that marriage produced. All those children (for whose maintenance his industry provided, and for whose education you were so carefully and so chargeably diligent) He hath now taken from you. All that wealth which he left, God hath suffered to be gone from us all; so that God hath seemed to repent that He allowed any part of your life any earthly happiness; that He might keep your soul in continual exercise, and longing, and assurance of coming immediately to Him.

I hope, therefore, my most dear mother, that your experience of the calamities of this life, your continual acquaintance with the visitations of the Holy Ghost, which gives better inward comforts than the world can outward discomforts, your wisdom to distinguish the value of this world from the next, and your religious fear of offending our merciful God by repining at anything which He doeth, will preserve you from any inordinate and dangerous sorrow for this loss of my most beloved sister. For my part, which am only left now to do the office of a child, though the poorness of my fortune, and the greatness of my charge, hath not suffered me to express my duty towards you as became me; yet I protest to you before Almighty God and His angels and myself to be as strongly bound to look to you and provide for your relief, as for my own poor wife and children.

For whatsoever I shall be able to do I acknowledge to be a debt to you, from whom I had that education which must make my fortune. This I speak not as though I feared my father Rainsford's care of you, or his means to provide for you; for he hath been with me, and as I perceive in him a loving and industrious care to give you contentment, so I see in his business a happy and considerable forwardness. In the meantime, good mother, take heed that no sorrow nor dejection in your heart interrupt or disappoint God's purpose in you; His purpose is to remove out of your heart all such love of this world's happiness as might put Him out of possession of it. He will have you entirely, and as God is comfort enough, so He is inheritance enough. Join with God and make His visitations and afflictions as He intended them, mercies and comforts. And for God's sake pardon those negligences which I have heretofore used towards you; and assist me with your blessing to me, and all mine; and with your prayers to our blessed Saviour, that thereby both my mind and fortune may be apt to do all my duties, especially those that belong to you.

God, whose omnipotent strength can change the nature of anything by His raising-spirit of comfort, make your poverty riches, your afflictions pleasure, and all the gall and wormwood of your life honey and manna to your taste, which He hath wrought whensoever you are willing to have it so. Which, because I cannot doubt in you, I will forbear more lines at this time, and most humbly deliver myself over to your devotions and good opinion of me, which I desire no longer to live than I may have.

XII

To Sir Robert Ker with my book *Biathanatos* at my going into Germany

[April, 1619]

Sir,

I had need do somewhat towards you above my promises; how weak are my performances when even my promises are defective? I cannot promise, no, not in mine own hopes, equally to your merit towards me. But besides the poems, of which you took a promise, I send you another book to which there belongs this history. It was written by me many years since, and because it is upon a misinterpretable subject, I have always gone so near suppressing it, as that it is only not burnt; no hand hath passed upon it to copy it, nor many eyes to read it; only to some particular friends in both universities, then when I writ it, I did communicate it. And I remember I had this answer, that certainly there was a false thread in it, but not easily found. Keep it, I pray, with the same jealousy; let any that your discretion admits to the sight of it know the date of it, and that it is a book written by Jack Donne, and not by Dr. Donne. Reserve it for me if I live, and if I die I only forbid it the press and the fire; publish it not, but yet burn it not, and between those do what you will with it. Love me still thus far for your own sake, that when you withdraw your love from me you will find so many unworthinesses in me as you grow ashamed of having had so long, and so much, such a thing as—

Your poor servant in Christ Jesus,

J. Donne.

XIII

To the Right Honorable my singular
good Lord the Marquess of Buckingham
[August 8, 1621]

May it please your Lordship,

Ever since I had your Lordship's letter I have esteemed myself in possession of Salisbury, and more than Salisbury, of a place in your service; for I took Salisbury as a scale of it. I hear that my Lord Keeper finds reason to continue in Westminster, and I know that neither your Lordship nor he knows how narrow and penurious a fortune I wrestle with in this world. But I am far from depending upon the assistance of any but your Lordship, as that I do not assist myself so far as with a wish that my Lord Keeper would have left a hole for so poor a worm as I am to have crept in at. All that I mean in using this boldness, of putting myself into your Lordship's presence by this rag of paper, is to tell your Lordship that I lie in a corner, as a clod of clay, attending what kind of vessel it shall please you to make of your Lordship's humblest and thankfullest and devotedest servant,

J. Donne.

XIV

To the Right Honorable Sir Robert Ker, at Court
[April 2, 1625]

Sir,

This morning I have received a signification from my Lord Chamberlain that His Majesty hath commanded tomorrow's sermon at St. James's; and that it is in the afternoon (for, into my mouth there must not enter the word, "after dinner", because that day there enters no dinner into my mouth). Towards the time of the service, I ask your leave that I may hide myself in your out-chamber, or if business, or privateness, or company make that inconvenient, that you will be pleased to assign some servant of yours to show me the closet, when I come to your chamber. I have no other way there but you, which I say not as though I had not assurance enough therein, but because you have too much trouble thereby, nor I have no other end there than the pulpit—you are my station and that my exaltation. And in both I shall ever endeavor to keep you from being sorry for having thought well of, or being ashamed of having testified well for

Your poor and very true servant in Christ Jesus,

J. Donne.

XV

To the Right Honorable Sir Robert Ker, at Court
[April 3, 1625]

Sir,

If I should refuse the liberty which you enlarge to me, of eating in your chamber, you might suspect that I reserved it for greater boldness, and would not spend it in this. But, in good faith, I do not eat before, nor can after, till I have been at home: so much hath my this year's debility disabled me, even for receiving favors. After the sermon I will steal into my coach home, and pray that my good purpose may be well accepted, and my defects graciously pardoned. Amen.

Yours entirely,

J. Donne.

I will be at your chamber at one afternoon.

XVI

To the Right Honorable Sir Robert Ker, at Court
[April 3? 1627]

Sir,

I was this morning at your door, somewhat early; and I am put into such a distaste of my last sermon as that I dare not practise any part of it, and therefore, though I said then that we are bound to speak aloud, though we awaken men and make them forward, yet after two or three modest knocks at the door I went away. Yet I understood after, the King was gone abroad, and thought you might be gone with him. I came to give you an account of that, which this does as well.

I have now put into my Lord of Bath and Wells' hands the sermon faithfully exscribed. I beseech you be pleased to hearken farther after it; I am still upon my jealousy that the King brought thither some disaffection towards me, grounded upon some other demerit of mine, and took it not from the sermon. For, as Cardinal Cusanus wrote a book, *Cribratio Alchorani*, I have cribrated, and re-cribrated, and post-cribrated the sermon, and must necessarily say, the King, who hath let fall his eye upon some of my poems, never saw of mine, a hand or an eye or an affection set down with so much study and diligence and labor of syllables as in this sermon I expressed those two points, which I take so much to conduce to his service, the imprinting of persuasibility and obedience in the subject, and the breaking of the bed of whisperers by casting in a bone of making them suspect and distrust one another.

I remember I heard the old King say of a good

sermon that he thought the preacher never had thought of his sermon till he spoke it; it seemed to him negligently and extemporally spoken. And I knew he had weighed every syllable for half a year before, which made me conclude that the King had before some prejudice upon him. So, the best of my hope is that some overbold allusions, or expressions in the way, might divert His Majesty from vouchsafing to observe the frame and purpose of the sermon.

When he sees the general scope, I hope his goodness will pardon collateral escapes. I entreated the Bishop to ask his Majesty whether his displeasure extended so far as that I should forbear waiting and appearing in his presence; and I had a return, that I might come. Till I had that, I would not offer to put myself under your roof. Today I come, for that purpose, to say prayers. And if, in any degree, my health suffer it, I shall do so tomorrow. If anything fall into your observation before that (because the Bishop is likely to speak to the King of it, perchance this night), if it amount to such an increase of displeasure as that it might be unfit for me to appear, I beseech you afford me the knowledge. Otherwise, I am likely to inquire of you personally tomorrow before nine in the morning, and to put into your presence then

> Your very humble and very true and
> very honest servant to God and the King
> and you
>
> J. Donne.

I wrote yesterday to my Lord Duke, by my Lord Carlisle, who assured me of a gracious acceptation of my putting myself in his protection.

XVII

To Mrs. Cokayne

[May, 1628]

My Noblest Sister,

In your letter from Bath you told me particularly how I might return an answer, that I presume you

intended it for a commandment that I should do so.
Therefore I write, though not therefore only, for though
my obedience be a good reason, yet I have another of
higher value, that is, my love; of which love of mine to
you one principal act having always been my prayers for
you. At this time I knew not how to express that love that
way, because not knowing what seasons of weather are best
for your use of the Bath, I know not what weather to pray
for. I determine my prayers therefore in those generals,
that God will give you whatsoever you would have, and
multiply it to you when you have it.

If I might have forborne this letter till tomorrow, I
could have had time enough to enlarge myself, for Saturday is my day of conversation and liberty. But I am now
upon Friday evening, and not got through my preparation
for my Paul's service upon Sunday. If you look for news
from hence, let my part (who knows but small things) be
this: That Sir John Brook is married to Sir William
Bam[fylde]'s third daughter. So, my noble sister, our
most blessed Saviour bless you with his best blessings, here
and hereafter.

Your very true friend, and brother, and servant,

J. Donne.

XVIII

To Mrs. Cokayne
[August 24, 1628]

My Noblest and Lovingest Sister,

Nothing returns oftener with more comfort to my
memory than that you nor I ever asked anything of one
another which we might not safely grant, and we can ask
nothing safely that implies an offence to God, or injury
to any other person. I fall upon this consideration now,
upon this occasion. Your letter, upon the two-and-
twentieth of August, which I received this day, lays a commandment upon me to give you an account of my state

in health. You do but ask me how I do; and if your letter had come yesterday, I could not have told you that. At my return from Kent to my gate, I found Pegge [his daughter] had the pox, so I withdrew to Peckham, and spent a fortnight there. And without coming home, which I could with some justice hope that it would spread no farther amongst them (as I humbly thank God it hath not, nor much disfigured her that had it), I went into Bedfordshire. There, upon my third Sunday, I was seized with a fever, which grew so upon me as forced me to a resolution of seeking my physician at London.

Thither I came in a day, and a little piece; and within four miles of home I was surprised with an accident in the coach, which never befell me before, nor had been much in my contemplation, and therefore affected me much. It was a violent falling of the uvula, which when Doctor Foxe (whom I found at London, and who had not been there in ten days before) considered well, and perceived the fever complicated with a squinancie [quinsy]: by way of prevention of both, he presently took blood; and so with ten days' starving in a close prison, that is, my bed, I am (blessed be God) returned to a convenient temper, and pulse, and appetite, and learn to eat, and this day met the acceptablest guest in the acceptablest manner, your letter, walking in my chamber.

All which I tell you with these particularities, lest my sickness might be presented by rumor worse than God hath been pleased to make it; for, I humbly thank Him, now I feel no present ill, nor have reason to fear worse.

If I understand your letter aright, much of your family is together. If it be so, entreat them, for your sake, to receive my service, which, by your hand, I present to them all. If they be otherwise severed, yet, in the ears of Almighty God, to whom, I know they all daily pray, my daily prayers for them all shall also meet them all; and that's the only service which I can promise myself an ability to do to God's Church now, since this infirmity in my mouth and voice is likely to take me from any frequent exercise of my other duty of preaching. But God will either enable me, or pardon me. His will be done upon us all, as His goodness hath been overflowingly poured out upon your poor friend and lovingest brother and servant,

J. Donne.

XIX

To Mrs. Cokayne, Occasioned by the Report of his Death

[1628]

My Noble Sister,

Though my man, at London, might have made such a return to your man's letter from himself, as might have given satisfaction enough, yet, because there were so many hours between his receipt of that letter and the return of the carrier as might admit that delay, he thought best to acquaint me with it. I am not sorry he did so, for I have found this rumor of my death to have made so deep impressions, and to have been so peremptorily believed, that from very remote parts I have been entreated to signify, under my hand, that I am yet alive. If you have believed the report, and mourned for me, I pray let that that is done already serve at the time that it shall be true. To mourn a second time were to suspect that I were fallen into the second death, from which I have abundant assurance in the application of the superabundant merits of my Saviour.

What gave the occasion of this rumour, I can make no conjecture. And yet the hour of my death, and the day of my burial, were related in the highest place of this kingdom. I had at that time no kind of sickness, nor otherwise than I had been ever since my fever, and am yet—that is, too weak at this time of the year to go forth, especially to London, where the sickness is near my house, and where I must necessarily open myself to more business than my present state would bear. Yet, next term, by God's grace, I will be there; at which time, I have understood from my Lord Carlisle's house, that the Dean of Exeter will be there, which hath made me forbear to write, because I know how faintly and lamely businesses go on by letters, in respect of conferences. In the meantime, my prayers for your happiness shall fill all the time of your true friend, and brother, and servant,

John Donne

XX

To Mrs. Cokayne

[1629]

My Noble and Virtuous Sister,

If I had had such an occasion as this to have written to you, in the first year of our acquaintance, I had been likely to have presented you with an essay of moral comfort. Now, my letter may be well excused, if it amount to an homily. My profession and my willingness to stay long upon so good an office as to assist you will bear it. Our souls are truly said to be in every part of our body; but yet, if any part of the body be cut off, no part of the soul perishes, but is sucked into that soul that remains, in that that remains of the body. When any limb or branch of the family is taken away, the virtue, the love, and (for the most part) the patrimony and fortune of him that is gone remains with the family. The family would not think itself the less, if any little quillet of ground had been evicted from it; nor must it, because a clod of earth, one person of the family, is removed. In these cases there is nothing lost; one part, the soul, enjoys a present gain; and the other, the body, expects a future. We think it good husbandry to place our children's portions so as that in so many years it may multiply to so much: shall we not be as glad to lay their bodies there, where only they can be mellowed and ripened for glorification.

The perverseness of the father put you to such a necessity of hiding your sons, so that this son is scarce more out of your sight, by being laid under ground, than he was before. And perchance you have been longer time, at some times, from meeting and seeing one another in this world than you shall be now from meeting in the glory of the resurrection. That may come sooner than you looked he should come from the Bath. A man truly liberal, or truly charitable, will borrow money to lend; for, if I be bound to assist another with my meat, or with my money, I may be as much bound to assist him with my credit, and borrow to lend. We do but borrow children of God, to lend them to the world. And when I lend the world a daughter in marriage, or lend the world a son in profession, the world does not always pay me well again; my hopes are not always answered in that daughter or that son. But, of all that I lend to, the grave is my best paymaster. The grave shall restore me my child, where he and I shall have but one Father and pay me my earth, when that earth shall be amber, a sweet perfume, in the nostrils of his and my Saviour.

Since I am well content to send one son to the Church, the other to the Wars, why should I be loth to send one part of either son to heaven, and the other to the earth? Comfort yourself in this, my noble sister, that for those years he lived you were answerable to God for him; for yet, he was so young as a mother's power might govern him; and so long as he was under your charge, and you accountable for him. Now, when he was growing into those years as needed a stronger hand—a father's care—and had not that, God hath cancelled your bonds, discharged you, and undertakes the office of a Father Himself. But, above all, comfort yourself in this, that it is the declared will of God. In sicknesses, and other worldly crosses, there are anxieties and perplexities; we wish one thing today, in the behalf of a distressed child or friend, and another tomorrow; because God hath not yet declared His will. But when he hath done that, in death, there is no room for any anxiety, for any perplexity, no, not for a wish; for we may not so much as pray for the dead.

You know David made his child's sickness his Lent, but his death his Easter; he fasted till the child's death, but then he returned to his repast, because then he had a declaration of God's will. I am far from quenching in you, or discharging natural affection; but, I know your easy apprehensions and overtenderness in this kind. And I know some persons in the world that I wish may live, especially for this respect, because I know their death would overaffect you. In so noble and numerous a family as yours is, every year must necessarily present you some occasion of sorrow, in the loss of some near friend. And therefore I, in the office of a friend, and a brother, and a priest of God, do not only look that you should take this patiently as a declaration of God's present will, but that you take it catechistically, as an instruction for the future; and that God, in this, tells you that He will do so again in some other of your friends. For, to take any one cross patiently is but to forgive God for once; but, to surrender one's self entirely to God is to be ready for all that He shall be pleased to do. And, that his pleasure may be either to lessen your crosses, or to multiply your strength, shall be the prayer of your brother, and friend, and servant, and chaplain,

John Donne.

XXI

To the Right Worshipful Sir George More, Knight.

Sir,

The business of this church and all other business which concerns me in this town determine [end] this week, so that I might be at my liberty to go to do the duty to my church in the country next week, but for the expectation of that £ 100 which you are to pay some days after that. If therefore it stand not with your conveniency to pay it before, because I presume you will be gone out of town before that 2nd of July, I am bold to entreat you to let me know by whose hands it shall be paid me then. For besides that it were a great disappointment of my necessary service in the country to be stayed any longer in this town, so not to receive it at it[s] day will put me to so great a trouble as to make my poor will anew and to substract from my other children their part of this £ 100. Therefore I humbly entreat you that I may hear from you before your going out of town, and rest your poor son-in-law and humble servant in Christ Jesus,

John Donne.

At Paul's house, 22 June, 1629

XXII

To my noble friend Mrs. Cokayne at Ashbourne.
Abury Hatch, 15th January, 1630/31

My noblest Sister,

But that it is sweetened by your command, nothing could trouble me more than to write of myself. Yet, if I would have it known, I must write it myself; for I neither tell children nor servants my state. I have never good temper, nor good pulse, nor good appetite, nor good sleep. Yet I have so much leisure to recollect myself, as that I can think I have been long thus, or often thus. I am not alive, because I have not had enough upon me to kill me, but because it pleases God to pass me through many infirmities before He take me either by those particular mercies in heaven. Therefore have I been more affected with coughs in vehemence, more with deafness, more with toothache, more with the vurbah [uvula?], than heretofore.

All this mellows me for heaven, and so ferments me in this world as I shall need no long concoctions in the grave, but hasten to the resurrection. Not only to be nearer that grave, but to be nearer to the service of the Church, as long as I shall be able to do any, I purpose, God willing, to be at London within a fortnight after your receipt of this, as well because I am under the obligation of preaching at Paul's upon Candlemas Day, as because I know nothing to the contrary, but that I may be called to Court for Lent service; and my witness is in heaven, that I never left out St. Dunstan's when I was able to do them that service, nor will now; though they that know the state of that Church well, know that I am not so bound, as the world thinks, to preach there; for I make not a shilling profit of St. Dunstan's as a Churchman, but as my Lord of Dorset gave me the lease of the Impropriation for a certain rent, and a higher rent than my predecessor had it at.

This I am fain to say often, because they that know it not, have defamed me of a defectiveness towards that Church; and even that mistaking of theirs I ever have, and ever shall endeavor to rectify, by as often preaching there as my condition of body will admit. All our company here is well, but not at home now when I write; for, lest I should not have another return to London before the day of your carrier, I write this, and rest

Your very affectionate servant, and friend and brother

J. Donne.

XXIII

To Mrs. Cokayne

[January, 1631]

My noble dear Sister,

I am come now, not only to pay a fever every half year as a rent for my life; but I am called upon before the day, and they come sooner in the year than heretofore. This fever that I had now, I hoped, for divers days, to have been but an exaltation of my damps and flashings, such as exercise me sometimes four or five days, and pass away without whining or complaint. But I neglected this somewhat too long, which makes me (though, after I took it into consideration, the fever itself declined quickly) much weaker, than, perchance, otherwise I should have been. I had Dr. Foxe and Dr. Clement with me, but, I thank God, was not much trouble to them. Ordinary means set me soon upon my legs, and I have broke my close prison, and walked into the garden; and (but that the weather hath continued so spitefully foul) make no doubt, but I might safely have done more. I eat and digest well enough, and it is no strange thing that I do not sleep well, for, in my best health, I am not much used to do so. At the same time, little Betty had a fever too, and, for her, we used Dr. Wright, who, by occasion, lies within two miles of us; and he was able to ease my sickness with his report of your good health, which, he told us, he had received from you. But I found it not seconded in your own letters, which I had the honor to receive by Mr. Hazard.

My noble sister, I am afraid that death will play with me so long, as he will forget to kill me, and suffer me to live in a languishing and useless age a life that is rather a forgetting that I am dead, than of living. We dispute whether the dead shall pray for the living; and because my life may be short, I pray with the most earnestness for you now. By the advantage of sickness I return the oftener to that holy exercise, and in it join yours with mine own soul. I would not have dignified myself, or my sickness, with saying so much of either, but that it is in obedience to your command that I should do so. And though there lies upon me no command, yet there lies a necessity growing out of my respect, and a nobler root, than my love to you, to enlarge myself, as far as I have gone already, in Mr. Hazard's business.

My noble sister, when you carry me up to the beginning, which it pleases you to call a promise to yourself, and your noble sister; I never slackened my purpose of performing that promise. But if my promise, which was, that I should be ready to assist him in anything I could, were translated by you, or your noble sister, or him, that I would give him the next living in my gift, certainly we speak not one language, or understand not one another, and I had thought we had; this which he imagined to be vacant (for it is not yet, nor any way likely) is the first that fell to me, since I made that promise; and, my noble sister, if a person of my place, from whom one scholar in each university sucks something, and must be weaned by me, and who hath otherwise a latitude of importunate friends, and very many obligations, have a living once in five or six years fall in his gift (for it is so long since I gave any) and may not make a good choice with freedom then, it is hard; yet it is not my fortune to do so now: for, now there is a living fallen (though not that), I am not left to my choice. For my Lords Carlisle and Percy have chosen for me, but truly such a man as I would have chosen; and for him, they laid an obligation upon me three years since, for the next that should fall; yet Mr. Hazard presses you to write for that, because he to whom my promise belongs hath another before, but doth he or his Lord owe me anything for that? Yet Mr. Hazard importunes me to press that chaplain of my Lord, that when he takes mine, he shall resign the other to him, which, as it is an ignorant request (for if it be resigned, it is not in his power to place it upon Mr. Hazard) so it is an unjust request, that I that give him fifty pounds a year, should take from him forty.

But amongst Mr. Hazard's manifold importunities, that I took worst, was, that he should write of domestic things, and what I said of my son to you, and arm you with that plea, that my son was not in Orders. But, my noble sister, though I am far from drawing my son immaturely into Orders, or putting into his hands any Church with cure; yet there are many prebends and other helps in the Church, which a man without taking Orders may be capable of, and for some such I might change a living with cure, and so begin to accommodate a son in some preparation. But Mr. Hazard is too piercing. It is good counsel (and as I remember I gave it him), that if a man deny him anything, and accompany his denial with a reason, he be not too searching, whether that be the true reason or no, but rest in the denial, for many times it

may be out of my power to do a man a courtesy which
he desires, and yet I not tied to tell him the true reason;
therefore out of his letter to you I continue my opinion
that he meddled too far herein.

I cannot shut my letter till (whilst we are upon this
consideration of reasons of denials) I tell you one answer
of his, which perchance may weaken your so great
assurance of his modesty. I told him that my often sicknesses had brought me to an inability of preaching, and
that I was under a necessity of preaching twelve or fourteen sermons every year, to great auditories at Paul's, and
to the judges, and at Court; and that, therefore, I must
think of conferring something upon such a man as may
supply my place in these solemnities; and surely, said I,
I will offer them no man in those cases which shall not
be at least equal to myself; and, Mr. Hazard, I do not
know your faculties. He gave me this answer, I will not
make comparisons, but I do not doubt but I should give
them satisfaction in that kind. Now, my noble sister,
whereas you repeat often, that you and your sister rested
upon my word, and my worth; and, but for my word and
my worth, you would not have proceeded so far: I must
necessarily make my protestation, that my word and my
worth is herein, as chaste, and untouched as the best
maidenhead in the world. For, my noble sister, goes there
no more to the giving of a scholar a church in London,
but that he was a young gentleman's schoolmaster? You
know the ticklishness of London pulpits, and how ill it
would become me to place a man in a London church that
were not both a strong and a sound man. And therefore,
those things must come into consideration before he can
have a living from me; though there was no need of
reflecting upon those things, when I made that general
promise, that I would assist his fortune in anything.

You end in a phrase of indignation and displeasure,
rare in you towards me, therefore it affects me; which is,
that he may part from me, as I received him at first, as
though I were likely to hinder him. The heat that produced that word I know is past, and therefore, my most

beloved sister, give me leave to say to you, that he shall not part from me, but I shall keep him still in my care, and make you always my judge of all omissions.—Your faithful friend and servant

J. Donne.

Bibliography

(Articles in the collections by Gardner, Kermode, and Spencer are not listed separately.)

Akrigg, G. P. V. *Jacobean Pageant, or The Court of King James I*. London, 1962.

Allen, D. C. "Donne on the Mandrake," *Modern Language Notes*, LXXIV (1959), 393-97.

Alvarez, A. *The School of Donne*. London, 1961.

Bald, R. C. "Donne's Activities," *Times Literary Supplement*, May 13, 1949, p. 313.

———. "Donne's Early Verse Letters," *Huntington Library Quarterly*, XV (1952), 283-89.

———. "A Latin Version of Donne's Problems," *Modern Philology*, LXI (1964), 198-203.

——— (editor). Robert Southwell's *An Humble Supplication to Her Maiestie*. Cambridge, 1953.

———. *Donne and the Drurys*. Cambridge, 1959.

Bennett, Joan. *Four Metaphysical Poets*. New York, 1960.

———. "The Love Poetry of John Donne: A Reply to Mr. C. S. Lewis," in *Seventeenth-Century Studies presented to Sir Herbert Grierson* (Oxford, 1938), pp. 85-104. Reprinted in *Seventeenth-Century English Poetry: Modern Essays in Criticism,* ed. William R. Keast. New York, 1962.

Bennett, R. E. "John Manningham and Donne's Paradoxes," *Modern Language Notes*, XLVI (1931), 309-13.

———. "Walton's Use of Donne's Letters," *Philological Quarterly*, XVI (1937), 30-34.

———. "John Donne and Everard Gilpin," *Review of English Studies*, XV (1939), 66-72.

———. "Donne's Letters from the Continent in 1611-12," *Philological Quarterly*, XIX (1940), 66-78.

———. "Donne's Letters to Several Persons of Honour," *Publications of the Modern Language Association*, LVI (1941), 120-40.

———. "John Donne and the Earl of Essex," *Modern Language Quarterly*, III (1942), 603-4.

Bowen, Catherine Drinker. *Francis Bacon: The Temper of a Man*. Boston, 1963.

Bredvold, Louis I. "The Religious Thought of Donne in Relation to Medieval and Later Traditions," in *Studies in Shakespeare, Milton, and Donne*, University of Michigan Publications, I. New York, 1925.

Bryson, John. "Lost Portrait of Donne," London *Times*, October 13, 1959, pp. 13 and 15.

Bush, Douglas. *English Literature in the Earlier Seventeenth Century*. Revised edition. Oxford, 1962.

Chamberlain, John. *Letters*, ed. N. E. McClure. 2 vols. Philadelphia, 1939.

Chambrun, Clara Longworth de. *Shakespeare Rediscovered*. New York, 1938.

Cheyney, Edward P. *A History of England from the Defeat of the Armada to the Death of Elizabeth*. Vol. II. New York, 1926.

Chute, Marchette. *Shakespeare of London*. New York, 1949.

———. *Ben Jonson of Westminster*. New York, 1953.

———. *Two Gentle Men: The Lives of George Herbert and Robert Herrick*. New York, 1959.

Coffin, Charles M. *John Donne and the New Philosophy*. New York, 1937.

Coffin, Robert P. Tristram, and Witherspoon, Alexander M., editors. *Seventeenth-Century Prose and Poetry*. New York, 1946.

Collmer, Robert G. "The Background of Donne's Reception in Holland," *Mississippi Quarterly*, XIV (1960—61), 51-57.

Cooper, H. "John Donne and Virginia in 1610," *Modern Language Notes*, LVII (1942), 661-63.

Crossett, John. "Bacon and Donne," *Notes and Queries*, VII (1960), 386-87.

Danby, J. "The Poets on Fortune's Hill," *The Cambridge Journal*, II (1949), 195-211.

Deas, M. C. "A Note on Rowland Woodward, the Friend of John Donne," *Review of English Studies*, VII (1931), 454-57.

Donne, John. *Complete Poetry and Selected Prose*, ed. John Hayward. New York, 1929, and later revisions.

———. *Complete Poetry and Selected Prose*, ed. Charles M. Coffin. New York, 1952.

———. *Poems*, ed. Herbert J. C. Grierson. 2 vols. Oxford, 1912.

———. *Poems*, ed. Herbert J. C. Grierson. London, 1929.

———. *Complete Poems*, ed. Roger E. Bennett. Chicago, 1942; reprinted, New York, 1958.

———. *A Selection of His Poetry*, ed. John Hayward. Penguin Books, 1950.

———. *The Divine Poems*, ed. Helen Gardner. Oxford, 1952.

———. *The Songs and Sonets*, ed. Theodore Redpath. London, 1959.

———. *The Anniversaries*, ed. Frank Manley. Baltimore, 1963.

———. *Biathanatos*. Reproduced from the first edition with a bibliographical note by J. William Hebel. New York, 1930.

———. *The Courtier's Library, or Catalogus Librorum Aulicorum incomparabilium et non vendibilium,* ed. Evelyn M. Simpson. London, 1930.

———. *Devotions Upon Emergent Occasions.* Ann Arbor, 1959.

———. *Essays in Divinity,* ed. Evelyn M. Simpson. Oxford, 1952.

———. [Juvenilia] *Ivvenilia Or Certaine Paradoxes and Problems.* Reproduced from the first edition with a bibliographical note by R. E. Bennett. New York, 1936.

———. *Paradoxes and Problemes.* London, 1923.

———. *Letters to Several Persons of Honour,* ed. C. E. Merrill Jr. New York, 1910.

———. "Two Unpublished Manuscripts of John Donne," M. de Havilland, *London Mercury,* XIII (1925), 159-60.

———. *Letter to Sir Nicholas Carey, Written from his House in London in the Early Summer of the Plague Year 1625.* Cambridge, Mass., 1930.

———. *Pseudo-Martyr.* London, 1610.

———. *Sermons: Selected Passages.* With an Essay by Logan Pearsall Smith. Oxford, 1919.

———. *Sermons.* Selected and introduced by Theodore A. Gill. New York, 1958.

———. *Sermons,* ed. George R. Potter and Evelyn M. Simpson. 10 vols. Berkeley, 1953—62.

Drummond of Hawthornden, William. *Conversations of Ben Jonson with Drummond of Hawthornden,* ed. R. F. Patterson. London, 1923.

Duncan, Joseph E. *The Revival of Metaphysical Poetry.* Minneapolis, 1959.

Duncan-Jones, E. E. "Donne's Praise of Autumnal Beauty: Greek Sources," *Modern Language Review,* LVI (1961), 213-15.

Eliot, T. S. *Selected Essays 1917—1932.* New York, 1932.

———. Review in *The Nation and The Athenaeum,* XXXIII (1923), 331-32.

Ellrodt, Robert. "Chronologie des poèmes de Donne," *Etudes Anglaises,* XIII (1960), 452-63.

Empson, William. "Donne the Space Man," *Kenyon Review,* XIX (1957), 337-99.

Explicator, I (February, 1943).

Fausset, Hugh I'Anson. *John Donne, A Study in Discord.* New York, 1925.

Finkelpearl, P. J. "Donne and Everard Guilpin: Additions, Corrections, and Conjectures," *Review of English Studies,* XIV (1963), 164-67.

Fitch, Robert Elliot. *Odyssey of the Self-Centered Self: Or Rake's Progress in Religion.* New York, 1961.

Gardner, Helen L. "Notes on Donne's Verse Letters," *Modern Language Review,* XLI (1946), 318-21.

———. *John Donne: A Collection of Critical Essays.* Englewood Cliffs, New Jersey, 1962.

Garrod, H. W. "The Latin Poem Addressed by Donne to Dr. Andrews," *Review of English Studies,* XXI (1945), 38-42.

———. "Donne and Mrs. Herbert," *ibid.,* 161-73.

Goldberg, B. Z. *The Sacred Fire: The Story of Sex in Religion.* New York, 1930.

Gosse, Sir Edmund. *The Life and Letters of John Donne.* 2 vols. 1899; reprinted Gloucester, Mass., 1959.

Gransden, K. W. *John Donne.* London, 1954.

Grierson, Sir Herbert J. C. "John Donne," in *The Cambridge History of English Literature,* ed. A. W. Ward and A. R. Waller, IV (New York, 1910), 225-56.

———. *Metaphysical Lyrics and Poems of the Seventeenth Century.* Oxford, 1921.

Hardy, Evelyn. *Donne: A Spirit in Conflict.* London, 1942.

Harrison, G. B. *The Life and Death of Robert Devereux Earl of Essex.* New York, 1937.

Heltzel, Virgil B. "Sir Thomas Egerton as Patron," *Huntington Library Quarterly,* XI (1948), 105-27.

Hickey, Robert L. "Donne and Virginia," *Philological Quarterly,* XXVI (1947), 181-92.

Hughes, Merritt Y. "Kidnapping Donne," *University of California Essays in Criticism,* 2d series (Berkeley, 1934), pp. 61-89.

———. "Some of Donne's 'Ecstasies,'" *PMLA,* LXXV (1960), 509-18.

Hunt, Clay. *Donne's Poetry: Essays in Literary Analysis.* New Haven, 1954.

Itrat-Husain. *The Dogmatic and Mystical Theology of John Donne.* London, 1938.

Jenkins, Elizabeth. *Elizabeth the Great.* New York, 1959.

Jessopp, Augustus. *John Donne Sometime Dean of St. Paul's A. D. 1621—1631.* London, 1897.

Johnson, Samuel. *Works,* VII. Oxford, 1825.

Johnson, Stanley. "John Donne and the Virginia Company," *ELH,* XIV (1947), 127-38.

———. "Sir Henry Goodere and Donne's Letters," *Modern Language Notes,* LXIII (1948), 38-43.

Jonson, Ben. *Works,* ed. C. H. Herford and Percy Simpson. 11 vols. Oxford, 1925—1952.

Kermode, Frank. *John Donne.* London, 1961.

———. *Discussions of John Donne.* Boston, 1962.

Keynes, Geoffrey. *A Bibliography of John Donne.* 3d edition. Cambridge, 1958.

Lear, John. "The Forgotten Moon Voyage of 1609," *Saturday Review,* May 4, 1963, pp. 39-46.

Le Comte, Edward S. *Endymion in England: The Literary History of a Greek Myth.* New York, 1944.

———. "Shakspere, Guilpin, and Essex," *Shakespeare Association Bulletin,* XXIII (1948), 17-19.

———. "The Ending of *Hamlet* as a Farewell to Essex," *ELH,* XVII (1950), 87-114.

Legouis, Pierre. *Donne the Craftsman.* Paris, 1928; reprinted, New York, 1962.

Leishman, J. B. *The Monarch of Wit: An Analytical and Comparative Study of the Poetry of John Donne.* 5th edition. London, 1962.

Lewis, C. S. "Donne and Love Poetry in the Seventeenth Century," in *Seventeenth-Century Studies presented to Sir Herbert Grierson* (Oxford, 1938), pp. 64-84. Reprinted in *Seventeenth-Century English Poetry: Modern Essays in Criticism,* ed. William R. Keast. New York, 1962.

———. *English Literature in the Sixteenth Century, excluding Drama.* Oxford, 1954.

Louthan, Donaphan. *The Poetry of John Donne.* New York, 1951.

Mahood, M. M. *Poetry and Humanism*. London, 1950.

Martz, Louis L. *The Poetry of Meditation: A Study in English Religious Literature of the Seventeenth Century*. Revised edition. New Haven, 1962.

McElwee, William. *The Wisest Fool in Christendom: The Reign of King James I and VI*. New York, 1958.

Miles, Josephine. *The Primary Language of Poetry in the 1640's*. Berkeley, 1948.

——. *Major Adjectives in English Poetry*. Berkeley, 1946.

Milgate, W. "Donne the Lawyer," *Times Literary Supplement*, August 1, 1942, p. 379.

——. "The Date of Donne's Birth," *Notes and Queries*, CXCI (1946), 206-8.

——. "Dr. Donne's Art Gallery," *ibid.*, CXCIV (1949), 194, 318-19.

Mueller, William R. *John Donne: Preacher*. Princeton, 1962.

Neale, J. E. *Queen Elizabeth*. London, 1934.

——. *Elizabeth I and Her Parliaments, 1584—1601*. London, 1957.

Newdigate, B. H. "Donne's 'Letters to Several Persons of Honour,'" *Notes and Queries*, CLXXX (1941), 441.

Nicolson, Marjorie H. *The Breaking of the Circle*. Evanston, Ill., 1950.

——. *Science and Imagination*. Ithaca, 1956.

Novarr, David. "Donne's 'Epithalamion Made at Lincoln's Inn,' Context and Date," *Review of English Studies*, VII (1956), 250-63.

——. "The Dating of Donne's *La Corona*," *Philological Quarterly*, XXXVI (1957), 259-65.

——. *The Making of Walton's Lives*. Ithaca, 1958.

Patrick, J. Max. Review of Harold Martin Priest's *Renaissance and Baroque Lyrics*, *Seventeenth-Century News*, XXI (1963), 4, 6.

Potter, George R. "Milton's Early Poems, the School of Donne, and the Elizabethan Sonneteers," *Philological Quarterly*, VI (1927), 396-400.

——. "John Donne: Poet to Priest," in *Five Gayley Lectures* (Berkeley, 1954), pp. 105-26.

Raine, Kathleen. "John Donne and the Baroque Doubt," *Horizon*, XI (1945), 371-95.

Ralegh, Sir Walter. *Works, VIII. (Miscellaneous Works.* Oxford, 1829.)

Reed, A. W. *Early Tudor Drama.* London, 1926.

Roberts, Donald R. "The Death Wish of John Donne," *PMLA*, LXII (1947), 958-76.

Rowse, A. L. *The England of Elizabeth.* New York, 1950.

——. *The Expansion of Elizabethan England.* London, 1955.

Rugoff, Milton A. *Donne's Imagery: A Study in Creative Sources.* New York, 1939; reprinted New York, 1962.

Sampson, J. "A Contemporary Light upon John Donne," in *Essays and Studies by Members of the English Association*, VII (Oxford, 1921), 82-107.

Shakespeare's England, ed. Walter Raleigh, Sidney Lee, and C. T. Onions. 2 vols. Oxford, 1932.

Shapiro, I. A. "John Donne and Lincoln's Inn 1591— 1594," *Times Literary Supplement*, October 16 and 23, 1930, pp. 833, 861.

——. "The Text of Donne's *Letters to Severall Persons*," *Review of English Studies*, VII (1931), 291-301.

——. "John Donne and Parliament," *Times Literary Supplement*, March 10, 1932, p. 172.

——. "Donne's Birth-Date," *Notes and Queries*, CXCVII (1952), 310-13.

——. "Walton and the Occasion of Donne's *Devotions*," *Review of English Studies*, IX (1958), 18-22.

Sharp, Robert L. *From Donne to Dryden: the Revolt against Metaphysical Poetry.* Chapel Hill 1940.

Simpson, Evelyn M. *A Study of the Prose Works of John Donne.* 2d edition. Oxford, 1948.

——. "The Biographical Value of Donne's Sermons," *Review of English Studies*, n. s., II (1951), 339-57.

Skinner, M. "John Donne Not in Germany in 1602," *Notes and Queries,* CXCVII (1952), 134.

Smith, Logan Pearsall. *The Life and Letters of Sir Henry Wotton*. 2 vols. London, 1907.

Sparrow, John. "John Donne and Contemporary Preachers: their Preparation of Sermons for Delivery and for Publication," in *Essays and Studies by Members of the English Association*, XVI (1930), 144-78.

Spencer, Theodore (editor). *A Garland for John Donne.* Cambridge, Mass., 1931; reprinted, Gloucester, 1958.

—— and Van Doren, Mark. *Studies in Metaphysical Poetry: Two Essays and a Bibliography.* New York, 1939.

Sprott, S. E. "The Legend of Jack Donne the Libertine," *University of Toronto Quarterly*, XIX (1950), 335-53.

Stein, Arnold. "Donne and the 1920's: A Problem in Historical Consciousness," *ELH*, XXVII (1960), 16-29.

Strachey, Lytton *Elizabeth and Essex, A Tragic History.* New York, 1928.

Terrill, T. E. "Notes on John Donne's Early Reading," *Modern Language Notes*, XLIII (1928), 318-19.

Thomson, P. "John Donne and the Countess of Bedford," *Modern Language Review*, XLIV (1949), 329-40.

Tillyard, E. M. W. *The Metaphysicals and Milton.* Cambridge, 1956.

Unger, Leonard. *Donne's Poetry and Modern Criticism.* Chicago, 1950.

Walton, Izaak. *Lives.* Oxford World's Classics, 1927.

Waugh, Evelyn. *Edmund Campion.* Boston, 1946.

Webber, Joan. *Contrary Music: The Prose Style of John Donne.* Madison, 1963.

Wedgwood, C. V. *The King's Peace.* New York, 1956.

White, Helen C. *The Metaphysical Poets: A Study in Religious Experience.* New York; reprinted 1956.

Whitlock, Baird W. "Donne's 'First Letter,' " *Times Literary Supplement*, August 22, 1952, p. 556 (inaugurating a debate that continues into December).

——. "The Dean and the Yeoman," *Notes and Queries*, n. s., I (1954), 374-75.

——. "John Syminges, a Poet's Stepfather," *ibid.*, 421-24, 465-67.

———. "Donne at St. Dunstan's," *Times Literary Supplement*, September 16 and 23, 1955, pp. 548, 564.

———. "The Orphanage Accounts of John Donne, Ironmonger," *The Guildhall Miscellany*, no. 4, London, 1955, pp. 22-29.

——— "Ye Curioust Schooler in Christendom," *Review of English Studies*, n. s., VI (1955), 365-71.

———. "The Heredity and Childhood of John Donne," *Notes and Queries*, VI (1959), 257-62, 348-53.

———. "The Family of John Donne," *ibid.*, VII (1960), 380-86.

———. "Donne's University Years," *English Studies*, XLIII (1962), 1-20.

Wiley, M. L. *The Subtle Knot: Creative Scepticism in Seventeenth Century England.* London, 1952.

Williamson, George. *The Donne Tradition.* Cambridge, Mass., 1930; reprinted New York, 1958.

———. "Libertine Donne: Comments on *Biathanatos*," *Philological Quarterly*, XIII (1934), 276-91.

———. "Textual Difficulties in the Interpretation of Donne's Poetry," *Modern Philology*, XXXVIII (1940), 37-72.

Wilson, F. P. "Notes on the Early Life of John Donne," *Review of English Studies*, III (1927), 272-79.

Wood, Anthony. *Athenae Oxonienses.* 2 vols. London, 1721.

Woolf, Virginia. "Donne after Three Centuries," *The Second Common Reader.* New York, 1932. Pp. 17-31.

Wright, Louis B. *Middle-Class Culture in Elizabethan England.* Reprinted Ithaca, 1958.

Index

295